Praise for [Brainiac]

"[Ken] Jennings recounts the whole roller-coaster experience.... *Brainiac* isn't really a memoir but a broader look at the culture of trivia competitions.... A smart new author."   —*Bookpage*

"*Brainiac* is, appropriately, part memoir, part response to what [Jennings] calls his "really weird" blip of minor stardom, but for trivia enthusiasts, the book shines brightest when shedding light on the secret history and subculture of trivia.... [He] is an astute, personable guide through this world."   —*Kirkus Reviews*

"Likely to become a bible for the thousands who want to replicate Jennings's amazing feat."   —*Contra Costa Times*

"*Brainiac* proves that [Jennings's] good nature and witty, self-deprecating humor successfully transfer from TV to print.... *Brainiac* is anything but trivial."   —*Seattle Weekly*

"Steeped in the world of trivia, [Jennings] offers an in-depth history of the young sport.... [He] informs and astounds us."   —*Booklist*

"Jennings is actually so effective in telling what it's like to be a *Jeopardy!* contestant that you can feel the tingling in the limbs and the perspiration forming on your hands."   —*Deseret Morning News*

"*Brainiac* is surprisingly entertaining, informative and very well written—just the right mix of autobiography, history, cultural commentary and humor."   —Harrisonburg *Daily News-Record*

"Though Jennings dominated [*Jeopardy!*] for months, the show does not dominate the book; he weaves his personal story into a broader assessment of the trivia phenomenon, past and present."
                              —*The New York Times*

"Jennings is hip enough to make fun of his freakish triviaphilia but savvy enough to indulge it too. . . . The world of trivia. It's a place where minutiae have a paradoxical grandeur and no fact is meaningless."

—*Time*

"Interactive and fun . . . recommended." —*Library Journal*

"Jennings could have written a quickie chronicle of his rise to *Jeopardy!* fame and riches, but *Brainiac* is much more—it's a look at trivia as a hobby, as a business, as a fascination for millions." —CNN.com

Brainiac

Ken Jennings

Brainiac

ADVENTURES IN
the Curious, Competitive, Compulsive
WORLD OF TRIVIA BUFFS

VILLARD
NEW YORK

To Mindy
For all the usual reasons
And six unusual ones

What shall I compare it to, this fantastic thing
I call my Mind? To a waste-paper basket, to
a sieve choked with sediment, or to a barrel full
of floating froth and refuse?

—LOGAN PEARSALL SMITH, *Trivia,* 1917

CONTENTS

Author's Note   xi

1.   *What is* AMBITION?   3
2.   *What is* AUDITION?   16
3.   *What is* ERUDITION?   28
4.   *What is* AMMUNITION?   50
5.   *What is* COMPETITION?   67
6.   *What is* IGNITION?   86
7.   *What is* COMPOSITION?   103
8.   *What is* FRUITION?   121
9.   *What is* TRANSITION?   133
10. *What is* COGNITION?   144
11. *What is* JUXTAPOSITION?   159
12. *What is* REPETITION?   176
13. *What is* TRADITION?   187
14. *What is* RECOGNITION?   210
15. *What is* DEMOLITION?   229
16. *What is* REDEFINITION?   240

Acknowledgments   249
Trivia Timeline   253
Notes   261

A book about trivia has, potentially, the same problem that rock criticism or a sex manual does: it's never as much fun as the real thing.

With that in mind, I've tried to sprinkle trivia questions throughout this book, so that the sufficiently nerdy reader can play along at home. A superscript number like this one[5] in the text doesn't indicate an endnote but, rather, identifies trivia question number 5 in a particular chapter. Each chapter has ten trivia questions embedded within it (except for Chapter 7, on the art of writing trivia, which has more, and the final chapter, which is essentially an epilogue and doesn't have any). Answers to each set of questions appear at the end of each chapter.

I've tried to make the trivia serve the book, rather than vice versa. As a result, the 170 trivia questions herein are not necessarily my 170 personal favorites, but rather they are the questions that filled a particular niche in the narrative. Trivia questions like "What did Einstein, Darwin, Poe, H. G. Wells, and Queen Victoria have in common, matrimonially speaking?"[1] or "What company released a February 2004 statement to customers in rebuttal to OutKast's hit song 'Hey Ya'?"[2] or "What two parts of the body are joined by the philtrum?"[3] might be aesthetically superior to some of the trivia to follow, but they didn't happen to fit the context of the chapters.

Since much of this book revolves around my 2004 appearance on the syndicated quiz show *Jeopardy!*, I thought it might be helpful to recap the rules of that game, to refresh the memories of readers who may not be regular viewers.

Jeopardy! is a straightforward game of questions and answers, in which three contestants try to beat one another to answering general-knowledge (but faintly academically oriented) trivia. The show's central gimmick is that the "questions" and "answers" are syntactically reversed.

Instead of asking, "Who was the only U.S. president to marry in the White House?" and expecting an answer of "Grover Cleveland," host Alex Trebek will offer a clue like "The only U.S. president to marry in the White House," and expect the response in question form: "Who is Grover Cleveland?" Contestants who forget the annoying "Who is . . . ?" tic may have their responses ruled as incorrect.

The game consists of two rounds, each played on a game board consisting of a grid of thirty TV monitors. The six columns of the board represent six categories: "Geography," "Classic TV," "11-Letter Words," and so forth. Each column contains five clues, arranged from top to bottom in increasing order of difficulty. In the first round, the clues are worth from $200 to $1,000. In the second round, or "Double Jeopardy," the dollar values double and range from $400 to $2,000 per correct answer. Contestants who buzz in but guess incorrectly are penalized the amount of the clue. The first contestant to buzz in with a correct answer is awarded the points, and selects the next clue of his choice.

Three clues in each game—one in the first round and two in the second—are preselected as "Daily Doubles," though neither the players nor the home audience know where on the board they will be found. The contestant who happens to select each Daily Double faces that clue alone, and can wager any or all of her current score on whether or not she will answer it correctly.

The *Jeopardy!* endgame is dubbed "Final Jeopardy." All three players participate, as long as they have finished the second round with a positive score. A clue category is revealed, and players can bet any or all of their winnings that they will know the correct answer to a single clue in that category, just as with the Daily Doubles. When the final clue is revealed, players have thirty seconds to write down their responses. The player who leaves Final Jeopardy with the highest score returns on the following show; the others go home with cash prizes.

Until recently, all winning contestants were retired after five games.

ANSWERS

1. Einstein, Darwin, Poe, H. G. Wells, and Queen Victoria all **married their first cousins.**

2. **Polaroid,** alarmed by OutKast's injunction to "shake it like a Polaroid picture," issued a February 2004 statement to customers, warning them that "if you shake it too vigorously, you could distort the image."

3. The philtrum is the groove between **your nose and your mouth.**

Brainiac

CHAPTER 1

What is AMBITION?

Here's some trivia for you. The red rock country of southern Utah is red for the same reason that the planet Mars has a pinkish tinge when you see it in the night sky: both are loaded with iron oxide, a.k.a. ordinary household rust. The shadows of these red desert crags are lengthening toward our car as it pulls into a dusty gas station on the Utah-Arizona border. The air smells of diesel fumes and sagebrush when I open the passenger-side door. My friend Earl Cahill unfolds himself from the driver's seat, relieved we've made it to this, our last chance at gas for fifty miles.

Earl is my old college roommate, and though he's a remarkable six-foot-nine in height, he's one of those giants who hope that by holding their head and shoulders at just the right dejected angle, they may somehow—if not disappear completely—at least give the appearance of being only six-foot-four or six-foot-five. He blinks into the setting sun through the shock of floppy brown hair hanging over his face, a face that bears the perpetually disappointed look of an English foxhound or a Cubs fan.

As I pump gas, we reenact the ritual of all road-trippers since the days of Jack Kerouac, and try to figure out how we're going to divvy up the trip's costs. Unlike our beatnik freeway forefathers, however, Earl and I are both computer programmers, and we're driving down to Los Angeles not to hear jazz or harvest lettuce or watch the sun set over the Pacific, but to try to land spots on *Jeopardy!*, America's most popular and most difficult quiz show. Appropriately, geekily, we are squabbling about the most *elegant algorithm* to calculate and divide up our expenses.

"How about this?" I offer. "There's two of us, so that vastly improves our chances that one of us will make it on the show, right? And as we know, that person is guaranteed at least a thousand dollars, even if he finishes in third place. So here's what we do: we split all expenses when we get back, but if one of us makes it onto the show, that person pays for the other's share of gas and other expenses from this trip."

Earl furrows his brow, suspicious he's being conned.

"It's no-lose," I persist. "If you get on the show, you pay for all expenses, but you still turn a big profit from your winnings. The one who doesn't get on loses nothing."

"Deal," he finally agrees. We shake on it as we switch spots and climb back into the car. It *is* a no-lose scenario, but I'm guessing that I'll end up being the beneficiary of my own plan. Earl, I figure, is exactly the type game shows look for. Besides being incredibly smart and, as he likes to put it, "sideshow-freak tall," he has a booming baritone voice and an eccentric way of speaking—an inside-joke-rich patois of computer-hacker lingo, *Simpsons* references, and, mysteriously, quotes from Merchant Ivory movies. He's exactly the kind of larger-than-life personality *Jeopardy!* needs—a lock to get on the show. I figure I've just negotiated myself a free trip to L.A.

But I admit to myself, I'm not just along for the ride as Earl's road-trip buddy. For as long as I can remember, I've dreamed of being on *Jeopardy!*, and Earl knows it. "You know, I keep telling myself that even if I fail the test, at least I can tell people I was the guy that got Ken Jennings on *Jeopardy!*" he says, as we pull back onto I-15 and drive off into the sunset.

I've been meaning to try out for *Jeopardy!* for nearly twenty years now, but I've loved trivia for even longer. My generation tends to think of trivia as an eighties craze, something we cherish nostalgically in the same neurons of our brain responsible for remembering Members Only jackets and Ralph Macchio. The watershed trivia year of my youth was clearly 1984, the year that the Alex Trebek version of *Jeopardy!* debuted on the airwaves and Trivial Pursuit sold twenty million copies, supplanting Pac-Man as *the* game craze of the era. But ask someone ten years younger what year trivia peaked, and her "final answer" would probably be 1999 or so, when *Who Wants to Be a Millionaire* became so explosively popular. Someone of my parents' generation might associate the word "trivia" with the vogue for college campus trivia contests in the late 1960s, while my grandparents would certainly remember America holding its breath as contestants sweated it out in isolation booths on the high-rated (and highly rigged) TV quiz shows of the 1950s. A scholar in the field might even point you back to 1927, when the best-selling book *Ask Me Another!* ignited the very first question-and-answer craze in America. If trivia is a fad, in other words, it's certainly a pesky one. Like the Terminator, Halley's comet, or genital herpes, trivia just keeps coming back.

And it's still around. In fact, though trivia isn't necessarily faddish at the moment, it's still somehow omnipresent. America plays hundreds of thousands of trivia games every day—in urban bars, on suburban coffee tables, on FM radio stations, on cell phones. Trivia appears on our beer coasters, under our Snapple caps, on our Cracker Jack prizes. It clogs our e-mail in-boxes and magazine article sidebars. It fills the blank space at the bottom of columns in the phone book. It pacifies us while we watch the cola-sponsored advertising on movie screens. It's the bumper that takes us to commercial on cable news and entertainment shows. It's such a familiar part of American life that we don't even notice it anymore, and yet there it always is. We live surrounded by trivia.

"Trivia," the word itself, predates 1984 and Trivial Pursuit, of course. In fact, it goes back millennia. Originally a Roman name for the goddess Hecate, in her role as guardian of the crossroads, "Trivia" derives from the Latin "trivium": a crossroads where "three ways" met. Centuries later, English writer John Gay named his most famous poem, a 1716 description of a walking tour of London, "Trivia," in honor of the same goddess. (Gay is better known for his satirical *The Beggar's Opera*, the musical work upon which Brecht's *Threepenny Opera* was based, which means he's also responsible for the pop song that was the number one *Billboard* hit of 1959.)[1]

The Latin word "trivium" is also our source for the adjective form "trivial," meaning unimportant or ordinary. It's generally believed that "trivial" came to mean commonplace because a "trivium," or public crossroads, was literally a "common place." Others claim that the adjective "trivial" derives from another use of "trivium"—in medieval universities, the course load was divided between the three-subject trivium and the four-subject quadrivium. The trio of courses in the trivium was always grammar, rhetoric, and logic, while the quadrivium was composed of home ec, driver's ed, wood shop, and band (oh, all right: arithmetic, geometry, astronomy, and music). The trivium contained the easier, more elementary subjects, thought to be less important than the advanced quadrivium, and, hence, "trivial."

In the twentieth century, the noun form "trivia" first began to be used as a derivative of "trivial" to refer to trifles, or things deemed unimportant. As early as 1902, popular essayist Logan Pearsall Smith (the brother-in-law, incidentally, of philosopher Bertrand Russell) published a collection of brief philosophical musings under the title *Trivia*. But the word didn't adopt its current usage—"questions and answers about unusual bits of everyday knowledge"—until the mid-1960s.

I've always felt it was a shame that the "trivia" moniker stuck to trivia so firmly. Referring to your hobby with a word that quite literally means "petty" or "insignificant" doesn't strike me as the best way to popularize it. Would football ever have caught on if gridiron fans had insisted on calling it "that stupid sport with the weird-shaped ball"? Do philatelists call postage stamps "little gummed squares that we pointlessly collect and pore over when we really should be out meeting girls"? And yet trivia fans happily adopt the language of the oppressor, tacitly but cheerfully agreeing that, yes, their tendency toward learning and knowing lots of weird stuff is completely valueless. Completely "trivial."

I first heard the words "trivial" and "nontrivial" in their scientific usage in the math and computer science classes I took in college. To math and computer nerds, a trivial problem is one with a ridiculously easy solution, one the teacher probably won't even bother to put up on the overhead projector. Science is, instead, about the pursuit of the unusual, elegant solution—the nontrivial one. For example, I remember learning once about "sum-product numbers," numbers equal to the sum of all their digits multiplied by the product of all their digits. There are an infinite number of natural numbers, said the instructor, but only three sum-product numbers. The number 1 is the trivial solution, the boring one: $1 \times 1 = 1$. The interesting solutions are the nontrivial ones—135, for instance (though there's one other):[2]

$$((1 + 3 + 5) \times (1 \times 3 \times 5)) = 135$$

For as long as I can remember, I've had the idea that trivia, despite its name, *is* elegant, complicated, fascinating, worthy of study—that trivia is, in a word, nontrivial.

My mom remembers the first trivia question I ever answered. I was four years old and sitting behind one-way glass at the University of Washington. The university, in conjunction with the Seattle public school system, was testing kids for placement in certain "gifted and talented" elementary school programs. So I got to spend the day stacking blocks and solving picture puzzles in dark little rooms lined with mirrors. Mom says she came back to the testing room to pick me up hours later, only to find that the grad students were having such a good time with the general knowledge portion of the testing that they'd let it go on far too long.

"Now, where did the Wright brothers' first plane flight happen?"[3] they asked as she walked in.

I was sitting in a tiny chair, playing with a train, seemingly oblivious to the test, and my mom didn't expect me to answer.

But I surprised her by getting the question right. Looking back, I don't know how a four-year-old would know *anything* about the Wright brothers. Some people apparently have a sponge-like brain that sucks up information and detail almost from birth, through some perfect-storm coalescence of curiosity, compulsiveness, and innate talent. These people are indiscriminate information gourmands, driven by inexplicable urges to scrawl every scrap of knowledge that comes their way onto their blank chalkboard of a brain. We did not choose trivia. Trivia chose us.

I can think of habits I've had since birth that, in hindsight, seem more like OCD symptoms than charmingly precocious childhood pastimes. I would sit in movie theaters long after the lights came up, carefully studying every name in the credits roll. I memorized all the patterns on the *Sesame Street* matching game in my closet, so I could beat my parents every time we played. I once spent an eleven-hour plane flight timing myself to see how fast I could name every country in the world in alphabetical order, from Afghanistan all the way to, well, to the very last one.[4] I remember, at four years old, being distraught that the surprise my parents gave us to celebrate my dad's graduation from law school was a mere trip to Disneyland (Disneyland! I ask you!) and not the item I'd had my eye on for months: the word game Boggle.

Though I obviously needed no encouragement, my parents encouraged me by finding me used copies of all the traditional accessories for the pint-sized trivia loudmouth: the *Guinness Book of World Records, Ripley's Believe It or Not!* paperbacks, a variety of poorly researched fact books featuring Snoopy. My parents were also very patient with the litany of trivia these gifts produced during long car trips. "Hey, Mom! Do you know what color a polar bear's skin is? No, black! Hey, Mom! Three-quarters of the dust in our house is from dead human skin cells, ewww! Hey, Mom! Guess how big the world's biggest pumpkin pie was. Not even close, 418 pounds!"

Surprisingly I survived many of these car trips without being beaten mercilessly. And when I didn't have all the answers, Dad, a science nut, was always ready with a helpful gee-Mr.-Wizard-that's-keen answer to childhood's many puzzling questions. What makes the sky blue? (Rayleigh scattering.) Why does a curveball curve? (The Magnus effect.) Where do babies come from? (Go ask your mother.)

Thanks in part to the Wright brothers, I suppose, I started kindergarten at a magnet school near our northeast Seattle home. Starting school was traumatic for me—not because I missed my mommy or couldn't remember which coat hook was mine, but because I knew I'd miss my beloved morning game shows. I spent my elementary school years perpetually pining for summer vacation, when I could catch up once again on *Wheel of Fortune, The $20,000 Pyramid,* and *Family Feud.* I was overjoyed in 1979 when my sister Gwyn was born: we were now a family of five—*the exact perfect size for a* Family Feud *team!* That could be *us* up there someday, being smooched by Richard Dawson wearing an atrocious light gray three-piece suit. To this day, my grandparents love to remind me how I used to phone them daily to give them the rundown on all the morning's game shows. I would run into our avocado-and-gold 1970s kitchen in my Underoos and clamber up on a stool to reach the telephone, just to recite the details of a particularly exciting *Password* matchup or *Pyramid* bonus round.

Two years later, my dad had a job offer at an overseas law firm and packed us all off to Asia, so I was living in Seoul when *Jeopardy!* came back on the air in 1984. With only one English-language TV channel to watch in South Korea—thank you AFKN, the Armed Forces Korea Network—everyone in my American school watched exactly the same shows at exactly the same times every day. AFKN showed *Jeopardy!* every afternoon around the time we all got home from school, and so, as weird as it sounds, the previous day's *Jeopardy!* was a big fifth-grade playground topic each day.

In sixth grade, we were assigned a class project to design games themed around endangered species preservation. Mine was Seal of Fortune, but I envied my friend Tom, who had been assigned a different animal and could call his game Jaguardy!, complete with that unnecessary exclamation point. The same year, a girl we knew caused a big stir when she brought to class a copy of the new, hot-off-the-press *Jeopardy!* book that had just been released Stateside, and many of us took turns going through the sample contestant tests in the back to see if we were *Jeopardy!* material. In the sixth grade! Some accident of U.S. Army television programming and typical elementary school obsessiveness had turned us into the Seoul Foreign School for Prepubescent Quiz Show Freaks.

I was, in short, a pretty nerdy kid. But I was not alone—countless trivia fans have described similar childhoods to me, hours spent indoors poring over world atlases and *The Baseball Encyclopedia* and Leonard Maltin's movie guide, and keeping shoe boxes full of note cards documenting trivial obsessions. I look back on it now with a curious mixture of bewilderment and nostalgia—was I ever really like that? As I entered adolescence and, eventually, adulthood, trivia became something childish and embarrassing that needed to be put away, like Saturday morning cartoons or a well-loved stuffed animal. I threw out whole boxes full of notebooks that I'd spent my childhood filling with lists: celebrity middle names, Olympic archery medalists, archived *Family Feud* questions, state birds. I quit buying *The World Almanac* when it came out every November. My subscription to *Games* magazine lapsed. Finally, my freshman year of college, I even fell out of the habit of watching *Jeopardy!*

It wasn't that I was suddenly too cool for trivia or, truthfully, very cool at all. Sure, I wasn't producing shelves full of *Quantum Leap* fan fiction or anything, but I still had plenty of nerdy pastimes: a vast collection of *Thor* and *Fantastic Four* comic books, my fantasy baseball team, speed-solving *The New York Times* crossword puzzle that ran every weekday in the student newspaper. But I'd started to see trivia mavens the way society at large sometimes sees them: as drips, oddballs, conversation killers. No one likes the guy with the immediate answer to every question or, worse, the dreaded follow-up "And-did-you-know?" factoid. And so I would hide tests that came back with A's on them, and soft-pedal corrections when forced to ("I almost think that rabbits *aren't* rodents, actually . . ."[5]), and let my Trivial Pursuit teammates talk me out of answers I knew were right. In college once, I overheard a girl from next door talking to Earl about the master's in math he was working toward, when he happened to mention that I was nearly done with my own degree in computer science. We had both known this girl for years.

"Wait, Ken's smart too?" she asked Earl, astonished.

I took it as a compliment.

Yes, I was on the down low: a deeply closeted trivia lover. But I'd never quite let go of my childhood fantasy of appearing on *Jeopardy!* As a kid, of course, this was a pipe dream: I was decades too young to even audition for the show. But when I was a teenager, *Jeopardy!* started an annual Teen Tournament, and when I was attending Brigham Young University, I got to know Jeff Stewart, who had won the *Jeopardy!* College Tournament as a BYU senior in 1994. Going on a game show started to seem like an attainable goal, something that happened to *real people I knew,* and not just to perky anonymous homemakers from Placentia or La Jolla or some other California city that only existed for me in game show announcer intros. Why couldn't it be me up there someday?

Jeopardy! never came to do one of their roving contestant searches in Salt Lake City, where I now live, so I decided that a Los Angeles tryout was my best bet. The show holds open auditions monthly in L.A., according to a book of *Jeopardy!* tips I found on a bookstore discount table one Friday evening, killing time before a movie. The slender paperback by Florida lawyer Michael Dupée, who won *Jeopardy!*'s Tournament of Champions back in 1996, was called *How to Get on Jeopardy!*

. . . and Win! The title spoke to me for some reason. As I paged through the book, gleaning it for helpful hints, I resolved never again to pass through Southern California without trying out. But this promise will prove harder than it sounds.

"How was work?" my wife, Mindy, asks me as I bang through the screen door. It's a cool April evening and Mindy is preparing dinner while she keeps one eye on our newborn, Dylan, who is gurgling in his baby carrier in the corner.

"Fine, I guess." I've worked as a computer programmer for a local health-care staffing company for the last few years, ever since my previous employer fell victim to the popping of the Internet bubble and stopped doing the little things that matter for its employees, like paying them. Now I spend my days writing software that helps get doctors and nurses placed in new jobs. It's a stable company and a nice group of people. It pays the mortgage every month on the little yellow-brick house we bought—our first—just before Dylan was born. And though I try not to dwell on it, it's incredibly dull work, made worse by the increasingly obvious fact that I'm a pretty mediocre computer programmer. The short attention span and encyclopedic memory that served me well in trivia are apparently a different set of mental muscles from the ones you need to write software eight hours a day. This bothers me, since I suspect that writing good computer code is probably a more accurate measure of real intelligence than knowing who hit the first home run in All-Star Game history[6] or which 1960s TV character was named Roy Hinkley.[7]

"I called *Jeopardy!* today," I add, trying to sound casual. "They're not doing tryouts the week we're in L.A. Their May tryout isn't until the week after."

Mindy can tell I'm disappointed. She dries her hands and comes over to me. "Oh, I'm sorry. You were really serious about auditioning, then?"

"It's fine. What are those bulb things you're slicing?"

"You've never seen fennel? It looks like celery and tastes like licorice. It's really good baked with a little olive oil." Automatically I find myself filing "fennel" away in my mind. You can take the boy out of the trivia, but you can't take the trivia out of the boy.

"I wish we could stay another week in California, but I don't want to leave Dylan with my mom for two whole weeks."

I pick up Dylan. He certainly takes after his father: about three-quarters of his body weight seems to be head, and three-quarters of *that* is ears. It's impossible to resent this obstacle to my lifelong *Jeopardy!* dreams as he sits in my arms, grinning up at me and blowing spit bubbles.

"Tell me if you think this is a dumb idea," I say to Mindy. "It's going to drive me nuts if I miss this audition by just a couple days. What if as soon as we get back from California I drive right back down to go to the tryout?"

To Mindy's credit, she doesn't remind me that this is a twelve-hour drive each way, or that *Jeopardy!* specifically tells people *not* to make a special trip for an audition, because the odds against making it onto the show are so astronomically steep: over thirty thousand would-be contestants try out for the show most years, competing for only four hundred spots. The exact odds are left as an exercise for the reader, but let's just say that getting into Harvard is about eight times easier.

"Do you think you can get off work for a second trip?" she asks.

"There's no way I'm going to ask for time off for a quiz show audition. I'll tell them it's a wedding or something."

"Then I think you should do it," she says, sliding a fennel-laden pan into the oven. I'm so relieved I could kiss her, and I do. "Can you find someone to go with you to share the driving?"

I'm already walking to the phone. "I'll call Earl."

Talking Mindy into my plan was the easy part, but I wonder if Earl Cahill isn't going to be a tougher sell. Earl, you have to understand, is pretty much anybody's idea of a genius. He's a concert pianist, a gifted photographer, a mathematician, and the best computer programmer I know. He wins our Oscar prediction pool handily every single spring. If you surveyed twenty people who know Earl, asking each of them for the name of the smartest person they know, nineteen would say, "Earl." The other guy would say something like, "You know, that really tall guy who used to live next door? Fixed my modem that one time? Burl or Merle or something."

But Earl is different from most trivia people I know in one important respect. Growing up in Cheyenne, Wyoming, he was never driven by that insatiable childhood compulsion to absorb knowledge. It was only later in life that he realized how many people mistook trivia recall for intelligence, and so he's been playing trivia catch-up ever since, determined to feel smarter if it kills him. One of the first computer programs he ever wrote, back when we were college roommates and he was starting to fiddle around with computers, was educational software designed to teach him all the capital cities of Europe. He didn't like not knowing which one was Bucharest and which was Budapest, so he wrote this program from the ground up and then spent days drilling himself on his own system until he knew all the answers. We both did the *Times* crossword puzzle every day, but only he would doggedly look up every word he didn't know. Earl wasn't born trivia-great, and he didn't have trivia greatness thrust upon him. Earl achieved it; he's the rare self-made trivia man.

As a result, he's always been a little thin-skinned about getting beaten at any intellectual pursuit by someone who didn't have to work at it as hard as he did. And since Earl and I are both pretty competitive people at heart (don't even ask about the notorious Scattergories Incident of 1998—"egg drop" is not a flavor of ice cream, Earl!), I'd understand completely if he turned me down flat. It *would* be pretty awkward if I passed the test and he didn't. "Well, thanks for chauffeuring me, Earl! Bummer about you flunking the test." Or, now that I come to think about it, what if he passes and I don't?

When he picks up the phone, I don't waste any time. "So, this is really weird, and you can say no if you want, but I think we should drive down to L.A. in May and try out for *Jeopardy!*"

The pause is almost imperceptible. "Sure. What day?"

We have liftoff.

Later that night, I trudge down to the basement, where there's a storage room full of cardboard boxes of books, still packed up from our recent move. It takes me quite a while to dig out *How to Get on Jeopardy! . . . and Win!* For the moment, I'm more concerned with the part of the title *before* the ellipses. Reading beside a sleeping Mindy in bed that night, I find that the bulk of the book is composed of practice quizzes. Most are on the tough topics that *Jeopardy!* writers tend to emphasize disproportionately: opera, ballet, gourmet food and drink (no fennel trivia, though). What country is home to diva soprano Kiri te Kanawa?[8] What kind of vegetable is also called an aubergine?[9] What's the alcoholic ingredient in a White Lady?[10]

I feel a little like Earl, force-feeding myself information I would never otherwise remember, and it makes me question the sanity of our upcoming *Jeopardy!* odyssey. Is all this headache going to be worth it, just for the infinitesimal chance of making it on the show, much less winning anything? I finally fall asleep with the book on my chest, still unable to quite remember which one is Nureyev and which one is Baryshnikov.

ANSWERS

1. Bobby Darin's **"Mack the Knife"** is from *The Threepenny Opera*. Mack himself is based on Macheath, the protagonist of John Gay's 1728 *The Beggar's Opera*.

2. **144** is, besides 135, the only nontrivial sum-product number. $((1 + 4 + 4) \times (1 \times 4 \times 4)) = 144$

3. The Wright brothers' first plane flight took place at **Kitty Hawk, North Carolina.**

4. **Zimbabwe** is the last country in the world alphabetically.

5. Rabbits are **lagomorphs,** not rodents.

6. **Babe Ruth** hit the first home run in All-Star Game history.

7. Roy Hinkley was the seldom-used real name of **the Professor on** *Gilligan's Island.*

8. Kiri te Kanawa is from **New Zealand.**

9. Aubergine is another word for **eggplant.**

10. **Gin** is the alcoholic ingredient in a White Lady.

CHAPTER 2

What is AUDITION?

I'm too young to remember the original version of *Jeopardy!*, which Art Fleming hosted on NBC from 1964 until the end of 1974, the year of my birth. As the story goes, Merv Griffin and his then-wife, Julann, were flying home to New York in 1963 when Julann suggested a novel reversal of a familiar quiz show concept: the host would provide the answer, and the contestants would need to reply with the appropriate question.

"Five thousand two hundred and eighty," said Julann to her husband.

"How many feet are there in a mile?" replied Merv, no *Jeopardy!* slouch even then.

A show was born.

The Griffins spent the next few months playing "What's the Question?," as they called it, with friends around the dining room table of their Upper West Side apartment. When Merv finally showed NBC the game, in a live run-through at Rockefeller Center, executives thought the questions and answers were way too hard, but a network assistant named Grant Tinker (later the president of NBC and Mr. Mary Tyler Moore) insisted that the show would be a hit.

Game shows had been in a fallow period for almost a decade, never having recovered from the infamous rigging scandals on such shows as *Twenty-One* and *The $64,000 Question* during the 1950s. But *Jeopardy!*'s successful decade-long run helped resuscitate the moribund genre, and when the show was reborn in 1984, with its format unchanged but now hosted by unflappable Ontario native Alex Trebek, it was an immediate hit yet again.

Two decades later, *Jeopardy!* is still the nation's top-rated quiz show, and has seeped into the popular culture—the American zeitgeist, a *Jeopardy!*-caliber nerd might say—in a way that no other game show really has. The same year that *Jeopardy!* returned to the airwaves, "Weird

Al" Yankovic commemorated his own game show suckitude by having announcer Don Pardo call him "a complete loser" in his song "I Lost on *Jeopardy!*" In the 1992 film *White Men Can't Jump,* Rosie Perez achieves her lifelong dream of appearing on *Jeopardy!* and kicks ass by knowing all five "Foods That Start with 'Q'," from "a custard pie often made with cheese and bacon"[1] to "a large edible clam of the Atlantic coast."[2] Dustin Hoffman, as the lead character in *Rain Man,* "definitely, *definitely*" refuses to miss his daily five-thirty dose of *Jeopardy!* And in *Groundhog Day,* Bill Murray expresses his ultimate boredom with his broken record of a life by watching the same episode of *Jeopardy!* over and over again until he can impress all the blue-hairs in his B&B by nailing all the right answers. Er, questions.

Jeopardy!'s success spilled over into TV shows as well. Cliff Clavin, the know-it-all mailman on *Cheers,* cleaned up on *Jeopardy!* when the categories turned out to be tailor-made for him: "Civil Servants," "Stamps from Around the World," "Beer," "Mothers and Sons," "Bar Trivia," and "Celibacy." But he lost by betting too much on Final Jeopardy: to the clue "Archibald Leach, Bernard Schwartz, Lucille LeSueur,"[3] Cliff lamely guessed, "Who are three people who have never been in my kitchen?" For a while, "the *Jeopardy!* episode" became a sitcom staple almost as essential as the "trapped in an elevator" episode or the "dates with two different girls on the same night" episode. During those halcyon days, *Jeopardy!*'s sitcom guests included Marge Simpson, *The Nanny*'s title character, Rose and Dorothy from *The Golden Girls,* and Thelma from *Mama's Family.* I had to look up that last one. Like everyone else in America, I've never seen an entire episode of *Mama's Family.*

These pop-cultural *Jeopardy!* cameos do have one thing in common, you'll notice: they're all around fifteen years old. (Tragically, even *Mama's Family* was canceled in 1990.) And that's to be expected: in the late eighties and early nineties, *Jeopardy!* was at the height of its iconic power. It's not that the show has declined since then. It's just that it's stayed exactly the same while hundreds of other programs have come and gone and the entire cast of *Law & Order* has turned over twice. People have come to count on *Jeopardy!* It's not even a program anymore, really. It's an institution.

It's also a daily habit among its faithful core of viewers, the ten million or so who watch the show night after night without fail. With its staid, repetitive format, *Jeopardy!* is possibly the least flashy show on television, so these viewers aren't watching for glitz or surprise. They're sure not watching it for the contestants or for the host, who—though I love 'em—sometimes seem to be locked in a desperate struggle to prove who can be less charismatic.

No, these regular viewers are watching for the trivia. They—we, I have to admit, having been a fan most of my life—shout out answers at our televisions with confidence. From the safety of our couches, we feel smarter with every answer we know, but go stealthily unpenalized for those we muff. The little ego-boost from a correct answer explains the whole human love for trivia. We love the endorphin rush, the I'm-smart feeling we get from unexpectedly producing an answer we had no idea we knew.

These nightly viewers are kids, college students, bright young professionals, and senior citizens—especially senior citizens, I'm not surprised to learn. *Jeopardy!*, with its unabashed inclusion of cognoscenti-only categories like "Ballet" and "Nuclear Physics" and "Art History," is the last vestige of another America: a brainier place, where science was going to solve all our problems and help us beat the Russkies, where high culture freely permeated the middlebrow sort. To a nation of grandparents nostalgic for a time when everyone listened to Toscanini on the radio, tired of having to watch people on TV win money for bungee jumping and eating goat rectums, *Jeopardy!* is sweetly cerebral relief piped in straight from the Eisenhower era, a time capsule from an age before America dumbed down.

"You look sort of nervous," I tell Earl. It's a month after I roped him into auditioning for the show, and we're inching through sultry, sluggish traffic on our way to the Culver City hotel where *Jeopardy!* is holding today's contestant search. We arrived in L.A. late the night before and spent a few restless hours on the living room floor of a Studio City apartment belonging to an old school buddy of Earl's—his debate team partner, in fact. In the last twelve hours, I've learned more than I ever wanted to know about the intricacies of junior college debate. Resolved: that you guys have to talk about something else at dinner tonight.

"I'm nervous," Earl admits.

"Are you afraid you're not going to pass?"

"Yeah," Earl says. "Ask me the rest of those science questions."

I pick up *How to Get on Jeopardy! . . . and Win!*, by now a creased, dog-eared shadow of its former self. On the drive down to California, we took turns poring over its pages to the point of car sickness. In the last five minutes of traffic alone, we've learned the longest muscle in the human body,[4] the musical term that's Italian for "detached,"[5] and the deepest lake in the United States.[6]

"Discovered penicillin."

"Dunno. Wait. Alexander Fleming."

"Correct! Discovered the neutron."

"James Chadwick."

"Yes. Discovered Uranus."

"Huh huh. You said, 'Uranus.'"

"Correct. We would have also accepted 'Who is William Herschel?'"

"Hey, here's a parking spot on the street. We won't have to pay ten dollars for hotel valet parking."

"Great. Pull over and quiz me on the opera questions again."

A phone call to *Jeopardy!* three weeks ago got us on the list for the ten o'clock tryout, but we've arrived half an hour early, so we're two of the first people milling about among the palm fronds and the Andrew Lloyd Webber piano music in the lobby of the Culver City Radisson. I make Earl hide the book we were studying from, not wanting to look like dorks, but I needn't have bothered: soon there's a steady stream of people entering the lobby clutching almanacs and whatnot. I smile when I see a woman frantically trying to absorb some last-minute information from that same *Jeopardy!* tie-in book that was such a hit in my sixth-grade classroom. A good crowd, maybe seventy-five people, has formed by the time we are ushered into the conference room where the audition will be held.

A dozen rows of folding chairs have been arranged on the conference room's ornately tiled burgundy carpet. The room is full, so Earl and

I sit down a few rows apart, in two of the remaining empty seats. I crane my neck curiously to look at the demographic of the room. There are plenty of the middle-aged white guys who make up *Jeopardy!*'s core contestant population, but on the whole, the room looks like America. I'm sitting right in front of the African American woman who was reading the *Jeopardy!* book in the lobby, and she's representative of a pretty good smattering of women and minorities. Everyone looks smart: lots of reading glasses and goatees and copies of *The Economist* and tweed with elbow patches. I start to feel a little performance anxiety. How can I compete against tweed with elbow patches?

Earl and I already know from our book that a written test will be our first hurdle today. Test-taking material is passed around, including a *Jeopardy!* ballpoint pen, which for most of us will be our only souvenir of the tryout. Very few pass the test, which is made up of fifty clues taken from the show's more difficult material. The contestant coordinators welcome us and ask if anyone has ever been on a game show before (there are a few *Millionaire* veterans, and one guy who was once on *The Match Game*) or if anyone has ever tried out for *Jeopardy!* before. A lot have. "Nine times, and I've always passed," someone volunteers. Nine times? I shoot Earl a look. I know that the odds are still against your making it onto the show even if you pass the contestant test, but *nine times*? Don't panic. Maybe this guy just isn't who they're looking for.

The test is projected onto a screen in front of the room, with the clues appearing on blue in the familiar white font used on the show (Korinna, for typography geeks). The clues are read in the (prerecorded) mellifluous tones of show announcer Johnny Gilbert, not by Alex himself. Prospective contestants have eight seconds to answer each clue before Johnny begins the next one. You write down your answers on a worksheet, and no, the staff explains, you don't need to answer in the form of a question.

I'm a little worried at the beginning of the test—I can't remember who succeeded Sandy Berger as national security adviser, and leave the very first question blank. But then there's maybe a dozen in a row that I know cold: Salvador Dalí! Hinduism! John Wilkes Booth! *The Merchant of Venice*! I start to relax enough that the first answer suddenly appears in my head unbidden, and I do a "I could have had a V8!" forehead slap and scrawl "Condoleezza Rice" in the space I left empty.

In some perverse way, I've always enjoyed being tested. The saw-dusty smell of a sharpened number 2 pencil, the chance to spell your name with the little bubbles on the computer answer sheet, the series of tricky, colon-heavy puzzles waiting to be solved. "ICONOCLAST : CONVENTION :: _____ : _____." It's not the kind of thing you can say at school without getting beaten up a lot, but deep down I always thought standardized tests were fun. The *Jeopardy!* test brings back the same feelings, except that—even better!—this time it's all about trivia. What human organ contains the nephrons?[7] What mother of Isaac is the most mentioned woman in the Bible?[8] Who is Melanie Griffith's *esposo*?[9]

As the test winds down, I know I didn't get every question—I'm blanking on something about a young country singer, another about a very fast kind of falcon, and I'm fairly sure I've confused Michelle Kwan with Kristi Yamaguchi. But I know the pass/fail cutoff is low enough to allow for a few brain-freezes. *Jeopardy!* doesn't announce where the cut-off falls, and the contestant coordinators reassure all the non-passers that they can go home and tell their friends they just missed it by one.

After we hand in our papers, the test-takers around me are all abuzz with the right answers to the questions I've missed (LeAnn Rimes! Peregrine falcons! *Kristi freakin' Yamaguchi!*), and it's rattling my confidence a little. Earl is having the same problem. He's sitting next to a college-aged kid who seems to be the cocky, ebullient type—the kind of guy who talks nonstop to every person who's ever been seated next to him on an airplane, even the ones just trying to read.

"I'm pretty sure I aced it," he's burbling. "After I got that *Oliver Twist* question—"

"You mean *Great Expectations*?" Earl replies.

"What?"

"It was about Pip and Magwitch. I'm pretty sure that's *Great Expectations*."

"Oh. Uh, right. Yeah, *Great Expectations*." That quiets him down.

While a few *Jeopardy!* staffers take the tests out to be corrected, two of the contestant coordinators entertain the nervous room by taking questions. Earl and I realize that if you haven't watched every single game of *Jeopardy!*, from the Art Fleming days right up until last night's broadcast, you're a little out of place in this bunch. People are trading references and in-jokes about *Jeopardy!* minutiae I've never heard of, not to mention some newfangled additions to the show. Alex shaved his mustache? There's a "Brain Bus" and a "Clue Crew" now? What is this, *Jeopardy!* or *Scooby Doo*? Earl and I chuckle nervously when we see everyone else laughing, trading sidelong glances and inwardly kicking ourselves for all that time we wasted in college foolishly *studying* when we could have been watching *Jeopardy!*

The test graders come back into the conference room, and everyone clams up instantly. The tension mounts as they hand the results to the contestant coordinators. We all try to act nonchalant, but there's a lot of nervous twitching of knees and feet going on. For the twelfth time, we're reminded that just by showing up today, we've proved ourselves, and don't feel bad if you didn't pass, and come try out again next year. Yeah, yeah, yeah, just read the names!

All my confidence has instantly evaporated: I'm convinced now that I've failed the test. What was I thinking, driving twelve hours for this?

But then there it is, "Ken Jennings." The second name read. Sweet relief. Of course I passed. I never doubted it for a second.

I'm expecting maybe five or six to advance out of this group, since I've heard the pass rate is so low. But five or six names have been read, and Earl's hasn't been one of them. Now there are nine passers. Now there are ten. Earl's trying to play it cool, but he's leaning forward, poised like a tackle on the line of scrimmage. His normally hangdog face now looks like the contorted close-up of all five Oscar nominees as the envelope is torn. Could he have not passed? The ride home is going to *suck*.

"Earl Cahill!" The eleventh name read, and the next to last, as it turns out. I clap so emphatically that people turn and stare.

"Congratulations, Earl!" a woman across the aisle whispers to me.

The twelve of us who passed move on up to the front of the room; everyone else drains sadly out the back. The *Oliver Twist* guy, who knew he'd "aced it," is among them, and I feel more than a twinge of remorse when I see his face. He looks like a kid who just let go of his brand-new balloon.

Now we have to use our shiny new *Jeopardy!* pens to fill out an extensive contestant information sheet. Mostly you have to say no to a lot of checkboxes. No, I'm not related to the CEO of Sony Television or to Alex Trebek. No, I haven't been on *Jeopardy!* before. No, I'm not running for public office. I waver a second before filling out the "Occupation" line. This could be my big chance to look interesting. Would *Jeopardy!* really hire a crack team of private eyes to shoot holes in my story if I wrote down "pet psychologist" or "magician's assistant"? Honesty wins out and I scribble down "software engineer," pained by a momentary vision of the tens of thousands of other hopeful young software engineers who have probably tried out for *Jeopardy!* in the past week.

The hardest question comes when they ask us what station we watch *Jeopardy!* on back home. Earl and I grimace at each other, embarrassed that *Jeopardy!* has finally stumped us completely. I write, "Your local Salt Lake City affiliate," but I don't think I'm fooling anybody. Earl leaves it blank.

The form also asks us to volunteer five "fun" facts about ourselves. If the fifty-question written test was the SAT of the *Jeopardy!* admissions process, these are the college essays. Our five facts will become the basis for our little interview segment with Alex, should we ever make it onto the show. If you've ever seen these strained little attempts to humanize the show's contestants, you know just how *not*-fun these fun facts usually turn out to be, but occasionally somebody will actually tell an anecdote right, or get a good line in. It's just hard to do so in your first ten minutes on national television. Earl and I knew this was coming, thanks to our helpful little book, and we spent our trip down trying to assemble a few anecdotes. Even with twelve hours of rehearsal time, we struggled a bit; I can only imagine how daunting this request must seem to a contestant coming in cold. "List the five cleverest, most charming things about yourself! Do it in one sentence! Be funny! And get them all down in a few minutes while we come around and take Polaroids of you!"

The contestant coordinators are Maggie Speak and Tony Pandolfo. Both are the kind of fun larger-than-life types that *Jeopardy!* thinks will inject life into a room of dull, nervous academics, like a balloon-animal-wielding clown trying to liven up a failed tenth-birthday party. Tony is a bearded, baldish guy with a dry sense of humor, instantly recognizable for his voice: thick New York accent and Harvey Fierstein gravel. He's in love with game shows, having spent his life working in them. In fact, he still plays in a regular poker game with Betty White; Bill Cullen's widow, Ann; *Password* inventor Bob Stewart; and other game show luminaries of yesteryear.

Maggie Speak is a five-foot-four whirlwind of energy with an ambulance siren of a voice and a big, boisterous laugh. Everyone is "sweetie" or "cutie-pie" to Maggie. She's a constant stream of helpful *Jeopardy!* advice, drill-instructor orders, funny jokes, unfunny jokes, and laughter at her own jokes (both varieties). In short, she's the perfect person to coax a little personality out of stiff, nervous *Jeopardy!* hopefuls.

The next test is a mock game. Being able to pass a very hard trivia test doesn't self-select for telegenic, outgoing people, it turns out. Who knew? So Tony and Maggie line us up, three at a time, on a practice buzzer system, and have us choose and answer actual clues from the show.

And they don't care, frankly, if we're answering the questions right or not. If only the real show were so forgiving. They just want to see if we can smile, speak up, respond quickly, and follow their buzzer coaching. *Jeopardy!* is a well-oiled machine, and they need people who are going to play by the book if they're going to get each game wrapped up in twenty-two minutes sans commercials. *Macht schnell!*

The staffers also role-play Alex's mini-interview with each contestant. In my imagination, Earl and I would be going up against a handful of lifeless, pasty bookworms who couldn't go half a sentence without saying the words "level nine cleric" or "Captain Picard." I'm about as far from telegenic as you can get, but stack me up against a group like that and I'd be Cary Grant! I'm disheartened to find that the twelve finalists are, for the most part, warm, gregarious people with interesting stories. One flew choppers in Vietnam. Another just got back from a semester digging wells in Africa. The only wet blanket is some poor guy who apparently couldn't come up with five fun stories about himself.

"It says here you like to read!"

"Yes."

"So, what are your other interests?"

"Uh, I . . . just reading. Reading mostly."

I'm not holding my breath to see this guy on the show.

My interview is pretty lame, something about our new baby that elicits a big "Aaaaaww" from Maggie. Still, America loves babies. Earl,

I think, is pretty funny, and I'm thinking—even hoping, to some degree—that he'll get "The Call" to be on the show before I do. But he's jumping all over himself for getting a movie question wrong during the mock game. "Not knowing who played the pitcher in *Bull Durham*!¹⁰ I've seen that movie twelve times!" he whispers to me.

"You did fine. Your interview was funny. That's the main thing."

Tony asks if there are any other questions. "How long will we be eligible in the contestant pool?" Just over a year. "What if you call us and we're not home or the machine picks up or something?" If we want you on the show, we'll find you, don't worry. "Does it disqualify you for the show if you're, for example, *very tall*?" That last one is Earl. He's told, encouragingly, that they just put the shorter folks up on boxes when one contestant is very tall. Apparently they tried putting the tall people in holes, but they kept tripping and falling. This answer cheers Earl up immensely.

And that's it. Don't call us; we'll call you. We leave the hotel pretty damn pumped, but it's not exactly the kind of thing where you can call somebody and gloat.

"Hey, guess what, I just passed the *Jeopardy!* contestant test!"

"Cool! When are you going to be on the show?"

"Well, probably never. If they choose me, maybe in a year or more."

"Oh! Um. Cool!"

In the drive-through of a nearby In-N-Out Burger, I do call Mindy, who lets out a little excited yelp for both of us when I tell her the good news.

Earl and I, exhausted from our late night of driving but too excited to relax, spend the rest of the day wandering around L.A. Normal people would be trying to see the sights, but instead we're trying to reconstruct the test in our heads to figure out exactly what our scores were. We finally decide that we each got somewhere between forty and forty-five out of fifty, which seems pretty good. In our one stab at tourism, we drive to Griffith Park because Earl wants to take some pictures, but the road up to the observatory is closed.

The next day, we're driving through the bleak Mojave again, our whirlwind tour completed—but this time we're both proud swimmers in the *Jeopardy!* contestant pool! We hold our heads high!

"So are you relieved you passed?" I ask Earl.

"Sure. Any dope could *not* pass that test. Your dog Banjo could. He might have a hard time turning the paper in, but he could sure fail it."

I know what he means. I'm fully prepared never to hear from *Jeopardy!* again, and to keep trying out every year until I'm the bitter "Nine times!" guy in the room. But it's still pretty cool to have passed the test once.

Back home, I try to tell as few people as possible about my trip. Still, I have to have the annoying "So when will we see you on the show?" conversation about twenty times. For a few months, whenever a long-distance number shows up in the caller ID on my phone, I wonder if it might be *Jeopardy!* But it never is. Nearly a year goes by, and our son, Dylan, sits up, then crawls, then talks, and then walks. I soon forget about *Jeopardy!* completely.

ANSWERS

1. **Quiche** is "a custard pie often made with cheese and bacon."

2. A **quahog** is "a large edible clam of the Atlantic coast."

3. Archibald Leach, Bernard Schwartz, and Lucille LeSueur are **the real names of Cary Grant, Tony Curtis, and Joan Crawford,** respectively.

4. The **sartorius,** located in the thigh, is the longest muscle in the human body.

5. *Staccato* is the musical term that's Italian for "detached."

6. Oregon's **Crater Lake** is the deepest lake in the United States.

7. The **kidneys** are made up of nephrons.

8. Isaac's mother, **Sarah,** is the most mentioned woman in the Bible.

9. **Antonio Banderas** is Melanie Griffith's *esposo* (Spanish for "husband").

10. **Tim Robbins** played the pitcher in *Bull Durham.*

CHAPTER 3

What is ERUDITION?

Earl and I first met in 1996, at a tryout for the Brigham Young University quiz bowl team. We both made the team, and together we spent our last three years at BYU crisscrossing the country, playing at weekend quiz tournaments at colleges and universities coast to coast. Quiz bowl is a team question-and-answer game played by squads from hundreds of universities and thousands of high schools nationwide. The questions cover just about every academic subject imaginable, from Vasco da Gama to Greek drama, the Bill of Rights to trilobites.

For many years, long after I'd renounced trivia and all its works, college quiz bowl was a bridge back to the fact-filled world of my youth. Finally I had an outlet for my bottled-up backlog of trivia. Earl and I, along with two other friends, made a decent quiz bowl team—BYU would routinely finish in the top ten at national championship tournaments. But it's been a long time since graduation. It's been more than five years, in fact, since I last held a quiz bowl buzzer in my hand, and I'm rusty. I've come to the placid pioneer town of Northfield, Minnesota, located just south of the Twin Cities on the banks of the Cannon River, to find out just how rusty.

The Laurence McKinley Gould Library is the academic center of Carleton College, one of tiny Northfield's *two* college campuses. (Local legend has it that "Northfield, Minnesota" was once the answer to a Trivial Pursuit question: "What's America's only town with two colleges and only one bar?" There are now five bars.) Laurence McKinley Gould himself, the library's namesake and the onetime president of Carleton, was also the second-in-command on Admiral Byrd's historic 1928 journey to the South Pole, I learn as I peruse a large display case in the library lobby. The case contains some of Gould's Antarctic memorabilia, including a stuffed emperor penguin named Oscar.

In a small classroom in one corner of the library, eight students sit grouped around two tables, each student holding a signaling device that looks as though it was cobbled together from an old guitar pedal. The foot-pedals are connected by cables to a lighted mechanism built into an open briefcase sitting in the middle of the table. A rush of adrenaline tingles all the way down to the "buzzer thumb" on my right hand. I feel like a long-retired ballplayer walking back onto the outfield grass. It's good to be back.

The briefcase device isn't a bomb. It's a quiz bowl buzzer system, though that was a frequent point of contention between me and airport security screeners back when I used to travel with the BYU team. The Carleton team has buzzers in hand because it's Monday night, a practice night for them. They're getting ready to run drills with some quiz questions, or "play some packets," in quiz bowl parlance.

"We'll warm up with a high school packet, toss-ups only," a sleepy-eyed man with a graying blond beard is telling the team as he shuffles some papers. I recognize Eric Hillemann, Carleton's coach and, back in my playing days, one of the best quiz bowl players in the country. He means that these will be questions written for high school play, and should be easy pickings for college-level players. A "toss-up" is just a garden-variety quiz bowl question, served up to both teams.

"Question one. Anne of Cleves and Catherine Parr—" He's interrupted by a loud buzz from the briefcase. A player has hit his pedal before I've even realized a question is being read.

"Henry VIII."

"Correct."

Okay, that one wasn't so hard. Henry VIII's wives. But as the questions get more difficult, the pace doesn't let up.

"The number *e* is so named because—" Buzz. Leonhard Euler.

"Located below the optic chiasm—" Buzz. The pituitary gland.

"When he was thirteen, his brother Ally died—" Buzz. Holden Caulfield.

"It was created by Namco programmer Toru Iwatani—" Buzz. Pac-Man.

In quiz bowl, you can buzz in and interrupt the moderator as soon as you know the answer—you don't need to wait for the end of the question. The Carleton team is on fire: they aren't even letting Eric get to the predicate of the question's first sentence before they pounce. It's one of the great mysteries of quiz bowl, the summer-lightning flashes of intuition you need to master its video-game speed. Call it what you will—nervous reflex, anticipation, precognition, Spidey-sense—but the best players can somehow buzz with their thumbs before their brains have quite caught up. Knowing the right answer isn't nearly enough, just as it's not enough for a football player to memorize the drawn-up plays. You also have to be in the zone and *execute*.

Of course, an obscene amount of esoteric knowledge helps too. This isn't your father's trivia. Each quiz bowl question is a lengthy, convoluted series of clues, sometimes as many as five or six sentences long. These sentences are arranged "pyramidally," meaning that the clues are impossibly obscure at the beginning ("In 1770, this woman's mother was the housekeeper to a Swiss physician named Philippe Curtius, who gave her lessons on art and anatomy"), and gradually work down to comparatively simpler ones by the end of the question ("For ten points —name this woman who, in 1835, founded her namesake London wax museum").[1] Speed is therefore crucial—you need to buzz as soon as you have a glimmer of an idea. This is trivia on steroids.

Eric ups the level of difficulty by switching over to some college-level question packets, but the pace doesn't slacken.

"His name derives from an intestinal beetle—" Buzz. Shaka Zulu, the eighteenth-century African chieftain, turns out to be the unhappy fellow.

"Its seventh section, 'Rotation of Crops'—" produces another immediate buzz. *Either/Or,* by Danish existentialist Søren Kierkegaard, is correct.

This level of play is, to me, mind-boggling. Even the easiest possible question on Shaka Zulu or Kierkegaard would be among the ultra-tough $2,000 material on *Jeopardy!* But these prodigies don't just know who wrote *Either/Or.* They know the names of its *individual chapter titles.* They don't just know who Shaka Zulu was. They know about the complicated intersection of entomology and etymology that gave him his name.

Despite its tiny size, Carleton has, for much of the last decade, fielded one of the best college quiz bowl teams in the country, with thirty-one tournament wins during that time span. This is all the more remarkable when you consider that there are no four-year eligibility requirements in quiz bowl. Many of the country's best teams are anchored by rudderless twelfth-year grad students who seemingly have been playing quiz bowl since the Ford administration. Carleton College, on the other hand, is a four-year school with no graduate programs—they're babes in the woods compared to some of these dinosaurs. And yet they win. Tonight at practice, Patrick Hope, the team's best player, is doing curls with the oversized second place trophy that the team recently won in New Orleans at quiz bowl's most prestigious national event: the NAQT Intercollegiate Tournament.

Coach Eric Hillemann is the biggest reason for the team's surprising success. At the high school level, quiz bowl "coaches" are often just glorified chaperones or the necessary faculty signatures on an entry form. Most college teams don't even have one. After all, what would a coach do in a quiz game? At a high school quiz bowl tournament, I once saw a "coach" call a time-out during a close match, lean over to his team, and say, "Guys, answer more questions. Okay, time in." That's helpful.

But Eric is a genuine coach. Though not outwardly a hatchet-faced Tom Landry type, he works his team hard. To attend tournaments, they need to attend practice twice a week, write a certain quota of questions per month, memorize lists of facts, and "certify" their knowledge in merit-badge-style tests. He's prepared over eighty of these forty-question fact sheets, summarizing areas of core quiz bowl knowledge: one on Civil War battles, one on Nobel Prize–winning chemists, one on the gods of Norse mythology, and so on. He does all this in his spare time as Carleton's campus archivist—he's the one responsible for that stuffed penguin I saw in the library lobby.

At practice tonight, he's constantly offering nuggets of information about the breadth of quiz bowl "canon," accumulated during his two decades of playing the game. "Here's how you remember the difference between Ayacucho and Chacabuco," he counsels his team at one point. "Those are the two battles of South American independence you *have* to know." Minutes later, he's wrangling with Courtney Colby, the only

female player in the room, on exactly which ethical principles of Confu-
cianism were introduced by the philosopher Mencius.

Toward the end of practice, he even fishes a five-dollar bill out of
his pocket and puts it down on the buzzer system in front of him. "I
don't even need to read this toss-up, because you're not going to get it."
Sure enough, nobody knows the name of the record-setting castaway
who floated in the South Atlantic for 133 days during World War II.
Deep down I'm a little relieved that even these trivia superheroes get
stumped sometimes, but I'd feel a little better if I had known the answer
and could have buzzed in confidently with "Chinese seaman Poon
Lim!"

"It's a strange subculture," Eric admits, in his equable librarian's voice.
"The real world would be shocked at the kind of obscure material that
quiz bowl teams will groan at as an 'old chestnut.'" We're chatting over
pesto pizza in the only restaurant we can find still open in Northfield at
nine o'clock on a weeknight.

Eric's been playing quiz bowl since 1983, when he was introduced
to the game as a grad student at the University of Wisconsin. The game
itself goes back thirty years earlier, to 1953, when the show *College Bowl*
first debuted on NBC radio. From 1959 on, with General Electric on
board as a sponsor and future *Password* fixture Allen Ludden hosting, it
ran on network television as *G.E. College Bowl*, becoming the first game
show ever to win a Peabody award. The game's format was simple: four
heavily Brylcreemed white people with big ears would be dispatched
from some college campus—say, the University of North Dakota—to
take on their buttoned-down counterparts from Rensselaer Polytechnic
or some such place. Any of the eight players could buzz in to answer
each ten-point "toss-up," an academically oriented question testing "the
quick recall of specific fact," as they often said on the show. A correct
answer would earn that team a "bonus" question, typically a multipart
affair worth between twenty and forty points. Winners received schol-
arship grants and the chance to return on the next program.

College Bowl left the airwaves in 1970, and though quiz bowl has persevered for thirty-five years as a campus activity for trivia nerds, it has fallen a long way from its well-groomed, brightly lit TV heyday. The games today aren't played on national TV. They're not even on local TV. The first tournament I ever went to with the BYU team, we got lost and spent an hour wandering around the campus of Iowa State, unable to find anybody at the university who even knew the event was going on. Quiz bowl tournaments are poorly funded, loosely organized fly-by-night affairs, held in the basements of dingy humanities buildings in the dead of night. Unlike Allen Ludden's guests, I never earned a $3,000 scholarship for winning at quiz bowl; the biggest prize I ever won at a tournament was a slim book of public-domain Walt Whitman poetry. It probably would have cost about $1.50 in the campus bookstore.

The competition has fragmented as well. Not unlike boxing, with its alphabet soup of organizing bodies and belts, the quiz bowl world is today divided into partisans of CBCI, ACF, and NAQT. CBCI, the College Bowl Company, is the corporate descendant of the 1960s TV show, and is still run by Richard Reid, the son of *College Bowl* creator Don Reid. For thirty years, College Bowl was the only show in town, but in the 1980s, players in the Southeast began to organize a circuit of homegrown, non-CBCI events, targeting quiz teams who wanted to play more often than the two tournaments College Bowl offered every year.

Just like any die-hard sports fans, quiz bowlers like to nitpick endlessly about subtleties of Their Game, and when CBCI wouldn't make changes to keep up with the player-friendly tournaments on "the circuit," teams started to gripe. College Bowl's entry fees were too high, they said. Its tournaments were often staffed by volunteers who had little experience moderating quiz bowl, and who were often out of their depth when it came to tricky judgment calls or long words. Players were peeved when College Bowl claimed legal ownership of any quiz game with a toss-up/bonus format, and required students running similar events to pay licensing fees. Mostly, though, people just disliked the questions.

College Bowl's questions, players grumbled to one another at tournaments and on Internet newsgroups, lacked clues, gauged difficulty poorly, and weren't sufficiently academic. One much-derided bonus awarded a team twenty-five points for identifying, after a list of super-fluous clues, a "curved yellow fruit" (the banana, it turned out). Questions were occasionally reused from past events. Worst of all, the questions sometimes came with tricks built in to discourage the best players from buzzing too quickly. "The players on these teams are so good that 90 percent of the time they could interrupt the question and give the correct answer if the questions didn't take those kinds of turns," Richard Reid told a newspaper reporter in 1987. "That wouldn't be fun to watch, so every now and then as I design these suckers, I say to myself, 'Watch this!' and wait 'til we're on camera. I got a lot of dirty looks this last tournament."

"It would be like a football team going to compete and you'd have a field with potholes and glass and referees who wanted to fix the match, calling made-up fouls against the better teams just to make it more in-teresting," recalls Bay Area lawyer David Frazee, Michigan's quiz bowl captain at the time. He used to write College Bowl thirty-page letters after each tournament, listing all the problems he saw with their ques-tions. Eventually these jeremiads became so well known that some began to call problematic College Bowl material "Frazee Unfair Ques-tions," or FUQs.

In 1996, following Frazee's team's win at Penn Bowl, then the largest non-CBCI quiz bowl event, he and many of the game's other best play-ers gathered in Room 1006 of the Philadelphia Sheraton and produced the quiz bowl equivalent of a manifesto. They would start their own company and write the material that CBCI wasn't providing. Knowl-edge would be rewarded. Questions would be linear and full of as many interesting facts as possible—no "curved yellow fruit" here.

Months of tussling over format, rules, and question distribution (what percentage of the questions were to cover which subject areas) would follow, but that meeting was the birth of National Academic Quiz Tournaments, or NAQT. "It was almost like being at the Consti-tutional Convention," Frazee recalls, without a trace of irony. "The pu-rity of the debate, and the passion of it, were great."

The game's powerhouse teams, including reigning College Bowl champion Virginia, soon began to de-affiliate from CBCI, announcing that they would instead compete only at national tournaments run by

NAQT or ACF—the Academic Competition Federation, another anti–College Bowl upstart. "Quiz bowl" became the new, genericized name for the game that players had once called "College Bowl," apparently the trivia equivalent of saying "photocopy" instead of "Xerox" or "plastic adhesive bandages" instead of "Band-Aids."

Today the three formats—CBCI, NAQT, and ACF—coexist fairly harmoniously, since College Bowl's legal threats toward copycats proved groundless. Though vociferous proponents still argue the superiority of their chosen format on the Internet, the point is really moot: each group fulfills a different niche. CBCI continues to run annual tournaments for the layperson, full of nonacademic questions on pop culture, current events, and general knowledge, aimed at players who pick up a quiz bowl buzzer only once a year. ACF, which uses an untimed format and relies on competing teams to submit their own questions to each tournament, has seen an "arms race" of increasing length and difficulty in its questions, making its material so abstruse that only seventeen schools sent teams to ACF's most recent national tournament. NAQT has tried to carve out a middle ground—more common-knowledge stuff than ACF, a fast-paced format, but with questions still fundamentally designed to reward expert knowledge. There's a fourth acronym to know as well: TRASH, or Testing Recall About Strange Happenings, is a group that holds quiz-bowl-style tournaments where all the questions concern movies, TV, pop music, and sports, instead of academic subjects. The acronym is a wink at long-ago complaints from ACF partisans that questions with pop-cultural elements were "too trashy."

The best way to understand the differences between these organizations is to look at sample questions from their events. Let's take the case of Chester Alan Arthur, the twenty-first president of the United States. Unless you're a particular fan of dead mutton-chopped Republicans, you probably don't know too much about the life and administration of Chester A. Arthur. Even in the rarefied intellectual air of *Jeopardy!*, they're not going to expect you to know too much about good ol' Chester, except maybe that he succeeded to the presidency after the assassination of fellow historical footnote James A. Garfield. Quiz bowl, of course, goes into quite a bit more depth. Here's a College Bowl question about President Arthur, from their 2002 intramural set:

> He's no longer remembered for the most lasting legacy of his presidency—calling the international conference that set the prime meridian, international date line, and twenty-four time zones around the world. For ten points—who called that Washington, D.C., conference in 1884?

This "toss-up" is actually a bit harder than many CBCI questions, but it has one essential thing in common with them: it really only consists of a single clue (and, eventually, a date). If you don't know which president was nuts about time zones, there's not much else to go on. This clue could easily be rephrased as a Trivial Pursuit question ("Which U.S. president called the conference that created the world's time zones in 1884?"), but quiz bowl diehards would say it makes for a bad quiz bowl question. Since all quiz bowl players worth their salt will know their presidential dates cold, all eight players in the room will probably be buzzing at exactly the same time, the second the moderator says "1884." The question rewards solely speed, not skill.

Here's NAQT's take on Chester A. Arthur, from a 2002 invitational tournament. We'll call this one *Arthur 2: On the Rocks*.

> Though he suffered from Bright's disease, he allowed himself to be considered for his party's nomination, but he lost to James G. (*) Blaine. Once known as a Stalwart, he declared his independence by signing the popular Pendleton Act. For ten points—name this New York politician who acceded to the presidency upon the 1881 assassination of James Garfield.

It's slightly longer than the CBCI question, but I count seven separate clues, so it's much more helpful than College Bowl's two-clues-and-a-cloud-of-dust version. It rewards incredibly esoteric knowledge at the beginning—"Bright's disease" is probably the Chester A. Arthur equivalent of knowing that Shaka Zulu was named for a beetle—but throws a bone to the rookie player at the end with the Garfield clue. The little asterisk is an NAQT innovation called a "power mark." Players who buzz and answer correctly before the asterisk (in this case, before the word "Blaine") will get an extra five points for their troubles.

It's actually hard to find an ACF question about somebody as elementary and *obvious* as Chester A. Arthur. Paging through the material used in the most recent ACF championship, I see question after question on things I've never even heard of: the Hampson-Linde refrigeration cycle, ex-presidents of Zambia, minor works of philosopher David Hume. I finally find this Chester Arthur question in a 2004 ACF regional tournament:

> Along with his secretary of the navy, William Chandler, he recommended appropriations to improve the U.S. fleet, and it was during his presidency that the coaling station at Pearl Harbor was acquired. He won the Lizzie Jennings case resulting in New York's forbidding segregation on public transport. This onetime director of the New York City Customhouse vetoed a bill excluding Chinese immigration for twenty years, but signed the Chinese Exclusion Act that banned them for ten years. Expected to be a defender of the Stalwarts, for ten points, name this president who disappointed Conkling by signing the Pendleton Civil Service Act after the assassination of his predecessor, James Garfield.

This 109-word Bataan Death March of a question is obviously not the kind of thing that a moderator can get through on one breath. Alex Trebek himself would probably have to stop for tea and scones and maybe a little nap somewhere in the middle. In fact, it reads more like a desk encyclopedia entry than a trivia question. And this is a *short* tossup by current ACF standards!

Finally, TRASH would never include a question about Chester A. Arthur. Instead, the question would be about Bea Arthur.

It's a fundamental tension in quiz bowl: Do you ask questions only about things that might actually come up in real life? If so, you run the risk of annoying longtime players, for whom "real life" is much too small a canvas. They will roll their eyes at the same old Chester A. Arthur clue for the hundredth time, and demand ever-more exotic delicacies of knowledge. But if you acquiesce, and start asking questions about the legendary first human of Madagascar mythology (Adriambahomanana, as players learned at the most recent ACF nationals), you confuse the hell out of beginners.

You also make quiz bowl a strange, hermetic pursuit, where players can quite competently answer questions on books they've never read, paintings they've never seen, and science they've never studied, merely because they've heard similar questions before. "Did they say 'Slavonic Dances'? Oh, that's always Dvořák. Say 'Dvořák.'" Dvořák himself, despite being a brilliant composer, might as well not exist outside a quiz bowl room. He's just an element you need to remember for a successful game, like a chess opening or a Scrabble word with lots of *Q*s and *Z*s.

"Have you ever read *The Last of the Wine*?" Rob Hentzel asked me the day before my trip to Carleton. Rob is the president of NAQT, and he spends upward of two thousand five hundred hours a year, barely compensated, writing quiz bowl questions and organizing tournaments. We'd been sitting in the living room of the Minneapolis home he shares with his wife, Emily, once the star of the Carleton quiz bowl team herself. In fact, Eric Hillemann was the "clergyman" who married Rob and Emily the year before, having purchased his clerical credentials online for five dollars. Between us, above the fireplace, was a framed parchment map whose contours I didn't recognize, until Rob explained that it was a map of the world in which he sets his ongoing Dungeons & Dragons campaign.

I admitted that I'd never read *The Last of the Wine*, though I remember—from quiz bowl, of course!—that it's a Greek historical novel by South African author Mary Renault.

"There's a point in there where the characters attend the Olympic Games, or maybe the Isthmian Games. I don't remember. But they're commenting on how the people who are winning the running titles now are just all legs. They have no upper body strength. They're not soldiers. All they have are these huge legs, so they can run really fast. And they're like, 'This is making a mockery of the Olympics! This is not what it's about!' It's supposed to be about well-formed, well-rounded citizen-soldiers who *happen* to be fast.

"I think the same thing about quiz bowl. It's supposed to be about well-formed, well-rounded citizens who happen to know a great deal about our cultural and intellectual history. And it has become, at its highest level, about people who verse themselves in the canon of things that happen to come up only in games, even if they're things that never come up in common conversation."

This isn't entirely true, of course. Talk to just about any veteran quiz bowler, and they'll volunteer how deeply their lives were changed by the cultural literacy that the game, almost despite itself, nurtures in its players. Rob himself was first persuaded to read a now-favorite novelist, Jane Austen, by the constant references to her works in quiz bowl packets. Subash Maddipoti, the University of Chicago phenom whose eleven toss-ups per game in the 2003 NAQT championship are considered the Wilt Chamberlain hundred-point game of the quiz bowl world, told me he discovered his passion for Renaissance art through quiz bowl. Craig Barker, the former University of Michigan quiz bowler and *Jeopardy!* college champ, uses historical anecdotes from quiz bowl to freshen up the AP History high school classes he teaches in his hometown of Livonia, Michigan.

Eric was a rock-and-roll fan who got turned on to Beethoven sonatas by quiz bowl questions on classical music. "My music collection is half-classical now," he says. But more to the point, it just pleases him to be at least vaguely knowledgeable about every aspect of the world around him. "I don't like to hear something and have no idea what it's about," he says. "I love getting all the references on *Gilmore Girls.*"

He also believes that the framework of knowledge he learned from quiz bowl has helped him to learn all kinds of other things more easily. "It's like your mind is a net, trying to catch all this information whizzing by. The more facts you know, the tighter the mesh of the net is, and the easier it is to retain the new things you're trying to learn." This rings true to me. I know from my experience with *How to Get on Jeopardy! . . . and Win!* that it's hard to sit down and memorize a list of facts about, for example, opera if, like me, you go in knowing absolutely nothing about opera. But if you already know a few little bits of opera trivia (Pavarotti, the William Tell Overture, "Kill the wabbit," etc.), the new information has something to cling to, barnacle-like, in your synapses.

Quiz bowl knowledge has proved profitable to its players in another arena as well: television game shows. You'll rarely hear it acknowledged on *Jeopardy!* or *Who Wants to Be a Millionaire,* but many of the elite winners on those shows got their trivia training in high school and college quiz bowl. One of the things that reignited my childhood dream of appearing on *Jeopardy!* was turning on the TV nearly every week and seeing a quiz bowl acquaintance of mine on a game show, whether answering in the form of a question, wanting to be a millionaire, or winning Ben Stein's money.

Eric Hillemann has been enlisted as a *Millionare* Phone-a-Friend lifeline by five fellow quiz bowlers, including Kevin Olmstead, the University of Michigan quiz bowl adviser who won a record $2.18 million jackpot on *Who Wants to Be a Millionaire* in April 2001. If not for Eric, Kevin might not have known, on his $250,000 question, who coauthored the book *Let Us Now Praise Famous Men* with Walker Evans.[2] I remember the sudden splash of realization I had as I sat at home watching Kevin's *Millionaire* triumph: the fifteen questions he had to answer may have seemed hard to the viewers at home, but it was all canonical quiz bowl knowledge. The capital of Nova Scotia,[3] the circumference of the Earth,[4] the inventor of the helicopter[5]—all things Kevin would have heard over and over in quiz bowl contests. I'm sure I wasn't the only quiz bowl player who started calling the *Millionaire* tryout phone line and looking up *Jeopardy!* contestant search schedules the day after Kevin Olmstead became a multimillionaire.

That knowledge overlap explains why quiz bowl has become a de facto farm club for the big-time game shows. After answering questions about quantum mechanics and Madagascan creation myths, the seemingly formidable *Jeopardy!* and *Millionaire* trivia look simple by comparison. When I took the written test at my *Jeopardy!* audition, I remember thinking how much more arcane and elaborate a quiz bowl question on each of the fifty covered subjects would have been. I felt like a runner who'd been training in high-altitude Mexico City, just to get his lungs in such superpowered shape that events at lower elevations seemed like a piece of cake.

Since quiz bowl is an activity designed solely so its participants can show off how smart they are, it was probably inevitable that it would attract its share of quirky or overbearing personalities. Some are obsessively competitive. To prepare for the national quiz bowl tournaments in 2003, Subash Maddipoti sat down and wrote eight thousand five hundred "lead-ins," or hypothetical beginnings to quiz bowl questions, so he could recognize them when they came up in game situations. It took him months. "It's an almost masochistic kind of pursuit," he says, "doing it until the point where it hurts."

Many are less than humble about their mental accomplishments. Call it Mensa syndrome. Subash calls his Chicago teammate, Andrew Yaphe, "the smartest person I've ever met in my life. Also the most egotistical person I've ever met in my life." Andrew is widely regarded as the single most talented quiz bowler ever to play the game, having won the last four ACF championships he played in, from 1997 to 2000. He's also a self-described "recluse" who, most days, does nothing but read books and write quiz bowl questions. The day I talk to him, I interrupt him in the middle of both the eleventh-century Japanese classic *The Pillow Book* and Prescott's *History of the Conquest of Mexico*. You know, a little light reading.

When I ask him if quiz bowl has helped him in other areas of his life, he seems amused by the notion that there could even *be* other areas of his life. "I don't know how it would affect my 'life.' There's not so many other things I do where it could possibly have a bearing." And he agrees with Subash's assessment of his ego: "I concede the point. I'm arrogant about questions I write. I'm arrogant about my relationship with people in the game. But I also feel like what I say is backed up by the things I've done."

Andrew is not alone: many, perhaps most, quiz bowl players have egos to match their trivia prowess. Hollywood may have persuaded you that nerds are mild-mannered, introverted milquetoasts, but that couldn't be further from the truth. In my experience, trivia geeks of all kinds are barely repressed *extroverts*, eager for any opportunity to dazzle you with their expertise. It could be the geek at the comic book shop holding forth on the properties of different colors of kryptonite, or the sports radio caller who has a theory on how the Padres are a *lock* this year, or the movie nut who wants to run down his personal top five favorite Tarantino lines with you. Quiz bowl players are no different: they want you to know how much they know. Gentle, witty self-deprecation is about as rare at these tournaments as a steady girlfriend, and straightforward discussion of one's own past miraculous feats and exploits is de rigueur. If a quiz bowl player volunteers to tell you the story of his "best buzz" ever, it's not going to involve a few bottles of Smirnoff Ice and a band that was, like, really jammin'. It's going to be about the time his team was down thirty points on the last question, and he "buzzed in" and answered "mitochondria" after just two or three words, and single-handedly converted the entire bonus question to win the game!

"You have two hundred people sitting in a room, and they're all used to being right," is how Craig Barker explains the endemic quiz bowl culture of braggadocio and one-upmanship. But there's still something endearing about it all, the personal highlight reel of someone who never made it onto one of his school's athletic teams but now has an outlet for his inner gritty competitor. And some of the "best buzz" stories *are* pretty great. At a Stanford tournament, I once answered a question after hearing only the first two words: "Twisted Kites—" (the answer is the rock band who first played together under that name in 1980).[6] But that's not even worth mentioning in these circles. Rob Hentzel is famous for his correct guess of "the Crimean War" after hearing only the first three words of the question: "Its pretext was—" in an Iowa State practice. His teammate Tim Carter once correctly answered a question after hearing only one word: "Hydrologically." (The answer: "Lake Michigan and Lake Huron," which, hydrologically speaking, are actually a single lake.)

Most famous of all is Emory University's legendary Tom Waters, quiz bowl's most dominant player for two decades, from the midseventies up until the midnineties. At the start of a 1979 College Bowl match, Tom told his coach that Emory's only hope of beating a quick Rice University team was to buzz dangerously aggressively on every question. On the very first question of the round, he was as good as his word, buzzing on the very first word the surprised moderator managed to get out: "Extremism." Tom's correct guess: Barry Goldwater, who famously said, "Extremism in the defense of liberty is no vice." Emory went on to defeat a shocked Rice team by over one hundred points.

Quiz bowl does have its peculiar personalities, but perhaps extremism in the defense of trivia glory is no vice either.

A month after my visit to Northfield, I'm back in the Midwest again. This year, NAQT's high school tournament is being held at an airport hotel outside Chicago, and I'm here to help moderate. This is only the second quiz bowl tournament I've attended since graduating from college five years ago. Even before we get to the hotel, I can tell I'm in the right place. Sitting behind me on the shuttle bus from O'Hare are four gangly teenagers, three with thin caterpillars of fuzz on their upper lips. "It seems like all the good fantasy authors are Australian nowadays," one is saying to his compatriots. A quiz bowl team, all right.

As we pull up to the hotel, another strikingly similar quartet is playing Frisbee out front, one wearing oversized 1980s headphones connected to his CD player. He makes an awkward dash for the Frisbee, but it goes sailing over his head and lands under the tires of the shuttle bus as we pull into the hotel driveway. "Wow, and I thought *we* were geeks," muses the Australian fantasy fan.

The hotel, as it turns out, is wall-to-wall with quiz bowl. Ninety-six teams are playing in this tournament, the largest NAQT event ever. That means forty-eight game rooms will be needed for the opening day of the competition, and so NAQT has taken over almost every conference room in the hotel, *and* converted an entire floor of guest rooms into game rooms by removing all the beds. As it happens, the hotel is also hosting some kind of national church conference the same weekend. Everyone who isn't a teenage geek in a "Gryffindor" T-shirt is a sweet old African American church lady in an elaborate hat.

Over the next two days, I moderate nineteen rounds of hot quiz bowl action. I am, somehow, even more intimidated than I was at Carleton. It's even more discouraging when high school kids, not college students, know all about things you've never heard of and can effortlessly rattle off, in warbly midpubescent voices, answers like "Nagorno-Karabash" and "Basil Bulgaroctonus" and "giberellic acids."

Everyone knows the team to beat is the fearsome foursome from Thomas Jefferson High, a science-and-technology magnet school in Alexandria, Virginia. In fact, there's a general feeling that it's going to take Tonya Harding–style shenanigans to get "TJ," as they're called, to lose even a single round. They've won NAQT's high school tournament each of the last two years, and have a thirty-seven-game winning streak going.

A year ago, they signed up for Buzzerfest, Princeton's annual university-level quiz bowl tournament, a first for a high school team. "The reason we did that was basically to get our hats handed to us if possible," says TJ cocaptain Sam Lederer. "There's a big danger, if you go undefeated all year, of thinking you're undefeatable. We wanted to make sure we didn't fall into that trap." Things didn't go quite as expected. Despite not fielding all their starters, TJ took second place in the tournament, their only two losses coming at the hands of the University of Maryland, one of the country's best college teams. Imagine a high school basketball team somehow being allowed to play in the NCAA tournament . . . and making the finals. "TJ was definitely legit," one shocked tournament organizer posted to an Internet message board the next day.

In every match I moderate for them that weekend, Thomas Jefferson doesn't disappoint. These high schoolers instantly recall facts I don't even remember learning in college. Joseph Banks was the longest-serving president of the Royal Society. Pepin the Short brought an army to Italy in 754 to fight the Lombards. Iodine is a purple solid at room temperature. While other teams win games with score totals around 280 points, TJ wins every game *by* at least 280 points. In one of their final play-off rounds, they spank Walton High of Marietta, Georgia—a top ten team nationally, mind you—885 to 95.

Even more remarkably, they're doing this on almost no sleep. TJ took a red-eye flight into Chicago in the wee hours of the morning. Their senior prom was the night before, and even the quiz bowl team— "grade-A nerds, nerds among nerds," admits Sam Lederer—wanted to go to prom. They seem like normal, unassuming guys, with refreshingly underinflated egos. Many quiz bowl players are obsessed with their individual statistics, but the TJ team adopts nicknames like Goose, Maverick, and Iceman (the pilots in *Top Gun,* a movie made before anyone on the team was even born) and rotates nicknames every match, so that individual statistics flatten out and become meaningless. It's a classy move.

In the tournament's final match, TJ squares off against Lakeside, a small Seattle prep school. Tournament handicappers are shocked. This year marks Lakeside's very first season of NAQT competition, and yet they've managed to finish the tournament undefeated—apart, that is, from two losses at the hands of Thomas Jefferson, a distinction they share, by the way, with nineteenth-century presidential runner-up Charles Pinckney. Lakeside, though, has no shortage of nerd cred in its history. Alumni Bill Gates and Paul Allen did their very first computer programming at Lakeside in the late 1970s, when they wrote a tic-tac-toe game on the school's minicomputer. And—holy trivia icon, Batman!—actor Adam West is a Lakeside graduate as well.

The final match takes place on a raised dais in the hotel's largest banquet room, with the tournament's other four hundred players and coaches, now eliminated from contention, looking on. The cavernous room is lit only by a brilliantly illuminated white oval hanging overhead, throwing a harsh glare and dramatic shadows on the faces of the eight competitors. The overall effect is straight out of the war room in *Dr. Strangelove*, lending the contest a strange, weighty air of geopolitical tension.

Everyone is expecting this match to be about as one-sided as the Anglo-Zanzibar War of 1896, history's shortest conflict. (Forty-five minutes. Hint: Zanzibar lost.) After all, when these two teams first met in the play-offs, TJ ran away in a 760–30 blowout, in which Lakeside managed to answer only a single question. But the rematch doesn't start out that way at all. This time, when TJ buzzes in uncannily early, it's *too* early— they're overeager and overconfident. They're making rookie mistakes. A wrong answer in quiz bowl is extraordinarily costly. It's not just the five points you lose, it's the missed chance at forty more points—ten for getting the toss-up correct, and a possible thirty points on the bonus. So TJ is understandably flustered when they "neg"—answer incorrectly—on three of the first six questions. The swamp whose name means "trembling earth" in Seminole is *not* the Everglades.[7] The twentieth-century Democrat who won only Massachusetts in his failed presidential bid was *not* Michael Dukakis.[8]

"Time out!" calls Sam Lederer, who is captaining, after the sixth toss-up. His theoretically unbeatable team is down 145–0, and the room is buzzing. "Stop negging," he whispers to his team. "That's all there is."

But TJ manages four more incorrect responses before the half. Confidence was the hair on this Samson, and their confidence is now badly shaken. On a question requiring teams to convert Roman numerals into binary notation, they forget to do the binary part of the math and give a decimal answer. "*Tosca*, that's wrong," answers a demoralized Jacob Oppenheim at one point, realizing too late that he's buzzed too soon on an opera question to which the answer turns out to be *La Bohème*. Each wrong answer is a gift-wrapped package for Lakeside, who has the chance to hear the question all the way to the end and gets a free guess at it, essentially a quiz bowl penalty kick. They don't always take advantage, muffing the *La Bohème* question and one on the name of the man who sculpted Mount Rushmore,[9] but they still lead 225–65 at the half.

Thomas Jefferson chips away at the lead throughout the second half. With just minutes to play, they answer three questions in a row (on Quakers, the Fourteenth Amendment, and *The Simpsons* villain Hank Scorpio) and are perfect on all three bonus questions, giving them their first lead, at 300–275. Lakeside calls their last time-out to regroup, and beats TJ to the next two questions, on electromagnetic induction and John Dean. With two questions remaining, the game couldn't be closer: 330–325. The room sits in rapt silence.

Thomas Jefferson beats Lakeside to the penultimate question, about the League of Nations, and then to the final question, about the measurement "pH." More important, they ace both bonuses, each one about a classic of Western culture: Shakespeare's *The Winter's Tale*, and the *Rocky* trilogy (though they nearly slip and call Clubber Lang, Mr. T's *Rocky III* character, Buster Lang). After a sloppy opening, they've played the last eleven questions of the game without a single incorrect answer, and converted an astounding 90 percent of their bonus points overall. It's their thirty-eighth straight NAQT match victory and third championship in a row. The crowd offers TJ a rousing ovation as they trade handshakes with Lakeside.

Perhaps quiz bowl will never again be a nationally popular spectator sport the way it was during the 1960s golden age of *G.E. College Bowl*. Certainly it's hard to play along at home with a game where the questions can be interrupted after the moderator has only read a few syllables, or where you need to understand words like "eutrophication" or "adiabatic" to even get the gist of a question. More to the point, *Jeopardy!* aside, does America even want to watch people be smart anymore? We'd rather laugh at the airheaded pedestrian telling Jay Leno that he thinks the U.S. national anthem is "American Woman." Watching some Poindexter pick out the finer points of Cavalier poetry or matrix algebra in prime time is just going to make us feel that much dumber by comparison, if it doesn't put us to sleep first.

Still, I was on the edge of my seat during Thomas Jefferson's championship comeback. Even when players answered before I understood the question, I was caught up in the horse race of it. "People have no problem watching a professional football game knowing they will never in their life ever catch a touchdown," argues David Frazee, who's still waging a lonely war to return quiz bowl to its former televised glory. "Why should that stop them from watching people answer quiz bowl questions they themselves could never answer?"

But even if quiz bowl never again finds an outside audience, it will always fill an aching void in the lives of its own tight-knit community. For many players, it's their safest haven in a world that always picked them last in softball and doesn't get their clever jokes about Linus Pauling or Piet Mondrian. Here their strange mutant power for trivia is not only accepted but valued. "It was just nice knowing, especially early on, that this was a place that I could go and be smart and not have people look down on me for it or get annoyed with me for it," says Craig Barker. It's a sentiment I've heard from many top quiz players in the past. I've often felt that way myself.

The next day, I'm back at O'Hare to catch my flight home. I pass a plaque honoring Edward "Butch" O'Hare, the navy pilot for whom Orchard Field was renamed in 1949 (hence O'Hare's cryptic three-letter code, ORD). O'Hare was shot down over the Pacific in 1943, the plaque tells me.

Suddenly I'm thinking like a quiz bowler. An airport named for someone who died in a plane crash? That would make a great quiz bowl question. It happens to me at least once a day, even now. You see or hear something new and you file it away under *T* for toss-up, solely because *that would make a great question*. "Everything's going to be worth ten points someday," Eric Hillemann tells his team.

Sometimes you see two related facts, and you start looking for a third, since quiz bowl bonus questions are typically three parts long. Are there two other airports named for plane crash victims? I think of one more immediately: Lyon Aiport in France was recently renamed for Antoine de Saint-Exupéry, author of *The Little Prince*. The third part to my imaginary bonus proves elusive—John Denver International? Amelia Earhart Airport? Rocky Marciano Field? My flight is already boarding when I finally remember the man for whom Oklahoma City's airport is named.[10] My quiz bowl compulsion momentarily sated, I walk happily down the jetway, headed for home.

ANSWERS

1. **Madame Tussaud** founded her namesake wax museum in London in 1835.

2. **James Agee** coauthored *Let Us Now Praise Famous Men* with Walker Evans.

3. **Halifax** is the capital of Nova Scotia.

4. The Earth is **24,900 miles** around at the equator.

5. **Igor Sikorsky** invented the helicopter.

6. **R.E.M.** used the name "Twisted Kites" at their first show, an April 1980 birthday party.

7. **The Okefenokee** is the swamp whose name means "trembling earth" in Seminole.

8. **George McGovern** won only Massachusetts in his failed presidential bid.

9. **Gutzon Borglum** sculpted Mount Rushmore.

10. Oklahoma City's airport is named for **Will Rogers.**

CHAPTER 4

What is AMMUNITION?

The phone on my desk at work rings, an unwelcome interruption. I'm a highly paid software engineer! How am I supposed to surf the Web and write e-mail all day if the phone keeps ringing? The last thing I expect to hear is: "Ken? Bob from *Jeopardy!* I just want to make sure our file on you is up-to-date." Bob proceeds to confirm with me that, in the eight months since my tryout, I haven't appeared on another game show, run for public office, purchased a professional sports team, overthrown any Central American governments, publicly joined the Church of Satan, and so on. I dutifully answer no to each question.

"In that case, we'd like you to come out and be a contestant. Our next tapings are February twenty-fourth and twenty-fifth." My eyes dart to my desk calendar. That's less than a month away! Why am I wasting my time reading blogs at work when I could be home reading the *Britannica*?

Bob rattles through some basic contestant information—where to stay, when to show up, what not to wear—all of which I scribble down without hearing a word. "And you know about our recent rule change, right?"

What rule change? Never mind the *Britannica*—why haven't I been taping *Jeopardy!* for the last eight months?

"We got rid of the five-day limit for returning champions. Now you can keep playing until you lose."

Yeah, like that's going to matter to me.

In *How to Get on Jeopardy! . . . and Win!*, Michael Dupée describes his demanding *Jeopardy!* training regimen. He spent hours every day studying newspapers and reference books. Instead of sinking into his couch every evening to watch the show, he taped each episode and watched it alertly, with his VCR remote in hand. After each clue, he'd hit the pause button to "ring in," pretend he was giving his answer and choosing the next category, and then unpause the tape. He even kept a scorecard of his right and wrong answers so that he could analyze his weaknesses. It's like a *Rocky* training montage, but with almanacs instead of boxing gloves! Perhaps he also watched the show with a cantankerous Irish "corner man" holding a "spit bucket," who rubbed him down and patched him up between rounds.

Up until now, when I read about Mike's *Jeopardy!* preparation, it always struck me as a trifle overzealous, or, to put it another way, "bat-shit insane." Scorecards and remote controls? Are you kidding me? But actually getting The Call myself has reduced me to a quivering blob of nerd Jell-O. I have only twenty-seven days before my long-repressed trivia savvy is going to be paraded before a national audience. I'm desperate enough to try anything.

"Where's Dylan's ring-stack toy?" I ask Mindy that night after dinner.

"What?" She's spoon-feeding applesauce to Dylan, or at least in his general direction. Somehow most of it is ending up in his hair.

"You remember that ring-stacking toy? It's yellow and you put rainbow-colored plastic doughnuts on it for some reason?"

"I'm familiar with the concept of Dylan's ring-stacking toy. I meant, what do you want it for?"

"Well, I'm going to start videotaping as much *Jeopardy!* as I can." In fact, I've discovered that I can tape *Jeopardy!* twelve times a week: five new shows, five syndicated reruns, and two older shows from the Game Show Network. I choose not to mention this part. "And I think I want to start watching the show standing up."

"Standing up?"

"Behind the recliner. It looks about the same height as the contestant podiums. To prepare me for the show."

"And the toy?"

"Looks like it's about the same size as the buzzer the contestants hold. I want to try different ways of holding it, and get used to pressing the button at the right time."

Mindy scrapes the last applesauce dregs from the jar. "Most of his old toys are in the spare bedroom." I wait for the look I deserve: the scowl, or at least the flicker of dawning so-this-is-how-it's-going-to-be-is-it? But she says only, "Are you going to start watching *Jeopardy!* right now?"

"Yes?" It comes out with a strange rising inflection, and I realize the implied question must be something like, "Are you okay with me turning into a total freak for the next four weeks?"

She tosses the empty jar into the trash. "Well, do you need me to come down with you and keep score?"

She's elbow-deep in applesauce, but I have my corner man.

I've been a future *Jeopardy!* contestant for less than a week when I get an e-mail that threatens to derail the whole thing. Matt Bruce is an old quiz bowl acquaintance of mine who now works for a Bay Area digital entertainment company. His trivia résumé includes winning a national quiz bowl championship while he was at Harvard. More recently, we've both been editing quiz questions for NAQT. His e-mail nonchalantly asks that I wish him luck, as he's headed to L.A. the following month to be a *Jeopardy!* contestant. We've drawn the very same taping day.

I already knew that the quiz bowl scene was fertile ground for game show aspirants, but I never expected this. Matt won a national championship with one of the best quiz bowl teams in the country. Given the choice of opponents between a veteran quiz bowl player like him and some unknown quantity of a player, I'd choose the devil I *don't* know every time. When I tell Matt that we're scheduled to tape the same day, his edgy e-mail response suggests he feels the same way about the co-incidence.

But I may have an out. Because of the scandals of the 1950s, quiz shows are so gun-shy about the possibility of cheating or collusion that they enforce all kinds of draconian measures on the contestants. Among these measures is a clause, in the contract Bob mailed me, requiring me to notify the show before playing against anyone I know.

When I call him back, Bob seems unsurprised by the coincidence, and just says he'll pass the question along to his boss. I wonder if quiz bowl and *Jeopardy!* are a small enough pond that this exact kind of collision has happened before. Within twenty-four hours, Matt gets a call pushing his *Jeopardy!* appearance back a week; we won't have to play each other. We both breathe easy.

Mindy turns out to be a born *Jeopardy!* coach, especially when we start in on the flash cards. I've been spending an hour a day watching *Jeopardy!*, standing behind my recliner spastically hammering the Fisher-Price logo on Dylan's toy. It's the stupidest I've ever felt in my entire life, if you don't count all four years of high school. But it's taught me a valuable lesson: *Jeopardy!*, like *Lucy* or *Bewitched*, recycles material.

"Every single show there's a question about world capitals or U.S. presidents or Shakespeare," I tell Mindy one night after *Jeopardy!* as she tallies my score. "I need to have those subjects down cold."

"You got fifty-two questions right that game, including Final Jeopardy," says Mindy.

"Really? Fifty-two? That's pretty good."

"Well, I gave you credit for the time you said 'James Earl Jones' instead of 'James Earl Ray.'"

"Oh, yeah. They totally would have taken that. . . . Listen, I feel good about the Shakespeare, but we should make flash cards on presidents and world capitals."

The only index cards I can find in my desk are bright pink, so the house is soon an inch deep in drifts of little pink squares. It looks like the Washington Mall the day after the cherry-blossom tourists have all left. Each square bears a likely *Jeopardy!* fact in neat block letters. By the end of the week, I have dozens of sets. World leaders paired with their countries. Colleges paired with their mascots and cities. Constitutional amendments paired with their numbers. Oh, and cocktails. *Jeopardy!* loves its "Potent Potables" category, where boozehound contestants finally get a chance to shine, but I'm a Mormon, and therefore a teetotaler. In my whole life, the closest I've come to having a drink was the bitter sip of "near beer" that Dad gave us as an object lesson once when I was about six. I don't remember too many *Jeopardy!* questions on nonalcoholic beer.

For the next month, every spare minute, in the car, around the dinner table, lying in bed, Mindy grills me with the flash cards.

"Gimlet," she'll say.

"Gin and lime juice."

"Benjamin Harrison."

"1889 to 1893."

Conversation around the house these days is pretty terse. It's like *Dragnet*, if both the cops were really into fruity cocktails and James K. Polk.

"Benjamin Harrison's First Lady?"

"Caroline."

"His vice president?"

I draw a blank. "William Wheeler?"

"No, Levi P. Morton. Millard Fillmore."

"1850 to 1853."

"Harvey Wallbanger."

"1833 to 1836."

"Very funny. It's a cocktail, not a president."

"Vodka and orange juice. No, wait. That's a screwdriver. Galliano! It has Galliano too."

Like a quiz bowl player who's never read all the novels he can answer questions about, I don't have the faintest idea who or what "Galliano" is. It's just an answer on a card. In fact, I don't really know what *any* of these drink ingredients taste like, unless it's a fruit juice or powdered sugar, but I'm getting pretty proficient at mixing them. If this whole *Jeopardy!* gig goes south, I can always tend bar somewhere.

Deep down I suspect that this may be an exercise in futility. Most *Jeopardy!* players last only one show, which means I'll probably only be hearing sixty-one clues, max. What are the odds that, in a universe of millions of facts, some pink factoid from our flash cards—the name of the Georgia Tech sports team,[1] the queen of the Netherlands,[2] the only Ivy League school in Rhode Island[3]—will come up in my game? Slim to none. But at least it gives me the comforting illusion that I'm as well prepared as possible. I don't think I could stand doing nothing. So we shuffle and drill, over and over, for weeks. I'm completely sick of it, and I'm the one who came up with the idea. I can only imagine how Mindy feels. She'd probably like a good stiff Harvey Wallbanger right about now.

———

This regimen is trivia in its most concentrated, unsweetened form: the idea that somehow it's fun to ask and answer general-knowledge questions about the world. Ideally there's something rewardingly clever or noteworthy about either the question or the answer, but in its barest form, trivia is just a pink square flash card. "Land of Enchantment?" New Mexico. "Thirtieth president?" Calvin Coolidge.

It seems self-evident that it's fun to try to remember general-knowledge facts. You might think that trivia would have existed since the dawn of time. Maybe cavemen didn't spend their rainy nights playing trivia games ("Og go for pink wedge. Ask Og Arts & Entertainment question!"), but what about later? You certainly wouldn't be surprised to hear that Renaissance men like Leonardo da Vinci or Benjamin Franklin enjoyed general-knowledge question-and-answer games with friends as they sat around their studio or laboratory or, in Franklin's case, possibly around a namesake stove, right?

But they didn't. Trivia as we know it today is purely a twentieth-century invention, like the airplane or the Flowbee, though its roots go back a little further. Periodicals from the 1700s reveal that our bewigged forefathers did enjoy plenty of geeky pastimes: word puzzles such as rebuses, charades, and anagrams, and math games that look suspiciously like middle-school story problems, with dreary openings like "Farmer Brown has a triangular field whose hypotenuse . . ." But trivia was not among these pastimes. The idea that it might be fun to ask each other, instead of algebra problems, "Which Roman emperor had a name that meant 'little boot?'"[4] or "What's the brightest star in the night sky?"[5] seems to have eluded them.

The earliest roots of trivia, in the sense of miscellaneous-and-not-entirely-useful-facts, date back to the "commonplace book" of ye olde England. In Shakespeare's time, a commonplace book was a rather dull thing, a personal journal of instructive moral quotes culled from one's reading. But at the dawn of the Victorian age, a commonplace book was becoming something a little less commonplace: a miscellany of random facts the writer happened to find interesting. A book like Sir Richard Phillips's 1830 *A Million of Facts* is half almanac (listing eclipses, weights and measures, and so on) but half trivia book as well. Tradesmen and farmers of the time had no practical need to know that "The oldest known painting in England is a portrait of Chaucer, painted in panel about 1390" or "A man is taller in the morning than at night, to the extent of half an inch or more, owing to the relaxation of cartilages." But such things amused Sir Richard and filled up column inches (the same purpose that little trivial facts and historical anecdotes were starting to serve in newspapers of the time), and so they made the cut.

It was not Sir Richard Phillips, but his copyist and protégé, John Timbs, who became the nineteenth century's go-to guy for trivia. Timbs was a London-born working-class boy, his parents having been "Italian warehousemen," as specialty grocers and importers were called at the time. At boarding school at age twelve, he already knew his calling was journalism: he printed his own school newspaper, which he sold to his fellow pupils for the price of a marble. Later, Phillips's patronage got Timbs jobs editing some of the most popular periodicals of the day, including the *Mirror* and the *Illustrated London News*, but Timbs's real love was trivia. In the parlance of his day, his pack-rat love of facts made him an "antiquarian," but this seems to have been just a handy Victorian euphemism for "directionless know-it-all."

Timbs produced an astonishing 150 books, most of them miscellanies of odd facts and anecdotes about whatever subject was bouncing around the inside of his skull at the time. The titles speak to the tremendous breadth of his trivial interests: *Nooks and Corners of English Life, Eccentricities of the Animal Creation, Wonderful Inventions, Historic Ninepins, Popular Errors Explained.* Timbs's most popular work was probably his 1856 *Things Not Generally Known: A Popular Hand-Book of Facts Not Readily Accessible in Literature, History, and Science,* whose title is as good a definition for "trivia" as I've ever heard. Timbs's paragraphs of arcane knowledge in *Things Not Generally Known* cover the entire span of human learning. "When Was the Umbrella Introduced into England?" "Fire-Proof Feats of the Ancients." "Architecture of the Beaver." "Cost of the Great Pyramid of Egypt." As to the latter, Timbs quotes an architect called Mr. Tite, who tut-tuts that the pyramid "could not now be built for less than thirty millions sterling!"

The book was a phenomenon, selling forty thousand copies in multiple editions. That number may not amaze you—one British supermarket chain sold more copies of the latest Harry Potter book in the first hour of sales alone—but keep in mind that Charles Dickens, the

John Grisham of his time, averaged only fifty thousand readers or so for the serialized versions of his insanely popular novels. Dickens's buddy Wilkie Collins, the man who wrote the first mystery novels in the English language, wrote an essay at the time in which he describes trying out some of Timbs's "things not generally known" at dinner parties. His fellow guests are, as you might imagine, flummoxed during the fish course to hear about the possible existence of mermaids, or to hear about the wavelengths of colored light as Collins admires a young lady's flowers.

Despite becoming a publishing megahit, despite educating tens of thousands of Britons on "The Antiquity of Soap" and "Napoleon's Bees" and "Heat from the Moon," despite his outpouring of dozens of similarly eclectic miscellanies, Timbs descended into poverty in his old age. In 1860, his publisher at the *Illustrated London News* died under bizarre circumstances, drowning in a shipwreck on Lake Michigan. Fired in the resulting management shuffle, Timbs refused a £40 yearly pension, feeling it was insultingly low. One acquaintance sardonically noted that, despite Timbs's heavy drinking from the "cheerful glass" late in life, he had developed "into a singularly sour and cantankerous individual." In his seventies, Timbs was one of the gowned "Poor Brethren," pensioners who resided in London's Charterhouse, an old priory that had been converted into a paupers' hospital. At his death in 1875, at age 74, the *Times* said that the prolific author had died still writing, "almost with his pen in his hand."

Timbs's quill is quite literally between his long, thin fingers in the painting of him held by London's National Portrait Gallery, done in 1855 by his friend T. J. Gullick. The portrait depicts him as a stocky, balding man with a weak chin and sad eyes, as if even in happier times he knows the fate that awaits the man of trivia who expects his mastery of minutiae to make him a success. His doleful gaze reminds me, not pleasantly, of my own youthful knack for trivia, and its disproportion to my later mediocrity as a software engineer.

Is there something about trivia that attracts the dabbler, the perpetual student, because it offers the illusion of real intellectual mastery? NAQT president Rob Hentzel calls this "quiz bowl disease" when he sees it on college quiz teams. "Typically quiz bowl players are the kind of students who excel as undergraduates. They're good at taking tests, remembering facts, solving little puzzles. But being good at quiz bowl doesn't necessarily mean you're going to go on to more meaningful achievement. These aren't the people who are going to do important research or get a novel published or start a company." I'm a little disillusioned by the idea. As a kid, I always assumed the know-it-alls on *Jeopardy!* were *obviously* the smartest people in America. If you were smart, that's how you showed it: by knowing all your state flowers and kings of Saxony. But what if Rob's right and that's a different, much shallower kind of intelligence? Is my mountain of flash cards all for naught?

Another sad story of Victorian-age trivia enthusiasm is Massachusetts educator Albert Plympton Southwick. Southwick was one of a handful of American trivia nerds who produced their own compilations of knowledge based on the commonplace books of Timbs and others, but he revolutionized the form with one inspired twist: a question-and-answer format.

Southwick was already a prolific author of little informational volumes in 1884 when he produced his most successful work, the memorably titled *Quizzism; and Its Key: Quirks and Quibbles from Queer Quarters*. He clearly thought of his six hundred numbered questions as a reference tool for the curious, not as the basis for a parlor game, but its resemblance to a twentieth-century trivia quiz book is uncanny. Not only did he use the word "quiz" in the title, a first as far as I know, but he included questions that were not of the open-ended, "How do grasshoppers breathe?" variety. Many of them look like modern trivia questions:

"What body of water is nine times saltier than the ocean?"[6]

"What is fool's gold?"[7]

"Who was born in Europe, died in Asia, and was buried in Africa?"[8]

The best facts, as in Timbs's book, are the ones you would never find in a Trivial Pursuit box. Southwick informs us that a Colonel Townsend of Dublin had the ability to stop his heartbeat at will and "at last lost his life in the act," that lightning turns milk sour, and that Adam, of Adam-and-Eve fame, was born on October 28, 4004 B.C. Adam is a Scorpio!

Quizzism apparently sold well enough to merit a sequel, the 1892 *Wisps of Wit and Wisdom; or, Knowledge in a Nutshell.* But for Albert Southwick, as for John Timbs, trivia didn't bring lifelong financial success. When he died of a heart attack in January 1929, Southwick was in a hospital on New York's Roosevelt Island, which was then Welfare Island, a squalid no-man's-land of prisons and asylums. Though Southwick was the scion of a respectable old New England family, by the time a distant cousin made arrangements to claim his body, the hospital had hauled it away with 167 other corpses to be dumped in the potter's field on Hart Island.

Though the lengthy subtitles and self-important introductions of Timbs's and Southwick's books trumpet their scholarly worth, it's clear from the books themselves that this was only camouflage. The books are pure pleasure reading. Who ever picked up an encyclopedia because they needed to know "Can toads live enclosed in stone and wood?" or "Is there any word in any language in which the letter *y* is doubled?" (No to both, incidentally.) Then as now, your standard reference books portrayed knowledge as spinach, something unpleasant but nutritious, necessary for fortifying young minds. These trivia pioneers saw knowledge as a light, airy dessert—pointless but pleasurable for its own sake.

Robert L. Ripley, their twentieth-century descendant, was the world's first true trivia celebrity. Ripley was an unknown cartoonist and a washed-up ballplayer in 1918 when his cartoon feature about unusual sports accomplishments, *Champs and Chumps,* first appeared in the *New York Globe.* Quickly renamed *Believe It or Not!,* the strip became a smash hit, eventually spawning successful books, movie shorts, and radio and TV shows. With his breathless captions describing absurd epitaphs, thirty-thousand-eyed dragonflies, and huge balls of twine, Ripley (and his tireless researcher, Norbert Pearlroth, who spent fifty-two years combing the New York Public Library for hard-to-believe exotica) popularized the idea that esoteric knowledge could be fun. Eighty million readers enjoyed the strip at its peak, and in the first three weeks of May 1932 alone, Ripley received over two million pieces of fan mail.

America's newspapers were the source of another important trivia precursor, now long extinct: the question-and-answer column. Perhaps you can still dimly remember a pre-Google era, a sad, primitive time when if you were unable to remember the source of a rock lyric or the

name of a TV character actor, you actually had to spend weeks bother-
ing friends and co-workers instead of taking twenty seconds to sate your
curiosity on the Internet. Things were even worse for someone living in
a Nebraska farmhouse in 1908, whose parlor contained no books other
than *The Farmer's Almanac* and a big family Bible. Where did you turn
when you couldn't remember the date of the Johnstown Flood, or
needed to find a long-lost cousin in Bangor, or didn't know how to de-
magnetize your pocket watch, or when the kids wouldn't shut up asking
how many leaves were on the apple tree out back? Who you gonna call?

In most cases, the local newspaper. Newspapers had been publishing answers to general-knowledge questions almost as long as there had
been newspapers at all, the *Athenian Mercury* having set up shop as a
question-answering rag in London way back in 1691. For the next
seven years, its contributors, who included *Gulliver's Travels* author Jon-
athan Swift, answered the "Nice and Curious Questions" of its coffeehouse readers in authoritative fashion. Most of these questions were
requests for romantic advice or help with scriptural conundrums: Ann
Landers meets Ned Flanders. "Whether a tender Friendship between
two Persons of a different Sex can be innocent?" "Where had Adam
and Eve their Needles and Thread, to sew their Fig-Leaves together?"
"Whether a Woman may be believed when she says she'll never
Marry?" "How may we convince the Heathen that our God is the true
God, and not theirs?"

But about a fifth of the six thousand questions answered by the
Mercury encompassed "natural philosophy," including matters of science, nature, math, and geography. These general-knowledge questions
often tackled the very same imponderable issues that pop-trivia books
do today. "Why looking against the Sun causes Sneezing?" "How came
the Spots in the Moon?" "What is the Strongest Creature in the Universe, given its bulk?" "Why do we commonly fart in pissing?"

But even the all-knowing Athenian Society never answered more
questions than Frederic J. Haskin, whose "Answers to Questions" column began running in American papers in 1911. Within a few years,
Haskin's D.C.-based "information bureau" was receiving, and answering, over a thousand questions a day. Some were eminently practical:
"My bathing cap has stuck together. How can I get it apart without
tearing it?—E.W." Some reveal America's foibles of the day: Haskin's

three most commonly asked questions concerned mining for gold, get-rich-quick patent applications, and which public figures of the time were Jewish. But most were pure trivia, obviously nothing more than idle personal curiosity or tea-table chitchat. What causes the holes in Swiss cheese? (Bubbles of carbon dioxide.) How many steps are there inside the Statue of Liberty? (Five hundred forty-six.) Who was the model for the Campbell Soup Kids? (Cartoonist Grace Drayton used her own face.) Incidentally, the apple tree out back probably has about fifty thousand leaves, kids.

By the mid-1920s, the stage was set for the birth of trivia. Newspaper readers were poring over Ripley's sparky did-you-know factoids and Haskin's seemingly bottomless vaults of knowledge. The crossword craze was sweeping the country, sharpening both the public's pencils and its appetite for new and different kinds of puzzles. Perhaps most important, the U.S. Army had begun its "Alpha" intelligence testing during World War I, and the nation was fascinated with the new idea of measuring brainpower by answering lists of questions.

Will Shortz, who edits crosswords for *The New York Times,* tells me the earliest trivia quiz he's seen in book form is from Ralph Albertson's 1925 *The Mental Agility Book.* Albertson was an odd duck, a Congregationalist minister who left his pulpit in 1895 to found Christian Socialist utopias in Georgia and Massachusetts, all of which soon failed. In the 1920s, he became convinced that puzzles and word games could provide a great educational service to America, and so he published a book of them. As an afterthought, in the back of the book, he provided a 602-question "General Information Quiz." Like other early trivia tests, the questions are surprisingly vague. What causes day and night? Who was Euclid? What is the government of Brazil? They sound more like *Jeopardy!* responses than actual trivia questions and, at least among my friends, would lead to bitter fights about answer acceptability around the Trivial Pursuit board. But otherwise, in subject matter and format, the questions are indistinguishable from a trivia quiz today.

Trivia hit the big time, for the first time, less than a year later. Justin Spafford and Lucien Esty were two out-of-work Amherst alumni in

Manhattan. Like many other trivia fans before and since, they were shocked to find that, despite their fancy new diplomas and broad liberal educations, the job world wasn't beating a path to their door. In their free time, which was plentiful, they quizzed each other on literature, and were surprised at how much they'd forgotten since college. They had so much fun with their question games that they began to compile quizzes to spring on others, and Viking Press, seeing the possibility for a sequel to the crossword craze of 1924, agreed to publish the finished collection of two thousand questions, under the title *Ask Me Another!: The Question Book.*

Today, nearly eighty years later, *Ask Me Another!* is still an entertaining read, mostly because of the book's most inspired quirk. The authors tried out all their quizzes on the intelligentsia of the day and recorded the celebrity scores, so the reader can pit his or her trivia skills against those of the president of Yale or the editor of *Life* magazine. Some of the book's trivia guinea pigs could still be the answer to trivia questions today: tennis ace Bill Tilden, Algonquin Round Tablers Dorothy Parker and Robert Benchley (who confesses his trivia addiction in the book's preface), behaviorist psychologist John B. Watson (who posted the book's worst score, a shocking 61 percent), and Harlem Renaissance luminary James Weldon Johnson (80 percent—suck that, Watson!). The best scores were earned by celebs who were given specialized tests in their areas of expertise. Sportswriter Grantland Rice got a perfect score on the sports quiz (sample question to make the kids giggle: How many balls does it take for a bowler to score three hundred?[9]), and theology professor Harry Emerson Fosdick did the same on the Bible quiz (sample question to make the kids giggle: What did Balaam's ass do that was unusual?[10]).

The book was published in February 1927, and immediately broke sales records, selling over one hundred thousand copies in the first month alone. By the end of the spring, Viking had sold a quarter of a million copies of *Ask Me Another!* and its hurriedly written sequel. By year's end, "ask me another" had become a catchphrase, Spafford and Esty had sold almost as many copies as *the* hero of 1927, Charles Lindbergh, had sold of his transatlantic memoir *We,* and almost every newspaper and magazine in America was running its own regular column of quiz questions. It was an age of fads—Charleston marathons, raccoon coats, flagpole-sitting—but, for a little while, trivia was the king of them all.

I've been cramming for only three weeks, but I already feel like my mind has been taken apart and put back together by aliens. Pink flash-card-wielding aliens. Every time I hear on the news about a new political appointee or celebrity death, it's followed by a strange tightness in my chest and a frisson of panic. *That could come up—I've got to remember that!* Another wave of panic follows when I realize I've already forgotten the last three facts that accompanied similar frissons. It's a little like the summer I played Tetris for six hours every day and started to see falling blocks every time I closed my eyes. My brain just feels fuller these days, now that I'm off the trivia wagon.

I wonder if I've hit the wall. Facts aren't nestling neatly in my mental mesh anymore. I've overstuffed the net and now I need elaborate mnemonic devices to retain them. To remember that a sidecar has a squeeze of lemon in it, I picture a gigantic lemon riding in a motorcycle sidecar. To remember that John Quincy Adams was elected in 1824, I concoct an elaborate story about the coroner Quincy, in the old Jack Klugman TV show, having to work a twenty-four-hour shift. Every mnemonic is clunkier than the fact it's supposed to retrieve—I'm like a forgetful man who keeps losing his wallet, so he ties an anchor chain to it. I'm pretty sure that, under harsh TV conditions, none of these mnemonics are going to pop to mind when needed. Sweating under the lights, I doubt I'll even be able to *spell* "mnemonics."

One night, a week before my taping, Mindy finds me hunched over the blue glow of the computer in our darkened family room, squinting at the tiny text on the monitor.

"Hey, you," I say, distracted. "Where's Dylan?"

"I put him to bed hours ago. It's after eleven. Are you coming to bed?"

"In a second."

She rests her elbows on my shoulders. "What are you looking at?"

"I found this website run by a woman who was on *Jeopardy!* a couple years ago. Actually, she writes the page as if it was her pet parrot who was on the show. She does, like, Abbott and Costello routines with him."

"How'd he do?"

"He was a one-day champion."

"Pretty good for a parrot."

"But she also keeps an archive of every question and answer from every *Jeopardy!* game this season."

"So you're studying up?"

"Even better. I'm keeping a running total of my percentages at hundreds of Daily Doubles and Final Jeopardy clues. I'm over 80 percent on the Daily Doubles. I figure this'll help me know how much to wager when I'm on the show."

She glances down at the pages full of tick-marks under my left hand and the flash cards littering the floor at my feet. "Honey, do you remember that scene in *A Beautiful Mind* where Russell Crowe's wife goes into his study and the walls are covered with all the crazy newspaper clippings and stuff and that's how she knows he's losing his mind?"

Subtle. "All right, I'll finish this tomorrow."

My eyes are tired. When I turn off the monitor, the reverse-image ghost of a *Jeopardy!* grid floats on my retinae, orangey pink instead of navy blue. We walk slowly upstairs.

"I don't want to look back and say, 'If I'd just been a little more prepared, I could have won,'" I try to explain to Mindy. "I'm just neurotic enough for that to bug me for the rest of my life."

It's true. *Jeopardy!*, by its own contestant rules, is a once-in-a-lifetime chance. If you get a cramp in the last mile of a marathon or don't quite make it up Everest, there's always next year. But you only get one shot at *Jeopardy!*, and odds are you're going to lose that very first game. *Jeopardy!* is a shark, mowing through America's self-declared intelligentsia with its huge, shiny teeth, claiming victims at the implacable rate of two a night (check local listings). You have to be in pretty good shape to escape the teeth for a night or two, but they get everyone eventually.

Minutes later, I lie in bed, staring at the ceiling. I'm exhausted, but there are two stacks of cards on my nightstand. Cabinet members and constitutional amendments, if I remember right. I reach out from under the comforter and shuffle them into a single deck. Ann M. Veneman. Poll tax. Prohibition. Income tax. Who's the secretary of education? I should know this, but the facts seem distant and fuzzy. Education. Books. Pages. Rod Paige!

Part of the pleasure of trivia is its unexpectedness. You turn over a conversational stone and there it gleams in the mud, unlooked-for: some wonderfully serendipitous fact. Jimmy Swaggart and Jerry Lee Lewis are first cousins! Koala fingerprints are identical to human ones! There's a crater on Venus named for Laura Ingalls Wilder! Purposefully cramming on the same trivia facts every waking hour of every day, on the other hand, sucks away all the fun.

As I listen to the faint sounds of running water in the bathroom, Mindy brushing her teeth, I have the overpowering sense of weariness that I used to get before exam week in college. Pass or fail, win or lose, at least it'll all be over in a week.

ANSWERS

1. The Georgia Tech sports teams are officially nicknamed "the **Yellow Jackets.**"

2. **Queen Beatrix** rules the Netherlands.

3. **Brown University** is the only Ivy League school in Rhode Island.

4. **Caligula** means "little boot" in Latin.

5. **Sirius** is the brightest star in the night sky.

6. **The Dead Sea** is nine times saltier than the ocean.

7. "Fool's gold" is **iron pyrite.**

8. **Alexander the Great** (among other people, I'd guess) was born in Europe, died in Asia, and was buried in Africa.

9. A bowler rolls **twelve balls** in a 300 game.

10. Balaam's ass **talked,** according to Numbers, chapter 22.

CHAPTER 5

What is COMPETITION?

Mindy and I drive down to sunny California, accompanied by my brother Nathan and his wife, Faith. We decide to spend the day before my *Jeopardy!* taping at Anaheim's most magical-est kingdom, Disneyland. Faith knows somebody who knows somebody who knows one of the Pirates of the Caribbean, or something, so we can get in free. This stop is pure nostalgia for Mindy and me. We visited Disneyland once while we were dating, and got scowled at by the pimply, costumed "cast member" who caught us making out on Mr. Toad's Wild Ride.

Since we have all-access passes, we decide to pop into the California Adventure park for the first time. In the late 1990s, Disney plowed up the venerable Disneyland parking lot (site of innumerable face-offs between tired, sweaty parents who couldn't remember if they'd parked in the "Goofy" or "Dopey" lot that morning) and built a California-themed amusement park there instead, with slightly more adult-oriented attractions than next-door Disneyland, and booze in the restaurants (the strongest thing you can get in the Magic Kingdom is the gag-inducing Dole "pineapple" whip outside the Tiki Room).

True to our predictions and many jokes on *The Simpsons*, California Adventure is both dull and empty. But tucked away in a corner of the park, we find an auditorium where thirty-minute sessions of *Who Wants to Be a Millionaire—Play It!* are held all day.

This replica of the once-popular TV property is misleadingly named, of course. Unless you show up already a millionaire in something (dollars, lira, pogs, head lice), you will leave the ride a non-millionaire as well, no matter how many questions you answer correctly. Players who make it to the high-pressure Hot Seat are awarded escalating "point" values, not dollars, and these Disney points are sadly nontransferrable to American currency in all fifty states. Except, that is, for backstage at *Millionaire—*

Play It!, where they are converted into "collectible" pins, lanyards, caps, and shirts, depending on how far you go. Players who make it all the way and answer the million-point question receive a three-night Disney cruise.

We decide to get in line for the next show. I'm excited for some free quiz show practice before my baptism by fire tomorrow on *Jeopardy!* Everyone else is merely being practical: in just over an hour, we've seen every other California Adventure attraction, so *Millionaire* it is! Like many Disney lines, this one has free entertainment to help you forget the grueling ninety-minute wait in the hot sun. *Unlike* most of the other lines, the entertainment here isn't being provided by the park.

Perched on a rockery is a spindly, bespectacled kid holding forth to a group of tourists, who listen in rapt attention. His easy, authoritative manner reminds me of Sunday school paintings I've seen of Jesus preaching to his disciples, except that in the paintings Jesus isn't wearing a checkered newsboy cap, sideburns, and a windbreaker.

"Ska fan at two o'clock," Nathan breathes into my ear.

But as we approach, I can tell that the kid is not preaching the gospel of ska. He's an even rarer, even more insidious breed: the game show freak. And he's got tips!

"On the 'Fastest Finger' question, use two fingers on the keypad, and just mash an answer as fast as you can. If you wait and actually try to figure out the answer, you'll be beaten by an eleven-year-old Nintendo freak. There's only twenty-four possible combinations, after all."

The gathered apostles, eager for a chance at the Hot Seat, nod sagely at his words of wisdom.

I'm impressed that someone loves the cash-free *Millionaire* so much that he comes to Disneyland every day to coach the newbies. I'm a game show fan too, but this is taking it to a whole new level.

We enjoy a little chuckle at Newsboy's expense, but once inside the purple-lit auditorium, I quickly sit us down in the exact same row he chooses, in case he knows something we don't. I'm not taking any chances. The stage looks great, exactly like the version I used to watch on TV during America's brief prime-time love affair with Regis

Philbin, right down to the swooping spotlights and ominous Casio orchestra hits.

The first Fastest Finger question, we're told, will determine which audience member will take the Hot Seat first. From then on, everybody will get to use the keypad in their seat to play along. Large monitors keep track of the top scorers at any given time—one of them will "get the chair" next. The Fastest Finger questions work just like they did on the show: four items are listed, which you need to put in some specified order. This one, luckily, turns out to be pretty easy:

Place these actions from a popular counting rhyme in numerical order:

    A. Pick up sticks   C. Lay them straight
    B. Buckle my shoe   D. Shut the door

You don't need Mother Goose or a rhyming dictionary to put the words that rhyme with "two," "four," "six," and "eight" in order. I mash "B-D-A-C" into my keypad as fast as I can, but there are hundreds of people in the crowd, so I'm not expecting to be the first.

And I'm not. But when the scores come up, I'm pleasantly surprised to see that I had the second-fastest time. Nathan is number nine, I notice, so when he starts elbowing me, I assume that's what he wants to show me.

Instead: "They're calling your number!" he says.

I check the board again. The guy whose number was ahead of mine turns out to be—yes, our checkered-hat friend, who is standing up in his seat, crossing his arms militantly in the shape of an *X*. I later learn that this cryptic protest isn't his show of support for Black Power—he's recusing himself from playing, as you're only eligible for the Hot Seat once every thirty days. The host and everyone else are now impatiently squinting up at me, the runner-up. I stumble out of our row and down the aisle into the waiting spotlight.

"Good job," says Newsboy, nodding at me as I pass.

People like Newsboy are the rule, I later learn, and I, as a casually visiting vacationer, am the exception at the California Adventure *Million-*

aire. Until the "ride" closed later in 2004, the Hot Seat was most often kept warm by locals who would spend all day there. Some would bring notebooks to record all the questions, since material sometimes repeated, especially at the lower point levels. They weren't there to win Disney cruises. They just loved game shows.

The object of their obsession is a comparatively young art form. The American game show is really only seventy years old, or, in other words, about fifty years younger than *The Price Is Right* host Bob Barker. Commercial radio broadcasts began around 1920, and *Ask Me Another!* debuted in 1927, but the two trends didn't meet up for another decade. In May 1936, *Professor Quiz* first aired from Washington, D.C., and within the year landed a nationwide spot on CBS. The Professor, a jolly vaudevillian, awarded silver dollars to members of his studio audience who could answer his trivia questions. His historic first question: "What is the difference between a lama with one *L* and a llama with two *L*s?"[1] The radio industry, then in its infancy, was hungry for novelty, especially the kind of low-budget novelty afforded by question-and-answer shows. In the next two years, over two hundred similar programs hit the airwaves, the reality show boom of that time.

These primitive quizzes, with unforgettable names like *True or False?*, *Ask-It Basket*, and *Answer Auction*, aged surprisingly well. In fact, with their rote question-answer-question-answer format, they don't differ substantially from today's trivia shows. There's rarely a high concept, or indeed any concept at all, in your basic quiz show. Trivia is trivia, apparently, and it doesn't need cosmetics or a fancy format to catch on.

Case in point: *Information Please*, the first radio trivia sensation, which bowed in 1938. It was plain question-answer-question-answer, with only a slight twist: the "contestants" were members of the audience, who sent in queries trying to stump a panel of Algonquin Round Table–era intellectuals, and won prizes (savings bonds and encyclopedias) if they stumped the Smart Set. *Ask Me Another!*'s success was almost certainly an influence on the program, since both the book and the show used some of the same literati as guinea pigs. At its peak, the show drew ten thousand letters and fifteen million listeners a week, and boosted annual sales of its sponsor, Canada Dry, by 20 percent.

Even more impressive was the caliber of guest panelist the show drew to sit alongside its regulars, who included concert pianist Oscar Levant and *Post* columnist Franklin Pierce Adams. Celebrities as diverse as Gracie Allen, Jackie Robinson, Sinclair Lewis, and Wendell Willkie all sat in. Sitting vice president Henry Wallace even appeared on a 1943 show, thus paving the way for Vice President Walter Mondale's historic appearance on *Match Game '78* (no, not really). The panelists had fun, but always in the midst of answering erudite questions about Shakespeare or medicine or Indonesian geography or whatever else was posed to them. Literary editor and *Information Please* host Clifton Fadiman believed that—even sixty-odd years ago!—his show was helping reverse the dumbing-down of America. "Suddenly, intelligent men and women were looked up to and emulated," he boasted about the rise of *Information Please*. So much for those who date the decline of Western civilization to that fateful Tuesday night in 1977 when *Three's Company* debuted.

In its fourteen-year run, *Information Please* aired over five hundred shows and gave away 1,366 copies of the *Encyclopaedia Britannica*. And its hit status helped other quiz shows take off: by the time America entered World War II, a quarter of all radio programs were game shows. Game show taglines became the catchphrase currency of the day: "Somewhere in this broad land, a phone is going to ring!" "I have a lady in the balcony, Doctor." "Wake up, America! It's time to stump the experts!" "You'll be so-rreeee!" Game shows even served the war effort: to promote Anglo-American cooperation, Manhattan literary gadabout Christopher Morley and Cambridge historian Denis Brogan spent their Saturday mornings pitching trivia questions across the ocean to each other via shortwave for the program *Transatlantic Quiz*. The final score for 1944: Morley 354, Brogan 341. USA! USA!

The ascendancy of the staid, brainy radio quiz well into the 1950s represents the longest sustained period of trivia popularity in American history. Instead of flaming out in a matter of months like *Ask Me Another!* had, radio trivia burned brightly for almost two decades. Rising dollar amounts helped keep the public's interest: on August 30, 1946, navy commander Jack Weiss won a record $5,220 on *Break the Bank* for correctly answering the jackpot question "Where is Lake Maracaibo?"[2] (Keep in mind that's $5,220 in 1946 dollars; add a zero to get the not-so-shabby equivalent in today's money.) Later that year, the Brooklyn public library system announced it would no longer help patrons answer radio quizzes, as the flood of questions was overwhelming its staff. "In some cases, [quiz questions] have resulted in actual impairment of morale," the head librarian sniffed. "The identification of 'Lemonade Lucy'[3] or the architect of the White House[4] . . . seems of small moment." He then returned to his various important card-catalog-related duties.

Even the decline of radio couldn't kill the quiz, any more than a hit play is killed when it moves from out-of-town previews in Connecticut to the lights of Broadway. Radio's slow death just moved trivia to a bigger stage.

Radio, of course, was soon eclipsed by an upstart fad, a big clunky box called "television." Television was a lot like radio, except that you could now actually *see* what Milton Berle looked like, thus frightening America's children for years. The game show, though perhaps the least visual programming genre in history, couldn't be any more inextricably bound to the birth of TV. On July 1, 1941, the same day that the FCC granted the nation's first commercial broadcasting licenses, NBC aired special TV versions of its popular radio hits *Uncle Jim's Question Bee* and *Truth or Consequences*. CBS followed a night later with its own television quiz, cleverly titled *CBS Television Quiz*. As long as there's been commercial TV, it's been showing quiz shows, a trend that continues today with *Millionaire* and *Jeopardy!* (or, as I like to call them, "Uncle Regis's Question Bee" and "Uncle Alex's Question Bee").

For the next decade, admittedly, old-fashioned quizzes took a backseat to game shows that offered lighter fare, such as word puzzles and parlor games. Television legends like Mike Wallace and Johnny Carson got their start at this time as genial game show emcees; Neil Simon was among the writers coming up with the harebrained stunts on *Beat the Clock*. Media scholar Thomas DeLong credits the postwar GI Bill with reviving interest in the good old-fashioned trivia program. A whole generation whose parents had never been to college was diving into academia headfirst, which meant that cultured and literary topics were increasingly fair game for TV. Unabashedly cerebral Ivy League–based quizzers such as Yale's *Answer Me This* and Penn's *What in the World?* started to fill the quiz void.

But what really goosed ratings was cold hard cash. In April 1954, just a month before it struck down school segregation in the landmark case of *Brown v. Board of Education*, the Supreme Court was asked to consider, of all things, the constitutionality of game shows. The justices ruled 8–0 that the FCC regulations that had hamstrung quiz shows' big-money prizes for years were illegal. Game shows were not a lottery, Chief Justice Earl Warren wrote, and the FCC rules violated broadcast-ers' First Amendment free-speech rights. With the money restrictions gone, it took CBS producer Louis Cowan less than eight months to de-velop the idea for the high-stakes quiz show that would become *The $64,000 Question*. His brainstorm would lead directly to the biggest media phenomenon of the 1950s, and then to the scandal that would kill off trivia in America for the next decade.

The $64,000 Question was the direct descendant of radio's *Take It or Leave It*, in which contestants faced a series of quiz questions for ever-doubling dollar values, with the option of quitting at any time instead of risking their winnings on the next question (a system echoed by *Mil-lionaire* decades later). On radio, the money escalated all the way up to a dizzying *$64*! Don't spend it all in one place, frugal forties housewives!

Cowan ratcheted up the tension by letting contestants sweat out their answers in soundproof isolation booths, giving them a week (in-stead of just a few seconds) to decide whether to risk their winnings on the next question level, and, of course, by adding three zeros to the prize money. When *The $64,000 Question* debuted on TV on June 7, 1955, it ushered in a new era of trivia-for-big-bucks. Viewers might still have been interested in playing along at home with their own knowledge of Chaucer or the Civil War, but they mostly wanted to know who would win life-changing amounts of money. The contestants were Mr. and Mrs. American Everyman, after all, playing in specialty categories they themselves chose. That could just as well be *you* up there in the booth, spouting off on your own personal trivia forte.

To a degree, that is. *The $64,000 Question* also revolutionized the quiz show by culling contestants from a lengthy search-and-testing process, instead of just yanking them from the audience, *The Price Is Right*–style. In other words, it was the direct ancestor of the grueling

Jeopardy! test that Earl and I took. The 1950s shows needed auditions to find contestants who could thrive on the show's tough questions, but eventually the auditions also turned out to be a great way for crooked producers to be 100 percent certain which answers their stars would or would not know on the air.

Multiplying the prize amounts by a thousandfold didn't quite increase audience share a thousandfold, but it came close. *The $64,000 Question* was the nation's top-rated show of the 1955–56 season, still the only Regis-free game show ever to have that honor. America's crime rate, telephone usage, and theater and restaurant attendance would all drop measurably on Tuesday nights, as an astounding 82 percent of viewers were tuned to CBS to see if the returning contestants would risk their fortunes on the next question, or call it a day. Revlon, the sponsor, saw its sales triple. The show's high-water mark came on September 13, 1955, when marine captain Richard McCutchen (specialty: gourmet cookery) became the first contestant to elect to risk his winnings on the dreaded $64,000 question. Fifty-five million television viewers were watching the standing ovation when Captain McCutchen confidently knocked down his seven-course meal of a final question, about a 1939 state dinner at Buckingham Palace.

The quiz show phenomenon brought trivia to an international audience for the first time, though the jackpots were much smaller. When Victor Bernardo won seven hundred dollars on the Argentine hit *Today We Have an Examination* (and what could be more fun than that title?) by knowing that a lararium was the niche where ancient Romans kept their domestic gods, he used his time at the mike to announce that he was donating the entire amount to his beloved Socialist Party. The unamused Perón government responded by shutting down the entire radio network for twenty-four hours. Britain's biggest quiz champ was the improbably named Plantagenet Somerset Fry, who won a record £512 in his specialty category of—what else?—European history. A Mexican man finally answered *The 64,000-Peso Question* in 1956, taking home the equivalent of five thousand dollars and quieting suspicions that the show was asking impossible questions to keep its own budget down. And on Italy's *Question* clone, *Leave or Double,* the biggest fan favorite was beauty queen Marisa Zocchi, the reigning Miss Tuscany, who elected to quit on the 2.5 million-lire question in her pet category, cycling. She couldn't risk her winnings on the final question, she said tearfully, because she needed the money to care for her poor ailing mother back home. The next day, Zocchi received a telegram from Egypt's ex-king Farouk, who had been listening to the broadcast and was so moved, he said, that he was sending her a messenger with a personal check to make up the difference.

On the home front, network programmers demonstrated their love for ingenuity and innovation by unveiling an ever-escalating arms race of copycat big-jackpot shows. *The $64,000 Question* begat *The $64,000 Challenge*, which begat *The $100,000 Big Surprise*, which begat *Break the $250,000 Bank*. But when people today talk about the quiz show hysteria of the 1950s, they don't remember the top-rated *Question*. Instead they probably picture the WASP patrician and the schlubby Brooklyn Jew facing off on NBC's own isolation booth knockoff, *Twenty-One*. The 1994 film *Quiz Show* (directed by Robert Redford, who received a fishing pole for his own 1958 appearance on the game show *Play Your Hunch*) cannily used the rigged quiz shows as a metaphor for America's gradual disillusionment with authority and received truth: the Kennedy assassination, Vietnam, Watergate. If not for Redford's film, the quiz show scandal would barely be remembered today, but when the scandal broke, it was the biggest news story in the country.

Twenty-One had bowed to low ratings and indifferent viewers in the fall of 1956, but it became must-see kinescope TV a few months later, when the affable Charles Van Doren began his fourteen-week run. Van Doren was a Columbia English professor whose Ivy League family included two Pulitzer winners. By the time he was finally defeated, in March of the next year, the clean-cut egghead was among the most famous faces in America. He won a quiz show record $129,000 (nearly a million in today's dollars), appeared on the cover of *Time* magazine, received thousands of fan letters a week, including movie offers and scores of marriage proposals, and landed an NBC consultant job for $50,000 a year, more than ten times what he was making teaching *Middlemarch* to Columbia freshmen.

But then cracks began to appear in the quiz show foundations. In 1958, backstage on CBS's *Dotto*, a contestant named Edward Hilgemeier snagged a small notebook that the returning champion had been studying carefully, and saw that it contained all the answers the champ was reciting onstage. A Reverend "Stoney" Jackson announced that the question that had won him a match on *The $64,000 Question* had been the same as a question he'd answered correctly in a pre-game interview. An artist named James Snodgrass even had the foresight to mail himself a registered letter containing the answers that *Twenty-One* had given him in advance to questions like "What are the names of the seven dwarfs?"[5] so that he'd have postal proof of the chicanery.

Most damning—and, luckily for Robert Redford, most cinematic—was the testimony of Herbert Stempel, the GI Bill student at the City College of New York who had been defeated by Van Doren after winning $49,500 on *Twenty-One*. Stempel raised ratings for the show, but mostly because his smug know-it-all manner grated on viewers, who tuned in hoping to see him lose. By an astounding (and scripted) coincidence, the well-bred white-bread Charles Van Doren edged Stempel after four unlikely tie games, which had pushed the stakes for the match up to $2,500 per point. In 1957, convinced the *Twenty-One* producers had reneged on their offer to find work for him in television, Stempel went to the papers with the show's dirty laundry. The eventual grand jury and congressional investigations led to the humiliation of the entire industry. True, quiz ratings had already been sagging—the victim, as with any TV fad, of too many competing look-alikes spawned too quickly. But the scandals effectively salted the earth for trivia. Low-key panel shows and word game shows replaced quiz shows for years.

As a result of the outcry, quizmasters and producers were drummed out of the TV business for decades. No one fell further than Van Doren, who spent a year protesting his innocence and dodging subpoenas before finally admitting his guilt to Congress. NBC and Columbia University both fired him. "I was involved, deeply involved, in a deception," Van Doren testified on November 2, 1959. "I have deceived my friends, and I had millions of them."

The standard line in the game show community is that producers like *Twenty-One*'s Dan Enright and *The $64,000 Question*'s Louis Cowan got a bum rap. "They thought they were producing entertainment," I've heard TV folks say. "They didn't see it as cheating." Maybe Dan Enright rigging a game show in Manhattan isn't as serious as, say, some dictator-for-life rigging an election in Zimbabwe, but he still knew what he was doing was wrong. The producers knew that the appeal of their shows lay in audiences *actually believing* the furrowed brows, the beads of sweat, the puzzled concentration. Trivia mastery was key to these shows. Audiences were playing along with the questions themselves, and wouldn't have settled for the simulacrum of intellect and suspense that they were, in reality, watching.

And it was a simulacrum. Stempel testified that producers rehearsed every pause, every wrong answer, every hem and haw, with key contestants. Not that these contestants weren't genuinely bright. Stempel had an IQ of 170, and complained loudly when producers made him flub answers he really knew—the location of the Taj Mahal,[6] in one show, or the winner of the 1955 Best Picture Oscar,[7] in his famous loss to Van Doren. Van Doren, for his part, had a master's degree in astrophysics in addition to a Ph.D. in English. He had tried out for the show genuinely thinking he could excel. He only agreed to the fix, he said, because the producers assured him it was the only way to get rid of Stempel and impress upon audiences the importance of education.

Should *real* trivia buffs have spotted the hanky-panky immediately? Surely the producers wouldn't be able to gauge the difficulty of every question correctly, and contestants therefore would have been muffing too-easy questions and nailing too-difficult ones left and right. Most of the subterfuge, though, was fairly subtle. *The $64,000 Question,* for example, would guarantee big winners by studying contestants' strengths and weaknesses closely, in order to pitch the big questions right in each player's wheelhouse. Captain McCutchen knew his French cooking, and the show knew that he knew it. It's often reported that, for his final question, he had to list the entire seven-course menu for a long-ago state dinner, which makes his achievement seem more improbable than it actually was. But that's not what happened: host Hal March listed the menu, and McCutchen merely had to *describe* the dishes and wines. His achievement may have impressed home viewers, but all he was doing was defining gastronomic terms such as "consommé" and "sauce maltaise." To him, the question was easy.

I watch old videotape of Stempel facing off against Van Doren, to see if I can detect the "fix." What's least plausible are the show's cooked "story lines," plots worthy of any pro wrestling promoter. Come on, Van Doren defeats Stempel after *four* tension-building tie games? Come on, Van Doren eventually loses (after three ties, mind you) to the wife of a previous contestant who is hoping to avenge her husband's loss? But the trivia itself is quite answerable. The multipart lists the contestants have to rattle off seem long and involved, but they're usually trivia chestnuts: the seven dwarfs or the wives of Henry VIII. Of all the questions in Stempel's final games, I only spot one that should have set off alarms. He flawlessly rattles off which islands were discovered on which of the four voyages of Columbus, a question at which even a hard-core quiz bowl player would scoff in disbelief.

It's fascinating to watch the two men stutter and grope for answers, since we know in hindsight that every beat was well rehearsed. Stempel is so aloof he's nearly robotic. I wonder if his blank Manchurian candidate stare is something his NBC "handlers" were trying to overcome, or if they themselves caused it by overprogramming him. Van Doren, on the other hand, has undeniable stage presence. And when he clutches for answers! He ruminates, he mumbles, he discounts possible but incorrect answers, he drops in asides about how he should or shouldn't know correct answers. It's Oscar-worthy!

The biggest giveaway for me is that both contestants give improbably complete responses to every question, middle initials and all, which you would never do with casually acquired knowledge. In *How to Get on Jeopardy! . . . and Win!*, I learned that you should always limit your answer to a famous person's last name only, thus avoiding the chance of screwing up the first name. Stempel and Van Doren didn't get that memo. On a Civil War question, instead of merely answering "Halleck," Van Doren says, "That was General Henry W. Halleck." When asked what happened to Jane Seymour, he says, "Died in childbirth giving birth to the future King Edward VI" instead of just "Died in childbirth" or "Died" or "Went on to star in *Dr. Quinn, Medicine Woman*." In hindsight, their belabored answers should have been a smoking gun. Fifty years too late, I've blown the lid off of these crooks!

Game shows today aren't booming the way they once were, and certainly never bounced back to their pre-scandal peak, but there are still those who love them obsessively. Wander through their Internet message boards and discover weeks-long conversations on the tiniest minutiae. Was it a mistake for NBC to change the set on the old Joe Garagiola *Sale of the Century*? Remember that episode of *Password Plus* where the judges shouldn't have accepted the clue "France" for the password "French"? Why didn't the revival of *Supermarket Sweep* keep the old theme music? How would you have tweaked the *Blockbusters* bonus round?

"You keep reading them because it's a train wreck; you just can't stop looking," says Cory Anotado. Cory's just a kid, a freshman at Philadelphia's LaSalle University, but he loves game shows, old-school or not. In fact, he runs "Buzzer," one of the larger game show blogs on the Web. "But then you have an opinion yourself, and you actually post on it, and it adds fuel to the fire."

One example: "People were getting argumentative about the style of numbers on the *Family Feud* displays. You know, on top of the board, the numbers that tell you how much money's in the bank?"

I nod. The number of hours of my childhood that went into watching *Family Feud* makes me one of these people. No ironic distance here.

"Well, there are two different styles of display that they used. In the '88 one, the zero is one row of lights too narrow, and the crossbar of the six is straight. As opposed to '92, where the width of the zero is correct and the six curves down."

"You actually have a preference?"

"Clearly the '92 one is better. I can't believe I just admitted that!"

Fans like Cory love arguing online—"I can see some of these people teaching college courses on bad *Pyramid* calls," he says—but they get together in person as well. These aren't glittering conventions where fans dress up like Monty Hall or like *Press Your Luck* Whammys. Typically they're informal gatherings in someone's basement, where friends play board or computer game versions of their favorite shows. The same impulse, no doubt, is what leads other fans to return to play a theme park version of *Who Wants to Be a Millionaire* over and over. There's no need for cash and prizes to be at stake; the play's the thing. These fans are more attached to the "game" than the "show."

The appeal is obvious. Game shows, unlike real life, are a tightly ordered universe where every rule is well established and explained to the contestants in advance. Every sound effect, every music cue, every tile turning over on the game board is impeccably choreographed, identically timed on every show, and the host's mastery over these elements is absolute. Players are either right or they're not, as the hidden answers on the game board will infallibly prove. Reassuring feedback, in the form of a giddy *ping* or a growling *buzz,* follows their every move. Questions always have answers. Puzzles always get solved.

I suspect that this is why trivia, in general, appeals to so many of us. Unlike life's messy questions and interwoven decisions, the answers in trivia are always clear-cut, as binary as an electric circuit. Right or wrong. One or zero. You can't be sure that you shouldn't have accepted that job in Fresno, but you can be 100 percent sure that the Munsters lived at 1313 Mockingbird Lane. You may never know if you handled things right with that girl who really liked you back in college, but you know for a fact that the word "Pennsylvania" is misspelled on the Liberty Bell. After all, the answer's right on the back of the card.

Game shows, like trivia, also offer a tidier alternative to life in that they reward nothing but skill and talent. In a world where the wrong people are forever getting ahead because of robber-baron ruthlessness, or accidents of birth, or coincidences of class or color or creed, quiz games offer a beguiling alternate reality where no one cares whether or not you went to Exeter or who married the boss's niece. It all comes down to who can solve the puzzle, or can match the stars, or knows the actual retail price of the floor wax. Nothing else matters. Could trivia be America's last meritocracy left standing?

It's no wonder that so many fans find the game show simplification of life so alluring, but none have been more successful in their passion than Bob Boden, the game show guru who mailed me videotapes of the Stempel–Van Doren showdown, so I could watch it for the first time. Bob grew up in New York, attending tapings of hit shows like *Password.* "But in the midseventies," he says, "the game shows had all moved to L.A., so I moved with them." While at UCLA, he began his remarkable climb from game show big fan to game show big cheese, rising from cue card boy to *The Price Is Right* intern to *Queen for a Day* production assistant. He wound up behind a desk overseeing daytime programming, and over the last two decades has worked on game shows across the industry: for ABC, Mark Goodson, a rehabilitated Dan Enright, Dick Clark, and the Game Show Network. He now runs programming for Fox's new reality channel.

Despite his corporate success, Bob is still just a game show fan at heart. In fact, he's a fan with, it's rumored, a remarkable collection of memorabilia. Knowing that I'm a recently reignited game show junkie myself, Bob has invited me to stop by and see his "museum" the next time I'm in L.A.

He and his second wife, Marla, welcome me into the living room of their home in the San Fernando Valley. Bob is an effusively friendly guy with a shelf of dark eyebrows protruding above a permanently creased grin. He has the robust glow of someone who's recently lost a lot of weight at the gym. We make small talk, but Bob is clearly more excited about dragging me to his office, in back of the house.

"You should be flattered," says Marla. "He's only cleaned it out once before, and that was for Dick Clark!"

I'm not really sure what I'm in for, as Bob leads me across a darkened patio and into his office. But when he flicks the light switch, I'm staggered. It's the glittering polyester-pastel game show equivalent of a pirate's hoard, with brightly colored set pieces, doodads, and merchandise stacked floor to ceiling. On almost every wall, there's something that gives me a little jolt of recognition from my childhood: the actual face-off podium from the Richard Dawson–era *Family Feud*, the giant *J* from the old *Jeopardy!* set, a deck of oversized playing cards from *Card Sharks,* the glistening silver $5,000 space from the *Wheel of Fortune.* All of these one-of-a-kind items were cajoled from producers, were rescued from Dumpsters, or, in a couple of cases, mysteriously went "missing" on their own. It's game show nerd-vana.

These knickknacks are, to game show fans, holy relics that should be in the Smithsonian right between Archie Bunker's chair and Dorothy's ruby slippers. "Mystery guest" sign-in cards from the syndicated *What's My Line?* A Plinko chip. One of Gene Rayburn's oddly thin *Match Game* microphones. Framed glossies of Wink Martindale posing with

Elvis, and Bob Eubanks with the Beatles. Lecterns from a revival of *To Tell the Truth* and from the more recent *Friend or Foe*. A posterboard clue from the old Art Fleming *Jeopardy!* game board, from the days before TV monitors. (It reads, "This was the only thing that remained in Pandora's box after she opened it.")[8]

What's next? The *Gong Show* gong? Alex Trebek's mustache? Paul Lynde hanging on the wall encased in carbonite?

Bob is enjoying my thunderstruck kid-on-Christmas-morning glee. "There's more in the garage."

Appropriately enough, Bob has some lovely parting gifts for me as we leave the reliquary. There's a Chuck Woolery bobble-head doll, an inflatable Whammy, a *Greed* tote bag, and a huge binder that probably weighs about as much at Pat Sajak. "It's every daytime TV schedule since October 1958, complete with Nielsen ratings," explains Bob. Apparently this is a lifetime pet project of his, and he probably thinks I'm one of the few people on earth who would understand it. As I thumb through the pages, I find that he's right. Look, there's the summer we came home from Korea and *Scrabble* was on half an hour earlier! Here's the fall when *Password Plus* was relaunched as *Super Password*!

"So what do you think it is?" I ask Bob as we say good night. "Why do game shows touch people so deeply?"

"Sometimes I forget, working in this profession, that we're a happiness factory. We make dreams come true." He smiles wistfully. "That's what keeps me going back to tapings of *The Price Is Right* year after year. The atmosphere in there is electric, as everyone waits to see whose name is going to be called. I get goose bumps. It's like nothing you've ever felt before."

It's just as electrifying when they actually call *your* name, I discover at Disneyland, though the thrill is soon replaced by panic and nausea. I stagger into the Hot Seat and give my name and vital statistics to a staffer. Wagnerian *Millionaire* chords thunder above.

The faux-Regis emcee introduces himself to me. The hosts here are friendly Disney employees who, for all I know, wander the park in Tigger costumes between *Millionaire* sessions. His name is also Ken, which leads to some goofy "Who's on first?" moments in our brief time together.

The early questions are easy, which is good, since you only have a few seconds to give your "final answer" at Disney *Millionaire*, unlike on the TV show, where you can hem and haw until Walt Disney starts to roll over in his freezer. You're meant to breeze through the first few, and I do. Cinderella's slipper was made of (B), glass. Practice makes (D), perfect. Ladyfingers are (C), cookies.

Instead of riling me up, the finger-snappin' fast pace somehow relaxes me. But then we get to the weeder questions, designed to make sure Michael Eisner doesn't give away more cruises than he's budgeted for. What was Lady Bird Johnson's real first name?[9] This one I actually know, from my recent presidential studies. Then: Coney Island is located at the southern tip of which New York City borough?[10] Except for trips to the airport, I've never been to the outer boroughs, and so I burn two lifelines here—"Ask the Audience" and "50–50." Now I'm left with "Phone-a-Friend," which has been retooled at the theme parks into "Phone-a-Stranger." All you get is the advice of some random California Adventure attendee in mouse ears who was dumb enough to be caught standing near a house phone. Since "Phone-a-Friend" is useless, I'm totally alone up here.

And that's when, like my quiz show forefathers before me, I get the $64,000 question. Well, the 64,000-point question. "In what country was famed lion tamer Gunther Gebel-Williams born?" A tough one, but it's considerably tougher for some poor schmo who's never heard of the eminent Mr. Gebel-Williams. Some poor schmo, for example, like me. Three of the choices are interchangeable European countries: Germany, Austria, Switzerland. For some reason, my brain frozen and time running out, I pick the outlier answer: (C), the United States. Maybe Gunther's stereotypically Germanic name is misleading. Maybe it's a trick question.

"C. Final answer."

Paranoia doesn't pay. Gunther was from Germany.

"I knew that one!" chirps my sister-in-law helpfully as I edge back to my seat. "I saw a thing on A&E about him."

Maybe quiz shows aren't *quite* a pure meritocracy. You can be as smart as you want, and you might still lose to someone who watched the right thing on A&E last night. Still, I'm now laden down with pins, a lanyard, a baseball cap, and a new polo shirt. Even if I crap out on *Jeopardy!* tomorrow, that's a pretty good haul.

The Hot Seat is now being filled by an effervescently happy ten-year-old girl with braces, whose dad is flashing her signals like a third-base coach. The crowd is cheering her on as they play along. The joy of trivia has been paired with something even more elemental: the vicarious thrill of wanting to see someone else win big. "Quiz" meets "show." Bob Boden was right: there's really no other experience quite like it.

"Good job," Newsboy leans over to say again, now that we're both Hot Seat warriors.

I feel as if we've bonded.

ANSWERS

1. A one-*L* lama is **a Tibetan monk.**
A two-*L* llama is **a pack animal of the Andes.**

2. Lake Maracaibo is in **Venezuela.**

3. "Lemonade Lucy" was the nickname of
Lucy Hayes, Rutherford B. Hayes's First Lady,
so called for her teetotaling ways (and White
House functions).

4. Irish architect **James Hoban** designed
the White House.

5. The seven dwarfs, as James Snodgrass was
instructed by producers to answer, are: **"Sleepy,
Sneezy, Dopey, Happy. [Pause.] The grouchy one,
Grumpy. [Pause.] Doc. [Pause.] Bashful."**

6. The Taj Mahal is in **Agra, India.**

7. *Marty* won the 1955 Oscar for Best Picture.

8. **Hope** was the only thing left in Pandora's
box after she opened it.

9. Lady Bird Johnson's real first name is **Claudia.**

10. Coney Island is in **Brooklyn.**

CHAPTER 6

What is IGNITION?

My first semester at college, a time when most new students do nothing dumber than sign up for a series of early-morning classes they will never actually attend, I decided to push the dumbness envelope a little, and jumped out of an airplane.

It was mostly my roommate's fault. He had been handed a flyer for the campus skydiving club and wanted to attend the first meeting. I went along for moral support. I can't remember what they said at the meeting, but it must have been 24-karat golden oratory, since it got my roommate to sign his name on the I-want-to-jump-out-of-a-plane list. This still doesn't explain why I signed up too. It must have been a testosterone thing. Nobody wants a scrawny diabetic guy from Yakima to be the alpha male in his dorm room.

Then, at the last minute, my roommate wussed out, suddenly deciding that the dive would be too "expensive." I suspect that by "expensive" he meant "terrifying." So I was the one left holding the bag, or in this case, the rip cord. My first dive was a tandem jump, in which you're strapped in a vaguely homoerotic position beneath a seasoned skydiver, who has to pull the cord and land and do all the hard stuff. Good thing, as I spent the whole dive, from wing-strut to crash landing, in a dazed state of severe sensory overload.

It's an indescribable feeling. The brain, overwhelmed by all the new things rapidly hurtling at it (chief among them the *ground*), says, "Well, that'll about do it for me," and checks out. For many divers, this lasts a few seconds before they snap out of it. But in my case, the fugue must have continued for the full jump. The whole ordeal seemed to last about ten seconds. I had momentary flashes of lucidity—awareness of rushing wind, admiration of the scenery, the jolt of the chute opening—during those brief intervals when my brain poked back in for a second, said, "Ah, you're still falling out of an airplane, then," and abruptly left again.

I mention this now not to show what badasses trivia buffs are, but because it was the only thing I've ever done that could have prepared me for my first *Jeopardy!* taping.

Mindy drops me off at the west gate of the Sony studios in Culver City. Back in Hollywood's Golden Age, these were the MGM studios; the tract homes across the street are all that's left of the old backlot where Gene Kelly sang in the rain.

As the guard at the gate checks IDs, I open the passenger-side back door to pull out the two spare changes of clothes that *Jeopardy!* asks you to bring.

The clothes aren't there.

"Mindy, what did we do with my clothes?" I ask in the rapidly rising inflection of rapidly rising panic. Note the grammatically correct use of the helpless-husband "we."

"What clothes?"

"I don't believe this. I must have left everything back at Ted's!"

There was only one thing I needed to remember, and it's still hanging in the guest room closet of my friend's house. I was so keyed up about *Jeopardy!* that I spent last night tossing and turning, until I finally forgot about sleeping and just lay there, visions of flash cards dancing in my head. And in the morning, my sleep-deprived brain forgot two shirts, two blazers, and a pair of pants.

Hoping to fetch the clothes in time, Mindy races back down the 405 at rush hour, muttering imprecations under her breath, albeit the G-rated Mormon kind. I sleepwalk onto a bus, which drives twelve other contestants and me to Stage 10, where *Jeopardy!*'s standing set is located. History floats around with the dust motes in this cold, musty-smelling soundstage, the very stage where Spencer Tracy filmed *Boys Town*, where Judy Garland filmed *Words and Music*, where Erik Estrada filmed *CHiPs*. As we file into the greenroom, I am conspicuously the only contestant *not* finding a place to hang a bulky garment bag. The day hasn't even started, and I'm already the kid who forgets his lunch box on the first day of school.

At first, the contestants are a nervous almanac-clutching group. Lots of edgy giggling and sidelong glances. Then Maggie Speak blows into the room like a burst of electric guitar feedback and puts everyone at ease with sheer volume, just as she did at my audition. A day of *Jeopardy!* tapings is a zero-sum game, of course—the better someone else does, the worse you yourself are likely to do. The aim of the contestant coordinators is to get the smartest people in America to forget this obvious fact. They don't want fistfights, or even the nearest nerd equivalent. So they try to foster a "We're all in this together!" attitude of group solidarity and camaraderie. It works. Within minutes, people are chatting amiably.

"How many surrealists does it take to change a lightbulb?" one woman asks no one in particular.

No takers.

"Three! One to hold the giraffe and one to fill the bathtub with clocks!" Some polite laughter ensues. "Oh, you don't know how great it is to finally be in a room where people are actually smart enough to get my jokes!"

I give us about ten minutes before the Monty Python sketch-quoting begins.

We sit down around a long table and start signing paperwork while Maggie begins her orientation spiel. We agree that *Jeopardy!* now owns everything related to our appearance on their show, and that we won't tell anyone the outcomes of our games until the shows air, over three months from now. I spot the words "felony" and "pursuant to sections" on one page, just as Maggie begins her lecture on how it's a federal crime to rig a game show (gee, thanks, *$64,000 Question*). As a lingering result of the 1950s quiz show scandals, we will be "under security" all day, which means we'll be supervised at all times. Even our potty breaks will be scheduled and monitored carefully. Apparently, appearing on a game show is a matter of the strictest national security.

All morning, I've been watching a woman sitting in a low armchair off to one side of the rest of the contestants. She rarely talks, wears a pleased, aloof expression, and nods knowingly at key points of Maggie's orientation. "This is Anne Boyd," Maggie now introduces her. "She's our returning four-day champion, and she's won—how much is it, Anne?"

"Oh, eighty-four thousand and something. I forget," Anne says demurely, smiling like the cat that just kicked the canary's ass at *Jeopardy!* Anne won each of her first four games in a runaway, or "locked game," in *Jeopardy!* lingo. In other words, her lead was so insurmountable going into Final Jeopardy that she couldn't be caught as long as she bet rationally. It's the goal of every *Jeopardy!* player, but I can't think of the last time I've heard of anyone doing it in each of her first four shows. Anne suddenly leaps ahead of the lightbulb-joke lady for the title of Least Popular Person in the Room.

There are thirteen contestants today, which might seem like ten too many for anyone with a passing knowledge of the *Jeopardy!* format. But *Jeopardy!* actually tapes five shows—an entire week's worth—in a single afternoon. Hence the required spare changes of clothes. If you win your game, you have no time to revel in your victory, call your mom, or do a Terrell Owens end zone dance. You and Alex are rushed backstage to change outfits—in separate dressing rooms, mind you—and as soon as your skirt is zipped or your tie is tied, you're yanked back on set to start all over again. Alex's clever introductory repartee pretends to the home audience that twenty-four hours have passed. ("On yesterday's show, folks—and it must have been yesterday, mind you, not ten minutes ago, because you'll notice that I'm wearing a blue tie now, and yesterday, as these photos reveal, I had a maroon one on. . . .") Five separate shows back-to-back makes for an exhausting day. It boggles my mind that, according to Bob Boden, Dick Clark taped *ten* shows a day back in his *Pyramid* heyday.

Susanne Thurber, *Jeopardy!*'s head contestant coordinator, walks us through the rules, and then we're trooped out of the greenroom for the first time, so stage manager John Lauderdale can walk us around the set. It seems slightly smaller in person. The camera must add ten pounds to things like plywood and blue polyethylene plastic as well. As I gape at the complex array of lights and cameras, it hits me for the first time that my big chance to look like an idiot on national TV is only hours away. Skydiving brain panic hits again. I take deep breaths and try to look calm.

John shepherds us behind our podiums and shows us how to use the light-pens that we'll use to write down our names and Final Jeopardy answers. Then we take turns playing a mock game onstage. This serves as a tech rehearsal for the TV crew, but it also helps accustom us to those tricky *Jeopardy!* buzzers, perhaps the most crucial element to winning the game. On TV, it's easy to see one contestant ringing in consistently and to think, "What's up with those other two?" Or, even worse, to see one contestant flailing fruitlessly away with his buzzer and to think, "Chill out, Poindexter. You're not in a mosh pit!" But the idea that exactly one contestant knows the answer to each question is just an illusion. Everyone on *Jeopardy!*, after all, has passed an incredibly hard test to be there. As a result, nearly all the contestants know the answers to nearly all the questions. All you get to see on TV is the one contestant who's figured out the timing well enough to beat the other two by milliseconds. *Jeopardy!* skill is largely buzzer technique, and the buzzer is a cruel and fickle mistress.

Here's how it works. You can't just start pressing the buzzer as soon as you know the answer. Once Alex Trebek finishes reading each question, a staffer sitting in front of the stage flicks a switch, activating rows of lights beside and below the game board. At that point, your signaling device is activated. Ringing in early actually deactivates your buzzer for a fifth of a second or so, long enough for somebody else to beat you. So ringing in too early is as fatal as ringing in too late. There's a narrow "sweet spot" somewhere in there, just like swinging a baseball bat or a tennis racket. The trick, I learned from *How to Get on Jeopardy! . . . and Win!* and from watching the show at home, is to ignore the lights. Just anticipate Alex's last word, wait a discernible pause—say, one extra syllable, giving the staffer a moment to flip his switch—and then hammer the button like crazy.

In my brief rehearsal play, I feel surprisingly comfortable. The top of the podium is the exact height of my recliner at home. The signaling device in my hand feels just like Dylan's ring-stack toy. I get beat to plenty of answers where all three of us were buzzing away at once, but sometimes I beat the other two as well. That's about all you can ask. Between the buzzer, the random draw of categories, and the hidden Daily Doubles, I realize, there are a lot of elements in *Jeopardy!* that have nothing to do with knowing the right answers. There's plenty of luck in play as well.

As my higher brain functions are still checking in and out, it's good that I at least feel comfortable and well rehearsed up here. But can you really win *Jeopardy!* on autopilot?

Back in the greenroom, I snag a doughnut and some pineapple from a table in the corner. To my relief, a page arrives with my clothes in tow. Mindy made the round-trip drive with minutes to spare. Maggie, meanwhile, is trying to coax energetic performances out of us with some last-minute cheerleading.

"This isn't *Masterpiece Theat-ah!*" she roars in a well-rehearsed bit. "A lot of people used to say the old *Jeopardy!* set looked like a library, but look at that new set. It looks like an eighties porno! *What?*" she continues, in protest of our nonexistent shock. "That's just what Jerry told me." Her joke's victim is Jerry Harvey, a sprightly Angeleno senior citizen who looks more like someone in his own eighties than someone who would know eighties porn. A good sport, Jerry chuckles along.

We learn how to keep the show moving briskly. We are to call categories and dollar amounts quickly, before Alex prompts us. We are to shorten long category names. We should applaud at the beginning of the show and smile at the end, especially if we win.

Maggie asks for a drumroll so she can announce the first contestant pairing of the day, the first two prospective sacrificial lambs on the altar of Anne Boyd. Please don't pick me. Please don't pick me.

"Jerry Harvey and Patti Gregg!" she announces. I sink back into my chair, relieved.

The remaining ten of us, momentarily reprieved, sit down in the reserved front row of the studio audience, waiting for our turn to be slaughtered one by one. I see Mindy, Nathan, and Faith sitting a few rows back, but we've been instructed not to even make eye contact with our loved ones. I can understand this, in light of the recent scandal on the British *Who Wants to Be a Millionaire?* where an army major won a million pounds thanks to some well-timed coughing by confederates in the crowd.

When the game begins, there are plenty of thumb spasms and whispered answers from the folks playing along on contestants' row, but I'm more interested in what's happening onstage. Anne starts slowly, which is heartening. Getting a few weeks off from the game must throw your buzzer technique off a bit. Jerry gets a big cheer from the crowd when he answers a question about UCLA's 1973 basketball MVP.[1] Alex asks about the cheering section, and Jerry explains that he runs the steps at UCLA's stadium every morning. The Bruins' track coach has given his team the day off so they can come cheer Jerry along. A row of lanky college kids, sitting right behind Mindy, whoops it up *Price Is Right*–style at their on-air mention.

Anne settles into a groove in the second round, and she's built up a commanding lead—$17,400 to Jerry's $8,600—when she finally finds a Daily Double, very late in the game. With just over twice Jerry's score, she bets only $200 on "Presidential Facts." This amount is the most she can bet without risking losing her "lock."

"A heating pad kept him warm during his second inauguration, the first one held in January,"[2] reads Alex.

After a long pause, and a prompt from Alex, Anne digs out the right response, and no doubt wishes she'd risked more. Still, there are only five clues left, and given Anne's big lead, the game seems over.

Then something strange happens. The very next question asks where in Washington, D.C., President Garfield was when he was assassinated, and Jerry beats Anne to the $2,000 answer: "What is the train station?" Maybe the oldster remembers the headlines firsthand. He picks the last $2,000 clue left on the board, trying to play catch-up. The category is "Gymnastics."

"Answer: the other Daily Double!" says Alex. "All right, we're almost out of time, Jerry. You trail Anne by $7,000."

Jerry squints at the scores and smiles. "Let's go for $10,000!" he says. It's a ballsy move: a right answer would give him a narrow lead, but a wrong one would leave him with only $600 and guarantee Anne's victory. The whole game will come down to this question, and the $2,000 squares typically contain the game's hardest material. No one on contestants' row wants to play a seasoned four-game champion like Anne, so we're all leaning forward eagerly in our seats. Let Jerry be a gymnastics lover as well as a track fan, I pray silently.

The clue: "Women performing this event with no equipment but a mat must make the moves to match the tempo and mood of the music."

I haven't even had time to puzzle out the answer myself when Jerry says, "What is the free exercise?"

Alex looks offstage, questioningly. John Lauderdale, the stage manager, gets a sign from the show's producers and stops tape.

There seems to be some question as to whether Jerry's answer is right or not. I realize now that the answer on Alex's card must be "What is the floor exercise?" and the judges want to make sure Jerry's answer is flat-out wrong. Typically, they'd wait until the next commercial break to do their homework, but this junction is so critical that they want to get everything right the first time.

Ten minutes drag by. Anne, Jerry, and Patti have been turned around so they can't see the game board and/or the debating judges. The contestant staff is vamping, trying to occupy them until there's a ruling. It's like a courthouse vigil. Everyone knows how important the judges' decision is: it will determine whether or not Anne's win is guaranteed.

Alex finishes conferring with a cluster of writers and producers, then walks back to his podium. As if nothing has happened, he picks up right where he left off. "Jerry, today it's more commonly known as the 'floor exercise,' but you're right! You add $10,000 and move into the lead." There's wild applause for Jerry, and now I'm clapping just as hard as the track team. Time expires, and the round is over. In an eleventh-hour comeback, Jerry now has a slender lead.

All ten of us on contestants' row are thinking the same thing: what we need now is an easy Final Jeopardy. In close games, easy Final Jeopardy clues favor the contestant in the lead. Hard clues favor the smart second-place contestant, who should make a small wager and hope that the leader is stumped.

Today, both players are smart. Jerry bets big hoping for the easy clue, and Anne bets small (in fact, $0) hoping for a hard one. The question Alex reads strikes me as the former: contestants have to name the three adjacent U.S. states whose names start with the same letter.[3] What makes it child's play is the category name: "The Midwest." *That* narrows down the answer space, as a quiz bowl player would say.

Jerry is grinning ear to ear as his correct answer is revealed and Alex announces his winning total: $35,201. There are surreptitious smiles among the remaining ten contestants as well. Anne is heading home; maybe we have a chance! She looks philosophical about the loss, but suddenly I feel sorry for her. She outplayed the competition handily, and still lost on a nightmarish eleventh-hour fluke. It could happen to any one of us. *Jeopardy!* giveth and *Jeopardy!* taketh away.

Half an hour later, Jerry is a two-day champion, thanks to a Final Jeopardy on "American Literature." He knew what 1850 title object was "so fantastically embroidered and illuminated upon her bosom"[4] and he's now racked up an impressive $70,000 haul—much more than Anne's per-day average during her streak. Have we just seen Tyson dethroned only to have to fight Holyfield instead?

"Our next two contestants: Julia Lazarus and Ken Jennings!" announces Maggie, after the remaining eight of us have been led back to the greenroom, chain-gang-style, for a potty break. We draw scraps of paper for our podium spot, and I choose number two, the middle podium. Trying to soothe my jangling nerves, I rationalize that the middle is somehow the "best" podium. I'll be right in the middle of the action! Maybe I can sneak a peek at my opponents' writing pads during Final Jeopardy, just like Cliffie did on *Cheers*.

I've been feeling a little befogged, a step slow, all day long, from a combination of nerves and sleep deprivation. But standing behind the podium, I really start to check out. I'm only vaguely aware of the makeup guy powdering my face, of the prop man sliding a black crate under Julia's feet to boost her up a few inches.

Julia is a pretty, blond fund-raiser for a Broadway theater company, and her wide, frozen smile suggests that she's as tense as I am. Jerry Harvey, to my right, seems completely at ease, and maybe even a little surprised at his own success. "If one of you wins this game," he tells me in his hoarse, homey voice, "that'll be just fine with me. I'm happy to have made it this far."

Julia and I tape our "Hometown Howdies," personalized greetings to air in our home markets during the days leading up to our airdate. I watched a few of them on the *Jeopardy!* website. Typically you give your name, occupation, and hometown, and then some dumb semi-joke playing on your name, occupation, or hometown. Mine seemed okay on paper, but when I deliver it to the camera, it seems lamer than Tiny Tim Cratchit, and twice as annoying.

"Hey there, Utah. This is Ken Jennings from Salt Lake City, and I hope the whole Beehive State will be 'buzzing' about my appearance on *Jeopardy!*" Did you see what I did there? "Beehive"? "Buzzing"? I wince on-camera at my own spiel, but there will be no retakes! The "floor exercise" controversy has already put *Jeopardy!* behind schedule, and Alex has Lakers tickets for tonight.

The stage cleared, John Lauderdale counts down the seconds. I wish I knew some secret Zen technique to slow my racing heartbeat and breathing. Why, oh, why didn't I spend my twenties studying martial arts in Tibet like Bruce Wayne did in *Batman* comics? I forcefully remind myself that being on *Jeopardy!* is the dream of a lifetime for me. Just try to have fun with it.

As tape rolls, I discover how closely *Jeopardy!* resembles skydiving. Even to the home viewer, *Jeopardy!* is a fast-paced show: it squeezes sixty-one questions and answers into every half hour, three or four times the pace of *Millionaire* and other trivia shows. But that crackling pace turns truly dizzying when you actually have to play the game and not just watch it passively from your sofa. Here it's not enough to shout out correct answers through a mouthful of Sun Chips whenever you happen to think of them. You need to be reading each clue as fast as you can as soon as it appears on the monitor, and to quickly gauge whether or not you have an answer. If you think you want to take a shot at it, you need to prep your thumb for the perfectly timed buzz. If you're correct, you'll need to choose another clue right away, so you should be keeping that decision in the back of your mind as well. *And* keeping an eye on the scores, if you can, *and* making strategic adjustments to your game when necessary. Just like jumping out of a plane, there's too much new and stressful input coming at you at once. Most *Jeopardy!* players can't believe how fast their game is over.

We applaud Alex Trebek as he enters. This is the first time I've seen him up close. I was sort of hoping he'd show up backstage, give us all a fist bump and a hearty "'Sup, playaz?" but, in reality, contestants are kept far away from anyone who might know the game material ahead of time, the host included.

And suddenly we're under way. Jerry chooses the "'Epi'sodes" category, about words that start with the prefix "epi-." I still feel like I'm playing on autopilot, like my brain is only half-conscious and my reptile hindbrain and spinal cord are doing most of the heavy lifting, but I beat Jerry and Julia to three of the early "epi-" clues, which helps my confidence. What is an epidemic? What is an epilogue? What is an epigram?

At the bottom of the category, I have my first *Jeopardy!* experience with a familiar quiz bowl feeling: buzzing not when you know the answer but when you *know that you will know* the answer. It's an odd feeling: the answer's not on the tip of your tongue yet, but a light flashes in the recesses of your brain. A connection has been made, and you find your thumb pressing the buzzer while your brain races to catch up. This happens to me when I see the clue for the $1,000 "epi-" word: "The best example of something."[5] Something there looks *familiar,* even if I don't quite have the word yet. Alex calls my name, and I grin dumbly and stutter for a second before the right answer comes out.

More often than not, though, I find my overmatched brain frozen on answers I would have nailed at home. I've played Scrabble a thousand times but suddenly can't be sure what the symbol on the board's center square is.[6] I can't remember which 2002 movie had the line, "There's a monster outside my room. Can I have a glass of water?"[7] though I saw it twice. To quote the ageless wisdom of Jeff Bridges in the movie *Tron:* "On the other side of the screen, it all looks so easy."

For some reason, it's important to me that I seem funny in my brief interview with Alex after the first commercial break. Julia has a killer story about pretending to be an invertebrate paleontologist at a cocktail party. No such urbane, cosmopolitan wit lurks in any of the anecdotes on *my* card, I'm painfully aware. I end up using my time to thank the kind strangers who gave me a lift when I ran out of gas in the Nevada desert once during college: two drunk teenagers and a truck driver named "Fuzzy." Luckily, Alex is funnier than usual. When I express doubt that these three Good Samaritans are regular *Jeopardy!* viewers, he huffs in mock outrage: "Are you saying that drunk teenagers and truck drivers don't watch *Jeopardy!*?"

"Not as funny as Alex Trebek." That will be the uninspiring inscription ("What is an epitaph?") on my tombstone.

Between some pretty accurate buzzer timing and Jerry missing a

Daily Double about Sam Walton, I have a $3,000 lead at the end of the first round. Not too shabby. In the second round, I run up a $14,000-to-$5,200 lead over Julia before she hits the Daily Double. I wince when I see the category: "Actresses & Playwrights." Julia *works* on Broadway. She bets a whopping $5,000, and of course knows which actress met Neil Simon when she was cast in his 1973 play *The Good Doctor*.[8] Equal time, *Jeopardy!* Where's my question about the Utah software industry?

The heat is on, but I manage to ace the category on people whose last names start with "H." The $1,600 question asks which U.S. president took office in 1877. I can't believe it! My mountains of flash cards actually paid off. "Who is Rutherford B. Hayes?" I state emphatically. Four weeks ago, I would have been fumbling for Benjamin Harrison or Warren Harding. I now lead $22,800 to $11,900. The locked game is tantalizingly close.

And then Julia Lazarus makes a Lazarus-like rise from the grave. She's obviously bright—in the first round, she beat me to three of the six tough $1,000 answers. The only thing holding her back, apparently, was buzzer technique. And she finally figures it out: she's been buzzing a fraction of a second too early. Now she's beating me to almost every answer. I'm frazzled anyway, and this is the last straw. I panic. My last three buzzes of the round are all dead wrong, while Julia is relentless. To add to her luck with the Neil Simon question, two of the five answers in the "Senatorial Successors" category happen to be her home-state senators. She has no problem telling Alex who succeeded Daniel Moynihan and Al D'Amato.[9] She probably voted for them.

By the time the board is cleared, putting me out of my misery, Julia is one clue out of first place: she trails $18,000 to my $20,000. Rutherford B. Hayes, of all people, provided me with my razor-thin lead. I feel terrible about all the times I gloated about his having lost the popular vote to Samuel J. Tilden. I'm so sorry, Rutherford.

"Final Jeopardy category today is: 'The 2000 Olympics,'" says Alex, with his trademark Canadian gravitas. I can't believe my good luck. I love the Olympics. During the last games, in Atlanta, I watched so many hours of Olympic coverage that I almost failed one of my summer classes.

Only—wait a second. The Atlanta games were in 1996. The 2000 Olympics were in *Sydney*, I realize to my horror. Mindy and I were on our honeymoon in London the exact two weeks of the Sydney games. I didn't see a single event.

Julia doesn't strike me as a huge sports fan either, but as long as she bets smart, the second-place player will always win a Final Jeopardy that stumps everyone. But even though I probably won't know the answer, I bet big. You always bet big from the lead, goes the conventional *Jeopardy!* wisdom. Much better to lose because you didn't know the answer than to lose because you knew the answer but didn't bet enough. If I made that mistake, even after my friends called off the suicide watch, I'd be kicking myself for life.

The commercial break before Final Jeopardy is usually the only time that the show stops tape. You're given as long as you want to do the math required to make your wager. I bet a whopping $17,201, enough to beat Julia should she ill-advisedly bet everything. I triple- and quadruple-check my math, having learned from the sad example of Brian Weikle, the *Jeopardy!* prodigy who lost the most recent Tournament of Champions by a piddling $200. Weikle got the final answer right *but did the math wrong,* mistaking an eight for a six on his scratch paper, a mishap that cost him almost $200,000. It was possibly the most fateful typo in human history since the so-called Wicked Bible of 1632, in which the Seventh Commandment was misprinted as "Thou shalt commit adultery."

Now that the breakneck speed of the game has eased up, I feel exhilarated rather than dazed. For all my panic, I played much better than I'd expected, without humiliating myself in any major way on national television. I suspect I'll get the upcoming question wrong and lose to Julia, but it's all for a good cause. I wouldn't have traded my honeymoon for anything, not even $37,201 and lovely parting gifts. Everything will be okay.

The final answer appears on the monitor with an authoritative *ping*.

"She's the first female track-and-field athlete to win medals in five different events at a single Olympics. Thirty seconds. Good luck."

The familiar *plink-plunk* of the *Jeopardy!* "think music" begins playing aloud in the studio. A mixed blessing: on the one hand, it's the only way for contestants to measure the elapsing thirty seconds. On the other hand, when concentrating with thousands of dollars at stake, this tune is incredibly annoying. I feel like there's a gang of elves with pickaxes hammering away on a glockenspiel *inside my brain*. Because it's been played thousands of times over the decades—in *Jeopardy!* games, in ads and on sitcoms as shorthand for deep thinking under pressure, during Major League Baseball pitching changes—this little thirty-second ditty has made around $80 million in royalties for its famous composer.[10] But right now, it's doing nothing but rattling me.

Final Jeopardy questions almost always have some trick element, some possibility of discovering the answer via a sudden "Aha!" leap of logic. But this question seems completely straightforward. All it takes is a passing knowledge of the leading lights of female track and field, and there aren't that many. Though I didn't watch the 2000 Olympics, I'm almost certain the big medal winner was Marion Jones. This was one of the biggest news stories out of Sydney. Wasn't it? No time for second thoughts: the kettledrums are thudding to a close.

Alex always starts with the player in third place. "Jerry Harvey, what did you put down? Which athlete did you think of?"

I'm confident that Jerry, the team mascot of the UCLA track squad, is going to know this answer cold. So I'm elated to see on his screen "Who is Marion Jones?"

"You are correct, and you add a dollar. You go to $7,401. Let's go to Julia Lazarus. Did she come up with Marion Jones?"

Julia's answer begins "Who is Gail" and then trails off. Right, Gail Devers, a UCLA alum herself. I'm glad I couldn't remember Devers's name thirty seconds ago or I might have second-guessed myself and put down the wrong answer. Sometimes ignorance *is* bliss.

Coincidentally, Julia and her husband were also on their honeymoon at the exact same time we were, and so she *also* missed the entire Sydney Olympics. She drops down to $14,801. A smart bet—she's still in second place.

"Let's go to Ken Jennings. An even twenty grand going into Final. 'Who is Jones?'"

Alex glances at the judges, unsure of himself. In the uncomfortable pause, I look down at my screen. Unlike Charles Van Doren and Herb Stempel, I've followed my quiz bowl training closely and stuck to the last name only. But to my horror, I realize I've been a little overzealous. "Jones" is such a common name that it looks like I had no clue about the answer and just took a stab at a random last name. "Who is Jones?"

"Who is Smith?" Am I going to lose this game on a brain-freeze and a technicality, just as Brian Weikle did?

I dodge the bullet; curt nods from the judges deem "Jones" to be answer enough. "We'll accept that," announces Alex, explaining that—luckily for me—there are no other prominent female track stars named Jones. "You've got $17,000 more for a $37,201 total, and you become the *Jeopardy!* champion!"

The adrenaline that's been flowing since the start of Final Jeopardy spikes goofily in my blood, and I'm euphoric as the crowd applauds. It's like the pineal-gland-melting experience of hearing your favorite guitar riff or watching your favorite team complete a Hail Mary touchdown, except that you're in the action—you *are* Eric Clapton or Randy Moss. The *Jeopardy!* music has begun and I'm shaking hands with Julia and Jerry when Alex saunters over to my podium.

"What, you didn't know her first name?" he growls.

We three contestants are brought downstage to stand with Alex and pretend to chitchat while the credits roll. This is each show's most awkward moment. All four of you are pretending to be at a jovial cocktail party when, in actuality, two of you are kicking yourselves for muffing your chance at *Jeopardy!* stardom and lamenting what might have been, one of you is gradually realizing you're going to have to go through the whole stressful ordeal again in about ten minutes, and one of you is wondering how much of the Lakers game you're going to miss.

Up in the crowd, Mindy is applauding wildly, and my brother gives me a big thumbs-up. I'm elated. It has nothing to do with the money, which hasn't really sunk in yet. It has nothing to do with the ego stroke of looking smart on national TV, especially since all I can think about are the answers I flubbed. It just feels good to have achieved something that I've been dreaming about since I was ten. Back then, I was so trivia-crazy that the people I watched behind the *Jeopardy!* podium were superheroes to me. Now I watch the show and I see mere mortals: soccer moms humoring their children, college professors hoping to scrape together a little extra money, terminally unemployed "freelancers" of one kind or another whose voracious reading and encyclopedic knowledge never helped them hold down a job for long. But when I was young, these people were gladiators, the best and the brightest, and the fame and glory they so obviously basked in were what first gave me the idea that all knowledge, no matter how trivial, was worth knowing.

I never really knew what to say when chin-chucking aunts and backslapping uncles asked me what I wanted to be when I grew up, but deep down, I realize, this is it. Just this.

I'm with Jerry Harvey. I don't care if I lose the next game. I'm just happy to have made it this far.

ANSWERS

1. **Bill Walton** was UCLA's 1973 basketball MVP.

2. **Franklin D. Roosevelt** was kept warm by a
heating pad during his 1936 inauguration,
the first to be held in January.

3. **Indiana, Illinois, and Iowa** are the three
adjacent U.S. states whose names start with
the same letter.

4. The 1850 title object "so fantastically
embroidered and illuminated upon her bosom"
is *The Scarlet Letter.*

5. "The best example of something"
is the **"epitome."**

6. There's a **star** on the square in the center of
the Scrabble board.

7. The line "There's a monster outside my
room. Can I have a glass of water?" is from
the movie *Signs.*

8. **Marsha Mason** met future husband Neil Simon
when she was cast in his 1973 play *The Good Doctor.*

9. **Hillary Rodham Clinton and Charles
Schumer,** respectively, succeeded Daniel Moynihan
and Al D'Amato as New York's senators.

10. **Merv Griffin** himself composed the theme
song to *Jeopardy!*

CHAPTER 7

What is COMPOSITION?

Somebody writes trivia. It doesn't just come forth, ex nihilo, fully formed, from a Parker Brothers printing press, from the lips of Alex Trebek, or from a flashing, whirring supercomputer of the kind that Captain Kirk could handily overload with illogical contradictions. Somebody has to sit down and physically write the questions.

This may seem obvious, but it's something we rarely consider. To paraphrase comedian Jacob Cohen (who was already in his forties, incidentally, when he adopted the stage name Rodney Dangerfield), trivia writers don't get no respect, no respect. Trivial Pursuit and other board games never credit the anonymous freelancers who toiled over their thousands of questions. The Daytime Emmys have specific writing categories for soap operas, children's shows, and family specials, but nothing for quiz shows: the oft-nominated *Jeopardy!* clue writers have to compete in the catchall "Special Class Writing" category against the literary lights who write for *The Ellen DeGeneres Show* and *The View*.

Nothing against those brave souls who have to get up at the crack of dawn to deliver talking points to a crabby Joy Behar or Star Jones, but trivia writing is in a whole different universe of difficulty. Writerly TV shows like *The West Wing* or *Gilmore Girls* are justly lauded by critics for their dense, verbose scripts, but my dizzying first game on *Jeopardy!* reminded me that nobody crams in more material per second than the *Jeopardy!* writers. *Gilmore Girls* is a silence-filled Pinter play, *The West Wing* a contemplative Bergman film, compared to the constant machine-gun rat-a-tat of the trivia on *Jeopardy!*

Yes, you will say, but surely trivia is easy to write. Life is full of facts, or at least it sure seemed that way in school. You pick some random facts, put a question mark on the end, and *ta da!* you've got trivia. It's like shooting *Rhincodon typus* (the world's largest fish) in a barrel.

But that's not true at all. Libraries may be full of facts, but finding beautiful trivia in those dry, dusty stacks is like panning for gold. The glittering grains are few and far between. As the introduction to one early trivia book says, there is a difference between "the flower of trivia and the weed of minutiae." Or, to put it another way, all trivia may be facts, but not all facts are capital-T Trivia. I can't spell out the difference, but I know it's there. "Comedian Albert Brooks attended Carnegie Tech in Pittsburgh" is a fact. So is "Comedian Albert Brooks is five-foot-ten-inches tall"—not that interesting unless you're his tailor. But "Comedian Albert Brooks had to change his name because he was born Albert Einstein"? Ah. That's trivia.

Who are they, these unheralded geniuses whose alchemy turns facts into trivia gold? *Jeopardy!* employs nine or ten writers and just as many researchers, but at tapings, I only catch glimpses of a few of them: bespectacled chiaroscuro faces lurking just offstage, ready to leap into action if a contestant says "Who is Johann Strauss?" when the answer is "Who is Richard Strauss?" But I can't talk to them. If I got within thirty feet, a burly Sony guard would probably come diving at me. To find people who write trivia for a living *and* who aren't legally enjoined from talking to me, I'll have to go elsewhere.

I find Martin Brown in Sausalito (Spanish for "little willow tree," incidentally), just across the Golden Gate Bridge from San Francisco. Martin's lived here almost fifteen years, since he left the Atlanta ad agency he ran, and moved out here to freelance as a writer and journalist. His career took an odd left turn while he was doing some work for John Gray, the author who, in 1993, shocked astronomers and anthropologists when he discovered that men and women, instead of being from Earth as long believed, were in fact from Mars and Venus, respectively. The book sold millions of copies and spun off a merchandising empire, which eventually included a popular board game. Martin ended up doing the game's "cardware" (the questions, in board-game-ese) and started a profitable new career writing trivia for game companies: the Top 10 Game, Who Said That?, the *mental_floss* game, the Snapple Real Facts game, and many more.

"How do you even define trivia?" ponders Martin expansively as he spears a piece of crab cake. "I like to use the example that, if we lived on the moon, *all* the problems of Earth would be trivia." We're in a sunlit waterfront eatery in Sausalito, or "Mayberry-by-the-Bay," as Martin calls it, as he points out every face that he recognizes in the small-town restaurant. He himself is a middle-aged man with a gaunt, friendly face and piercing, watery blue eyes. He loves trivia. We met only minutes ago, and he's already told me that "Calcium ions are what make lobster antennae oscillate." I normally save that kind of thing for the second or third date.

There is skill, he says, even artistry, in crafting a piece of information, even an interesting one, into an entertaining, playable trivia question. He just got back from a Grand Canyon trip with his son, during which he prodded his son to try a little trivia exercise. "Here's a baseball fact. The Shot Heard 'Round the World was hit by Bobby Thomson for the New York Giants in 1951, against the Brooklyn Dodgers, in the final play-off game to determine which one of those teams was going to go to the World Series. So, there's a lot of facts in there. How do you present those facts? How do you write the question?"

His son tried, "The Shot Heard 'Round the World was hit by what baseball player?"

But, Martin pointed out, you could also make the question easier or harder. "What team won the National League pennant when Bobby Thomson hit the Shot Heard 'Round the World?" is easier. So is "What nickname is shared by a 1775 rifle volley at Concord and a 1951 home run at the Polo Grounds?" Or you could make it harder. "Who was pitching for the Dodgers when Bobby Thomson . . ." (Ralph Branca.) "What was the score when . . ." (4–2.)

"There are a hundred different ways to approach how difficult that question is going to be. It's almost like I took your finger and—" He mimes turning a vise. "Does it hurt now? Does it hurt now? You can ratchet it up."

One crack of the bat, a glint of sunlight off the steel of the upper deck, and a single event, a single fastball high and in, spawns hundreds of possible trivia questions, branching off backward and forward in time. What famous Russ Hodges radio call followed the home run, and was only saved because a Dodgers fan, of all people, taped the game?[1]

As his team slouched off, what baseball legend stayed on the field and made sure that Thomson touched every base?[2] What comedian threw up on his buddy Frank Sinatra's shoes in the stands the very moment that Thomson hit his homer?[3] What future Yankees Hall of Famer was born the same day as Thomson's home run?[4] What movie character is killed while listening to the game in his car?[5]

Facts abound, but the trivia writer has to boil them down into the best questions possible. A thousand different decisions might go into a simple one-line question: the form isn't long, but it's demanding. It's a little like writing a poem in a rigorous straitjacket of a verse form, like a villanelle or a haiku. Everything must be accurate. Every syllable counts. And for all that work, trivia writers might get a measly buck or two a question.

"Of my freelance work, I am paid at the lowest level for the work that I do on games. If I'm getting five bucks a card, I might as well be serving coffee at Starbucks," Martin says ruefully. "On the other hand, it's often the most fun that I have."

After lunch, we talk trivia as he gives me a driving tour of Marin County. The sight of the towering redwoods, or the view of the Golden Gate Bridge from the bluffs above Tiburon, seem to bring out Martin's philosophical side. Like me, he doesn't think much of the name "trivia."

"What's trivial to one person, it's really meaningful to another," he says. Calling it trivia "shortchanges it. It also gives a lot of people an excuse for why they don't need to have knowledge about it.

"Why, for example, is there any benefit in knowing—here, let me do a little design for you." He fishes out a pen and peppers a scrap of paper with seven dots. "What's this?"

"The Big Dipper."

"Now what's the benefit in knowing that in another, I don't know, million years, the Big Dipper will look like *that*?"

He shows me what he's drawn on the back of the paper. Millennia of "proper motion," a phenomenon first discovered in 1710 by Edmund Halley, have distorted the Dipper unrecognizably. It's now a crooked letter *M* stretched like taffy.

He answers his own question. "To me, the benefit is knowing that the sky that I look up and see and the stars that I see are not the stars that the dinosaurs saw. And the stars that people living on this planet three million years from now, that they see, will not be the stars that I saw. Now there's a lot of people, high school students, who'll say, 'Well, why does that matter to me?' Well, it matters because you understand that the universe is not a constant. It only seems like a constant, my friend, because your life is a"—he snaps his fingers—"in time. So when you realize that, you connect to it something bigger. It's the same thing that spirituality gets people. It connects them to something bigger."

The spiritual power of trivia. Somehow, as we stand silently considering the ageless coast redwoods, it almost makes sense.

If anyone could make a living writing trivia, Ray Hamel could. It's a Friday morning, and Ray has just packed his nine-year-old son off to school when I pull up in front of his home, a ranch-style house with pumpkin-colored siding in suburban Madison, Wisconsin. The light blue sedan parked in the driveway has a vanity license plate that reads "TRIVEA."

"TRIVIA with an *I* was taken," explains Ray, in a placid, good-natured voice with a slightly flat Midwestern accent. He's a relaxed sandy-haired fella with a wry chipmunk smile. "Trivia paid for our driveway too. When I got the book deal, that meant we could have cement, not asphalt."

For six years, Ray wrote the "Noodle Nudgers" trivia quizzes on the *New York Times* website, which were eventually published in book form. He's written trivia for radio, for magazines, and for the Internet. But despite this success, Ray still holds down his day job. He and his wife are both reference librarians at the University of Wisconsin. Ray works at the school's primate research center.

It was the UW-Madison's 1940 research on rhesus monkeys that led to the discovery of the "Rh factor" (short for "rhesus") in human blood groups, which I think is sort of interesting. Now that I'm constantly attuned to the trivia around me, I'm turning the Kinsey Report upside down. Unlike the average American male, I now think about *trivia* every seven seconds.

Ray, like me, can't remember a time when he wasn't a trivia sponge. "My mom used to say they didn't need to buy the *TV Guide,* because I knew the entire TV schedule by heart." In college, he started writing quiz questions for a La Crosse, Wisconsin, bar, and won so many radio call-in trivia prizes for his dorm that the station asked him to start hosting his own trivia show. He's run trivia newsletters and college trivia tournaments. The walls of his basement are lined with literally thousands of trivia books and games. He even lectured on trivia at the Smithsonian in 2000.

I ask him what he looks for in a great trivia question. Like Martin, he cites the problem of gauging difficulty, of making a question easy enough to be accessible, but tough enough so that listeners still have to scratch their heads. Trivia's not fun unless it falls right in that twilight zone between easy and never-heard-of-this.

But mostly, he says, he looks for "something I haven't heard before. The novelty of a question."

I know the feeling. The longer you play trivia, the more jaded you get. Sure, there was once some thrill in knowing that John Adams and Thomas Jefferson died on the same Fourth of July, or that Tom Selleck had to give up the role of Indiana Jones in order to play *Magnum, P.I.,* but once you hear those questions a few times, they're old news. You come to crave fresh trivia faster than the universe provides it.

"So how do you come up with novel questions?"

"You take two elements that you wouldn't have thought had a commonality and put them together and then you go, 'Oh, yeah, that's pretty cool, there's a connection there that nobody's seen.'"

Ray's right. In an area where all the good trivia has been stripmined, creating *new* connections between old trivia facts is often the only option. Sure, the encyclopedia can tell you that playwright George Bernard Shaw won the Nobel Prize for Literature in 1925. Movie reference books will tell you that Shaw won an Academy Award in 1938 for helping adapt his own play *Pygmalion* to the screen. But only a trivia buff will pore through pages of lists of Oscar winners and Nobel laureates and confirm for you that, yes, Shaw is indeed the only one ever to receive *both* a Nobel Prize *and* an Oscar. A trivia fact is born.

When Ray confused *Pride and Prejudice* with *Northanger Abbey* in one of his *New York Times* trivia questions, he got a few angry letters. I've written my share of questions for quiz bowl tournaments, and when I make a mistake, the worst-case scenario is some huffy humanities grad student in an Escher T-shirt bitching me out after the game. But when you're writing for a top-rated quiz show, the stakes are a tad higher. Huge sums of money might hinge on a trivia question you wrote.

"Those were really stressful times," says Bobby Patton, of his years as a writer and a researcher for *Who Wants to Be a Millionaire*. I've caught up with him in New York, in the Sixth Avenue office building where he now writes for a new reality show. I don't know what I thought a quiz show writer would look like, but Bobby's not exactly the tubby comic-book-store-owner type. Rather, he looks like he should be fronting an emo band: shaggy Beatle cut, big ears, sensitive good looks. Red socks are the only band of color in an otherwise all-black outfit.

Bobby wrote for *Millionaire* at the height of its fame, when it held the top spot in the Nielsens and ABC was airing the show—I don't even know how this is possible—137 times a week. Trivia gets serious at that elite level, especially when it's a struggling network's biggest cash cow. "For one thing, they were real gung ho about security," Bobby says. "They were so worried about quiz show scandals that the only people allowed in the writers' room were writers and researchers. We had to sign confidentiality agreements. We weren't allowed to talk to anyone on the production side." ABC's director of programming would even show up on Fridays to lecture the writers before they left for the weekend. "She would say, 'You can't tell anyone where you work.' She was real over-the-top about it. If anybody asked, we just worked at ABC in production." And should you be caught or killed, the secretary will disavow any knowledge of your actions. . . .

The network was tough on the trivia as well. Questions couldn't just be tossed off: a complicated database was set up to ensure that no fact or specific subject matter could be used twice. At first, this was no problem. "But it got to a point where, whatever you searched on, it was already in there," says Bobby. Writers had to crank out a quota of twenty-five questions a day, and that was nearly impossible when every subject had already been taken.

But nothing worried the show runners more than question accuracy. Every question had to be triple-sourced by a team of researchers. There was no wiggle room for ambiguity. "The head writer was a lawyer who went to Yale Law School," so every question had to be as precisely worded and as airtight as a legal contract. "All the questions had to be 'pinned' to one thing."

" 'Pinned'?"

This is *Millionaire* lingo for making sure that a question is specific enough that alternate answers are impossible. "Who first proposed daylight saving time?" though a common enough trivia question, is not "pinned." The answer could be a variety of German, American, or British thinkers, depending on how you define your terms. You "pin" this question by rewriting it with more specific facts: "Who first proposed daylight saving time in his 1784 essay, 'An Economical Project'?"[6]

The tiniest slipup in wording could lead to a multimillion-dollar lawsuit, as the *Millionaire* producers well knew. The show had already seen a couple contretemps of contestant complaint in its first year—whether Lake Michigan or Lake Huron is bigger depends on whether you're measuring area or volume, and whether Scorpio comes before Aquarius or after it depends on whether you're talking about the calendar year or the Zodiac cycle—when Rick Rosner sat down in the Hot Seat on July 27, 2000. Rosner was an oddball, a bouncer/nude model/cosmologist who spent much of his twenties and thirties going back to high school time and time again, in a variety of wigs and disguises, obsessed with "getting it right" this time. Well, Rosner would also want a do-over when it came to *Millionaire*. His $16,000 question was the following:

What capital city is located at the highest elevation above sea level?[7]

A. Mexico City	B. Quito
C. Bogotá	D. Kathmandu

Rosner may be unusual, but he's also unusually bright. In fact, he's a former editor of *Noesis,* the official newsletter of the Mega Society, a high-IQ organization that takes Mensa's self-congratulatory ninety-eighth-percentile ethos into the stratosphere. To join the Mega Society, you must be in the 99.9999th percentile of intelligence, or, quite literally, one in a million. I'm not sure what their membership is like, but since fewer than three hundred Americans are even mathematically *eligible*, they probably don't need that big of a clubhouse.

But on this day, Rosner's one-in-a-million mind let him down. His final answer was Kathmandu, Nepal, which is actually at the *lowest* elevation of the four options. Rosner went home with only $1,000.

Unfortunately for *Millionaire* writer John Sellers, who penned this question, it turns out that La Paz, one of the capitals of Bolivia, is even higher than any of the options listed. If the question had said "*Which* capital city," there would have been no problem, but the choice to use "What" turned out to be a fateful mistake. Rosner claimed he'd been cheated, because the best answer to the question, "La Paz," hadn't been listed. He began to send letters to *Millionaire* and ABC higher-ups, in which he demanded a "do-over." He surveyed dozens of *Millionaire* games to determine that this $16,000 question was unusually hard. He provided research suggesting that the curvature of the Earth meant that city elevations were never measured accurately. He assigned every city in the world—I'm quite serious here—an "overall Obscurity Rating," to demonstrate that Kathmandu, the wrongest answer on the list, really was an "inordinately attractive answer."

Millionaire routinely brought players back when the producers agreed that a question had been ambiguous, but, in this case, they must have felt that the difference between "what" and "which" was too slender a thread to hang a grievance on. Rosner sued in Los Angeles County court, but his vague notions of fair play and "getting it right" butted headlong into an ironclad *Millionaire* contestant contract granting ABC "final and binding" say on the correctness of questions and answers. The judge granted the show's motion of summary judgment, which was upheld on appeal. Case dismissed.

The whole four-year imbroglio was the result of the three-letter difference between "what" and "which." Trivia writing is serious business when you hit the big time.

The money was good, though. Freelancers like Martin Brown may sometimes work for near-minimum wage, but *Millionaire* writers—at the time a pretty equal mix of TV comedy writers and "puzzle people" from the Scrabble tournament/crossword constructor circuit—made Writers Guild minimum. In other words, their weekly salary was about what I get for a year's worth of freelance writing and editing for NAQT.

Speaking of big money, Bobby mentions that he wrote the million-dollar question that made Nancy Christy the show's first woman millionaire: "Who did artist Grant Wood use as the model for the farmer in his classic painting 'American Gothic'?"[8]

"So what's that like, watching someone's financial future hinge on trivia you wrote?"

"Whenever a high-money-level question would come up, and it would be one of my questions, I would feel so bad if they didn't get it right. When you're writing the questions, when you're putting down the three false answers, you feel like you're trying to trick them, you know?"

"Not at all!" says a voice behind us. "I felt like I beat them! I felt good!"

Ben Gruber has entered the room. A big bear of a guy with a shaved Michael Chiklis dome and a sheepish grin, Ben wrote for *Millionaire* as well. Now he's working down the hall on the pilot for another quiz show. *Millionaire* wasn't Ben's first game show experience—he started out as a production assistant on the kids' geographic quiz *Where in the World Is Carmen Sandiego?*, so you might recognize him from his on-air appearances as a space alien, a chicken, a shark (recurring), and a giant piece of cake.

Bob and Ben start to rehash some of the high-level stumpers they wrote, questions that determined the fate of would-be millionaires. Some of these questions rank among their all-time favorites. In *Halloween*, Michael Myers's creepy visage is just a painted rubber mask of what celebrity?[9] Which club did Alan Shepard use for his famous golf shot on the moon?[10] What were the names of Rocky Balboa's turtles?[11]

I pop Ben and Bob the big question: What makes a good trivia question? What were they shooting for in the best *Millionaire* material they wrote?

"If you have a piece of information, you want to draw out the best possible question and answer from it," suggests Bobby. "On *Millionaire*, sometimes you'd get stuff back and the note would be, 'This is good material, but the question is who-gives-a-shit.' But you could reposition the question and then it'd be much better."

"You can ask questions about anything," says Ben, "but some of them just feel so random. There's no good reason to ask that."

So a question should let you know why it's asking something important, and not just a random fact? Interesting, I think. Trivia fails unless it's clearly not trivial.

The more trivia facts and questions I examine, the more I see that they do tend to fall into distinct categories. I don't mean categories of topic—the blue wedge of Geography versus the orange wedge of Sports & Leisure—but a whole new taxonomy, based on the *styles* of the questions themselves, what it is that makes them askable and interesting. In each of these styles, one could write questions on any subject, from the Pet Shop Boys to the sunspot cycle to Haitian voodoo rituals. The nine most common styles would probably be as follows:

THE PLAIN VANILLA RECALL. Your basic garden-variety trivia question. Either you have the answer in your memory bank or you don't, period. What did the *M* stand for in Richard M. Nixon?[12] What was the name of Captain Ahab's whaling ship?[13] What football great was nicknamed "Sweetness"?[14]

PLAIN VANILLA WITH HOT FUDGE. Plain vanilla is pretty boring call-and-response much of the time, but since that's what most trivia is, sometimes you need to disguise it, to tart it up with nonessential (but more interesting) facts. *Jeopardy!* does this all the time. It's boring to ask "Which state is nicknamed the Golden State?" time and time again, so you add another California clue that's not helpful at all, but which gives the home viewer an extra, interesting tidbit. "This Golden State is named for a mythical island from a 1510 Spanish romance," or "This Golden State produces 90 percent of America's broccoli."

THE SUPERLATIVE. It's obviously more trivia-worthy to be the first or best or most of something than a runner-up. "What U.S. national park is both the first alphabetically *and* the easternmost?"[15] "What land mammal has the longest tail?"[16] "What's the world's best-selling copyrighted book?" In their crudest form, these are a particular favorite of young boys who have just received a copy of the world's best-selling copyrighted book, the *Guinness Book of World Records,* and want to quiz you on that book's semi-famous superlatives—the crazy guy in Nepal with the four-foot fingernails, for instance, or those fat twins on the motorcycles.

THE UNIQUE ONE. Even more superlative than the Superlative. "What's the only planet of the solar system named for a goddess, not for a god?"[17] "What's the only mammal that can't jump?"[18] "What's the only TV-series-turned-movie to be nominated for a Best Picture Oscar?"[19] The word "only" has a refreshing, authoritative ring that gives you the impression you're learning something important. The questions visibly crumple when the answers are no longer unique. "Which seven planets of the solar system have moons?" "Name all the types of mammals that can't use a TV remote control." "What twenty-six boring corset movies have been nominated for Best Picture Oscars?"

The problem with the Unique One is that determining uniqueness can be incredibly labor-intensive. That damn question about the only mammal that can't jump? I've seen it dozens of times, and yet I'm still skeptical. Did a crack team of Trivial Pursuit researchers track down *every other species of mammal* on the planet and ask them politely, one at a time, to do a little jump, so that they could tick off a little box on a form and move on to the next species? "All right, thank you, Chihuahua, you can stop jumping now. Call in the chimpanzee, and tell the chinchilla and the Chinese water deer they'll be next!" I tend to take questions like this with a grain of salt, or, as I like to call it, a grain of "the only mineral directly consumed by man."

THE HUGE NUMBER. It's apparently been decided that any fact with an eye-poppingly big number makes for fascinating trivia. You see them everywhere. There are eight billion jillion tons of concrete in Hoover Dam. There are eleventy thousand different words for "hockey" in the Canadian language. It would take you thirty-seven zillion years to get to the Sun on a Segway.

I always feel like I'm missing out on the mind-blowingness of facts like these. First of all, how do you even visualize nine-zero numbers like that? "What, you can't picture a trail of Starburst wrappers going around the Earth sixty million times? Okay, just picture something so big it goes around the earth thirty million times. Got it? It's pretty big, right? *Now double it!*"

But the real problem comes when quiz rookies try to turn these exorbitant numbers into trivia *questions*. "How many tons of concrete are there in Hoover Dam? Oooh, no, I'm sorry. You were four tons off. The answer is eight billion jillion." Interestingly, questions like this do come in handy in at least one scenario: they're often used as the tiebreaker in British-style pub trivia, where nice big numbers about the area of the biggest waffle ever baked are pretty much guaranteed to eliminate ties at the top.

THE MEANINGLESS COINCIDENCE. Abraham Lincoln and Charles Darwin were born on exactly the same day in 1809, just hours apart. Buzz Aldrin's mother's maiden name was Moon. The four Best Supporting Actress Oscar winners from 1978 to 1981 all had the initials M.S.

These remarkable facts are clearly not the result of any kind of design or meaningful pattern. Baby Abie and young Charles Darwin were not the subjects of a sinister hospital baby-swap; they were born an ocean apart (though Darwin would probably find it interesting that Lincoln was once called "a well-meaning baboon" by no less an authority than Union general George McClellan). And unless NASA and the Academy of Motion Picture Arts and Sciences had some *strange* selection criteria for Apollo astronauts and Oscar winners, the other facts are equally coincidental. They may not be important or meaningful, but they're fun and they're rare, and they remind us that truth can be stranger than fiction.

THE ELUSIVE EVERYDAY DETAIL. How many rays make up the Statue of Liberty's crown?[20] What color are the two Gs in the Google logo?[21] Which Beatle is barefoot on the cover of *Abbey Road*?[22]

These little stumpers are a particularly malevolent and irritating form of the art, the Pauly Shore of the trivia kingdom, if you will. You've seen the Statue of Liberty, the Google logo, and *Abbey Road* hundreds of times, and yet memory doesn't always give us the photographic specificity that these (usually visual) trivia questions demand. And so questions like these are inevitably followed by groans, hair-pulling, and forehead-thumping. When Elusive Everyday Detail questions deal with currency, as they often do ("What building is pictured on the back of a twenty?")[23] there's also the bonus fun of watching the quiz players try to surreptitiously fish coins and bills out of their pockets without anyone noticing.

British quiz veteran Rob Linham once told me that the best trivia question he ever wrote hinged on an Elusive Everyday Detail, though with the added plus of temporary humiliation for anyone who dared to answer it correctly. The fatal question was simply, "What color is Viagra?"[24]

THE TRICK. The trick trivia question comes from a rich schoolyard tradition, going all the way back to gems like "Is it legal in California to marry your widow's sister?" or "If a rooster lays an egg on the top of a peaked roof, which side will it roll down?" You're frantically combing your brain for esoteric knowledge about marriage laws and poultry, but the questioner is just waiting impatiently to ridicule you. "Ha, made you think! Anyone with a widow is already dead!" Or, "Roosters don't lay eggs, idiot! Hens do!"

It may be dumb, but this kind of trivia question has really caught on. *Jeopardy!* goes back to the well of their "Stupid Answers" category altogether too often. When the makers of a recent edition of Trivial Pursuit had to choose one question out of four thousand eight hundred to put on the back of the game box, they chose a Trick: "What fitting name was given to a dinosaur discovered near Muttaburra, Australia?"[25]

That said, I actually like trivia that, in addition to requiring real knowledge, makes the listener think about the question in an offbeat, unexpected way. "Other than Germany, what nation currently has a head of state who was German-born?"[26] Easy enough if you happen upon the right angle, impenetrable otherwise. Ray Hamel's favorite trivia question requires both esoteric knowledge and an eye for tricks: "What two U.S. presidents were named Thomas?"[27]

THE PUZZLER. Not overtly deceptive like the Trick, but just as diabolical. The goal of this kind of question is to ask something *nobody* knows the answer to, but to include just the right clues so that, with a little bit of common sense, deduction, or lateral thinking, the listener can have a sudden "Aha!" flash of insight and get to the answer. When you ask "At what university was Gatorade invented?" you don't expect the listener to know the corporate history of Gatorade, Inc. You're expecting their train of mental thought to go down this track: Gatorade . . . Gators . . . University of Florida!

These don't work on *Millionaire* or in other multiple-choice formats. If the correct answer is an absolute this-one-*must*-be-right "Aha!" moment, it's hard to come up with three fake answers that deliver the same convincing blast of certainty. On *Millionaire*, all four choices should sound equally plausible . . . or implausible.

Jeopardy!, on the other hand, loves the Puzzler, especially for Final Jeopardy questions, where the contestants have a full thirty seconds to try to duplicate the writers' deductive process. Sometimes coming up with the right response in Final Jeopardy is a matter of reframing the clue in the right way. When I hear, as I do in my seventh game, "This title character, who debuted in 1999, was created by former marine biology educator Steve Hillenburg,"[28] I'm supposed to mentally rephrase this to, "What pop-cultural icon is an obscure underwater creature?" Sometimes it's a matter of following the chain of clues: when they ask, "Experts believe that sixteenth-century Dutch growers, through breeding, gave this vegetable its color to honor their ruling house,"[29] they expect you to begin by figuring out the right ruling house, then moving on to the color, and finally to the vegetable. And sometimes it's just hard work and good luck. When *Jeopardy!* asks a doozie like, "Of the Social Security Administration's top ten boys' names in 2000, the two, ending in the same letter, on a list of the twelve apostles," [30] there's clearly no way to know that fact off the top of your head. Instead you have three overlapping lists to mentally compile in thirty seconds: apostles' names, popular baby names, and names ending with the same letter. It's a race against the clock to see if you can find the one place where the three circles overlap. The question rewards speed more than skill, though you do need factual knowledge as well. If you're unlucky and attack the names in the wrong order, you will answer "Who are James and Judas?" (as I almost did) and lose a ton of money.

Those nine templates show how trivia writers choose and shape topnotch trivia. Some are ways to frame facts so that the listener has a more interesting time digging out the answer. Some are ways to pick facts that have something uniquely question-worthy about them, so that listeners feel satisfaction instead of who-cares? apathy. Maybe the best test of a well-composed trivia question is how you feel when you *don't* know the answer. Anybody can enjoy getting a question right, even if it's poorly written or dull. It's fun to show what you know. But the ideal trivia question is so good that you even enjoy getting it wrong: you liked the mental exercise of rooting around for the answer, and you like the surprise of hearing the right answer after you gave up.

Ancient philosophers and medieval alchemists believed that, in addition to the obvious four elements making up the universe (earth, air, fire, and water), there was a fifth essence that permeated all creation and lent nature its highest power. This theory never really had anything going for it in the way of supporting evidence, but before it went the way of disco, it did give us our word "quintessence"—"fifth essence," get it? It also gave us the awesome French sci-fi epic *The Fifth Element*, but that's beside the point.

I took apart trivia questions and interviewed trivia writers hoping to find the "quintessence," the life-giving force, that makes trivia tick. I wanted to hold in my hand the mysterious Element *X* that differentiates a humdrum run-of-the-mill fact from the kind of sparkling, brilliant, memorable fact that spawns trivia questions, the hidden factor that separates trivia from minutiae.

Well, defining "good trivia" turned out to be elusive, but the more trivia I look at, the more I realize that, like Supreme Court Justice Potter Stewart said about porn, I know it when I see it. And at least you don't need to hide trivia under your mattress so your mom doesn't find out.

ANSWERS

1. Russ Hodges's famous call **"The Giants win the pennant!"** (repeated four times) is only remembered today because a Dodgers fan, of all people, taped the game.

2. **Jackie Robinson** stayed on the field and made sure that Thomson touched every base.

3. **Jackie Gleason** threw up on his buddy Frank Sinatra's shoes in the stands the very moment that Thomson hit his home run.

4. Future Yankee Hall of Famer **Dave Winfield** was born the day of Thomson's homer.

5. In *The Godfather*, **Sonny Corleone** dies listening to the radio broadcast of the 1951 pennant game.

6. **Benjamin Franklin** first suggested daylight saving time in his 1784 essay "An Economical Project."

7. Of those four answers, **Quito, Ecuador,** is located at the highest elevation above sea level.

8. Grant Wood used **his dentist** as the model for the farmer in his classic painting *American Gothic*.

9. In *Halloween*, Michael Myers's creepy visage is just a painted rubber mask of **William Shatner.**

10. Alan Shepard used a **six iron** for his famous golf shot on the moon.

11. Rocky Balboa's turtles were named **Cuff and Link.**

12. The "M" in Richard M. Nixon stands for **Milhous.**

13. In *Moby-Dick*, Ahab was captain of **the *Pequod*.**

14. Chicago Bears legend **Walter Payton** was nicknamed "Sweetness."

15. **Acadia National Park** is both the easternmost national park and the first alphabetically.

16. The **giraffe** is the land mammal with the longest tail.

17. **Venus** is the only planet of the solar system named for a goddess, not for a god.

18. The **elephant** is the only mammal that can't jump (according to the often-asked question, anyway; I'm skeptical).

19. *The Fugitive* is the only TV-series-turned-movie to be nominated for a Best Picture Oscar. (Note to show-offs: *Marty* was a special and *Traffik* a miniseries.)

20. The Statue of Liberty's crown has **seven** rays.

21. The two *G*s in the Google logo are **blue.**

22. **Paul McCartney** is the one Beatle who's barefoot on the cover of *Abbey Road*.

23. **The White House** is pictured on the back of a twenty-dollar bill.

24. Viagra is **light blue** (um, I hear).

25. The dinosaur discovered near Muttaburra, Australia, was creatively named **Muttaburrasaurus.**

26. Because the head of state of **Vatican City** is always the reigning Pope, it is currently the only country besides Germany to have a German-born head of state.

27. The two U.S. presidents named Thomas are **Thomas Jefferson and Thomas Woodrow Wilson** (who went by his middle name).

28. **SpongeBob SquarePants** was created by former marine biology educator Steve Hillenburg.

29. The **carrot** was bred by Dutch growers to honor their royal family, the House of Orange.

30. **Matthew and Andrew** are the popular baby names that end in the same letter of the alphabet and also belonged to two of the twelve apostles.

CHAPTER 8

What is FRUITION?

Between the blistering, bewildering game pace and the five-shows-a-day taping schedule, *Jeopardy!* moves pretty fast sometimes. If, after the first game, I'm no longer in aghast, hyperventilating shock, my brain is still just barely keeping up with all the input: the neon and sound effects and answers and questions and more answers and questions. By the time I can finally freeze-frame the experience to examine it, like a purple cartoon blur resolving itself into the gracefully curvilinear pose of the Road Runner frozen in midair (*Ding! Accelerati Incredibilus!*), two days have passed and I'm in a car heading back to Utah having somehow won eight games in a row. The five-game limit rule was removed only months ago, so eight wins is enough to give me the title of all-time regular season *Jeopardy!* champ.

Some of these wins are decisive, mostly the result of the formidable home-field advantage that comes with the champ's podium on *Jeopardy!* Every game under my belt makes me feel a little more relaxed, a little more confident, and a little more familiar with the buzzer timing. The two challengers, though, are always deer in the klieg lights—wide-eyed, thumb-spazzing innocents—which doesn't seem quite fair. To quote Matthew McConaughey in *Dazed and Confused*, on a slightly more statutory subject: "I get older; they stay the same age."

Even so, plenty of these games are close. Even the lock games, which probably look like runaways on tape, feel casual and precarious in the studio, where I'm painfully aware of all the incidents and accidents that could have derailed them. The outcome of my first game hinged entirely on a track star's first name, after all. In game after game, the pattern continues: tiny events, the *Jeopardy!* equivalents of a butterfly somewhere in Asia flapping its wings, conspire to grant me lucky escapes from strong players. If Paula Filson from Powell, Ohio, had known what island owns Gavdos, Europe's southernmost point.[1] If Deirdre Basile of Ridgefield, Connecticut, hadn't switched categories in midstream, robbing her of an easy Daily Double about the literary protagonist who lived on Asteroid B-612.[2] If Mary Ann Eitler of Alexandria, Virginia, had bet more on an easy Daily Double about Mikhail Gorbachev, or if Michael Cudahy of Hollywood, California, had beat me to a $2,000 clue we both knew about the mascot of the Duke basketball team.[3] If any one of these questions had fallen differently, I would have been sent packing.

Thirty short hours ago, my *Jeopardy!* goal had been to finish a game in the black, so I wouldn't be one of those hapless players who gets yanked unceremoniously from Final Jeopardy for having a negative score. This wasn't exactly pessimism—more like waving the torch of lowered expectations into the darkness, trying to dispel the specter of future disappointment. But it was also a recognition of the fact that playing *Jeopardy!* is, going into it, a black box. You have no idea who you'll be playing, what the categories will be, how your buzzer skills will hold up, or who will find the Daily Doubles. And every game produces twice as many losers as winners.

After my eighth game, Susanne Thurber had come up on the stage holding an envelope for me. Sadly, it didn't contain a check for $266,158 (minus 7 percent for California state tax, which *Jeopardy!* withholds). Winners and runners-up alike have to wait as long as six months for their prizes. Instead, the envelope held my return itinerary to L.A. the following week, for the show's next taping.

"We'll see you next Tuesday," Susanne said brightly. I'd forgotten this tidbit from the contestant orientation: all *Jeopardy!* contestants are responsible for paying their own way out to California, including plane tickets, hotel, and rental car, but if you have to fly out more than once (for example, if you keep winning), *Jeopardy!* at least pays for the additional plane ticket.

I stare out of the car window at the sunbeaten creosote bush scrub of the Nevada desert. "How am I going to get off work next Tuesday?"

I ask Mindy, whose turn it is behind the wheel. "The contract I signed says I can't tell anyone the outcome of my games until they air."

Neither Mindy nor I can really grasp that we've just won over a quarter of a million dollars. Even after we give Uncle Sam his 35 percent and California its 7 percent and tithe 10 percent to our church, that's still a pretty good chunk of change, but it doesn't seem real at all. I'm used to seeing *Jeopardy!* winnings as points on a scoreboard, not as actual dollars that you can spend in stores. Somewhere between Barstow and Baker, we decided we'd splurge on a trip to Europe in the summer. Mindy served an LDS mission in Paris, where I've never been, and I was a missionary for two years in Madrid, where she's never been. We'll show each other around. Beyond that, it's still just Monopoly money.

"You'll have to tell Glenda that you're still winning." Glenda's my boss. "She can cover for you. It'll just be one day. Unless . . ."

"Unless I win five more? I don't think we really have to worry about that."

Mindy won't be able to come with me next time unless we find a babysitter for Dylan. But if I'm to keep my winning streak secret, we can't tell a soul (with the necessary exception of my boss) that I'm returning to California. Life under a *Jeopardy!* confidentiality contract, we realize, is a little complicated.

Despite what I was always taught by Sunday school teachers and TV after-school specials, our tangled web of lies seems to hold up okay. We find a friend of Mindy's who didn't know in advance about my *Jeopardy!* tape dates, and she agrees to babysit Dylan. My boss tells everyone at work that I have the flu. In the age of the cell phone, it's easy to pretend we're still in Salt Lake City even when my parents call while we're stuck in traffic on the San Diego Freeway. But the whole charade is exhausting. This must be what it feels like to be a secret agent, or Spider-Man.

The next time I step into the Sony parking garage, there's a familiar face waiting for me. The short, stocky guy with the cherubic smile is quiz bowl veteran Matt Bruce. I had completely forgotten that his tape date had been pushed back to today because of me. And here I still am. How awkward.

"Will Ken and I be allowed to play each other?" Matt asks Maggie in his distinctive voice, a clipped, calmly considered falsetto that always reminds me of a 1950s switchboard operator, or the computer on the starship *Enterprise*.

"No," Maggie reassures us. "Once Ken's not playing anymore"—nobody ever says "loses" at *Jeopardy!*—"you'll get your shot."

Five games later, Matt's still waiting impatiently, and I have to race Mindy to the airport. When I won the fifth game, *Jeopardy!* ripped up my plane ticket so I could stick around for tomorrow's taping, but Mindy decided she needed to get back home to Dylan.

Dylan, by the way, is a trivia nerd in embryo. I know he's only a year and a half old, still chubby-cheeked and falling down every ten seconds and as bald as Gavin McLeod, but the signs are all there. A year earlier than most kids, he's started following every sentence he hears with a genuinely curious "How come?" His memory is equally precocious. If he's heard a Dr. Seuss book once or twice, he can then grab the book and "read" big chunks of it out loud to himself, from memory. He knows every Muppet on *Sesame Street*, every locomotive on *Thomas the Tank Engine*, every word to his favorite song (currently "The Lion Sleeps Tonight"). Curiosity, memory, and a love for exhaustive, exhausting detail—that's the trivia trifecta right there.

This isn't tiresome parental boasting, either. It's concern. It might seem odd to worry about a toddler because he loves to learn, but I know from talking to my own parents that rearing a pint-sized know-it-all isn't all fun and games.

"Dylan remembers every word he hears," I'd mentioned a few Sundays ago, over at my parents' house for dinner. "Yesterday he pulled one of his *Sesame Street* CDs off of the shelf and asked Mindy, 'Mom, is that Tony Bennett?' And it *was* a picture of Tony Bennett, on the back cover. I think I mentioned the name to him weeks ago, just once. That was all it took."

"Welcome to my world," said my mom. "Welcome to *my* early parenthood days."

When the University of Washington ran me through their tests the year before I started kindergarten, she says, I was already reading at a seventh-grade level and doing math at a fifth-grade level.

"So did that worry you?"

"Sure. At three years old, you'd take books and go sit in a corner for hours and just . . . absorb. We were afraid of creating a kid who would be a behavioral problem in school. You don't want your child to be odd."

Well, it's obviously too late for me, but I don't want Dylan to grow up odd either. I grew up in the sheltered bubble of expatriate life: a tony private school filled with competitive kids-of-internationalists already studying Princeton Review manuals in sixth grade, miles of ocean keeping us blissfully unaware of the latest trends of American media and fashion, and almost no access to the commonest touchstones of mild teen rebellion (pot, fake IDs, 7-Eleven parking lots). But even inside this cocoon, I was keenly aware of the hierarchies of popularity that regiment every high school, and I knew that I personally spent a little too much time in the library to ever hope to climb too high on that cafeteria-table totem pole. If Dylan has inherited my nerd genes, how much worse will it be for him in the U.S. public school system?

Hacker-turned-essayist Paul Graham has also wondered why brains are the high school equivalent of leprosy. "Why don't smart kids make themselves popular?" he asks. "If they're so smart, why don't they figure out how popularity works and beat the system, just as they do for standardized tests?"

His answer is that nerds don't *want* popularity. The rules of the popularity contest are a constant burden, and the smart kids just don't have the time or the inclination. Even given the choice, they'd stay in the chess club. What's more, it doesn't matter, since the smart kids are the ones who will come out on top when everyone graduates and realizes that real life is nothing like high school. In other words: "That's all right, that's okay, they're gonna work for us someday!" as the old Harvard football cheer goes.

I'd like to believe Graham's theory, but I know from experience that if there's one variety of nerd who sometimes unwittingly brings his isolation upon himself, it's the trivia know-it-all. Most of the contestants I meet on *Jeopardy!* are successful, interesting people, but from time to time there's an unbearable show-off, not happy to be in a room of smart people unless he can establish that he's the smartest. You can tell them by their stage-whispered responses to other players' *Jeopardy!* clues, or their habit of automatically adding a date and a name to any song, album, book, or movie that you mention. If you say "The Lion Sleeps Tonight," they have an uncontrollable Tourette's-like need to reply, "The Tokens, 1961!" If they don't know the date, they will make one up. They remind me why I decided, back in junior high, that I was done with trivia. What if I started acting like *that*?

Not that every trivia buff turns out like this, and not that Dylan deserves daily bullying during his Clearasil years even if he does. But there's a fine line between the joy of knowledge and the joy of being smarter-than-thou.

The night after driving Mindy to the airport, I drive Matt Bruce and his girlfriend, Julia, back to their hotel. I figure it's the least I can do: Matt never got to play, which means that he and Julia flew down here, missing work, for nothing, not even a third-place booby prize. And it's all my fault, as Julia reminds me, lips pursed, half- (or maybe third-, or quarter-) joking.

I fly back to L.A. the next two Tuesdays as well. *Jeopardy!* doesn't usually tape this often, but this time of year they're building up a backlog of shows before their summer hiatus. Sometimes Mindy comes with me for the first day of taping, but she always flies home before the unexpected second day. After all, surely I'll lose this time, we tell each other.

It's unusual, to put it mildly, for a contestant to be spending this much time in the *Jeopardy!* studio. Typically a player will be on set for an hour or two at most—to the production crew, contestants are just an endless assembly line of interchangeable parts. But instead of treating me as some kind of sideshow freak or VIP, everyone is being careful not to even mention the oddity. They don't want a whiff of scandal or accusations of favoritism from other contestants, so I'm never going to get my name on a dressing room door or fly down to L.A. on Merv's private jet. I'm just another contestant. And so my bizarre longevity becomes the elephant in the room that nobody talks about but everybody fixates on.

If anything, everyone is so careful not to act any differently toward me that my treatment is unusually harsh: all *Jeopardy!* contestants are equal, but some are more equal than others. For my last game of one long taping day, for example, I change into a necktie that, I learn when I arrive at my podium, doesn't "read" well on-camera—it produces a shimmery moiré pattern. I have a spare tie in my blazer pocket, just in case, and offer to change. To save precious minutes, the stage manager brings me to the backstage mirror where Alex adjusts his Perry Ellis suits, instead of taking me back to the greenroom. The tie problem is solved, but by the time I get back to the podium, all hell has broken loose. Letting me use Alex's mirror turns out to be a game show security breach on the level of the Pentagon Papers. The producers, joined by the independent auditor who monitors *Jeopardy!'s* treatment of contestants, are up in arms, openly chewing out the production crew *and* the contestant coordinators for their lapse in protocol. Contestants are not supposed to be that far upstage! What if the questions and answers had already been on Alex's podium?

I feel even guiltier than I did about the Matt Bruce incident, and play a terrible game, barely escaping with the win. My worst moment was probably this non sequitur:

"'Negative Thoughts' for $1,600, Alex."

"Winston Churchill told inquiring reporters, 'I think' this two-word phrase 'is a splendid expression,'"[4] Alex reads.

Buzz. "What is 'Iron Curtain'?"

This is what is known in quiz bowl circles as a "bad buzz." I saw something in the question that looked vaguely familiar, remembered that Churchill had coined the two-word phrase "Iron Curtain," and reflexively buzzed without "checking my work." My answer is idiotic: it doesn't fit the category, and makes no sense whatsoever in context. At least I'm in good company: the most famous "bad buzz" in quiz bowl history was probably one by none other than Matt Bruce himself, who once confidently answered, "Crack cocaine!" to a tournament question for which the answer turned out to be "Pecan pie." So close!

It's on my return visits to *Jeopardy!* that I start to notice something funny about the other contestants. Sarah Jane Woodall, a photographer from Vegas, isn't exactly the Platonic ideal of a *Jeopardy!* contestant—the fishnets, miniskirt, baby tee, big hair, and chewing gum see to that. More interestingly, I discover as I talk to her, she tried out for *Jeopardy!* less than a month ago. I waited nine months, and Sarah Jane gets The Call in a week or two?

I notice this more the more contestants I meet. Many of the women tried out just weeks ago. Most of the men, though, have been waiting six months to a year. I assume that *Jeopardy!* likes to have at least one woman playing on each show, but that the men-to-women ratio at the tryouts doesn't easily permit this. The contestant pool is always a little shallow on the female end.

Jeopardy! is no stranger to tricky gender politics. A 1993 tell-all by disgruntled ex-*Jeopardy!* producer Harry Eisenberg claimed that producers switched Daily Doubles and Final Jeopardy categories around to favor less "male" categories. "Science Fiction" became "National Parks." "Michael Jordan" became "Mikhail Baryshnikov." My personal favorite: "Airports" became "Alice B. Toklas." Eisenberg's examples were damningly specific, but *Jeopardy!* loudly disputed the charge, and the accusations went mysteriously missing in the second edition of his book.

Anecdotally, I can see that *Jeopardy!* still makes efforts to include their idea of female-skewing categories in the mix. For every sports or beer category, there's a "lifestyle" category on food, or fashion, or "chick flicks." Science, which I suppose is a stereotypically "male" category, is so underrepresented on *Jeopardy!* that the Kansas Board of Education might as well be vetting the questions.

But Beverly Herter, whom I play a week later, disagrees: she thinks that the clues on *Jeopardy!* still give men a leg up. "There is an inherent bias from the fact that the writers are, by and large, white males," she tells me via the Internet, after our game. In fact, she sees a wide range of categories as problematic, from military history to space, because they favor men. "As the mother of two children, one boy and one girl, as well as someone who volunteers in their schools twice each week, I can tell you without doubt that boys are more interested in some subjects—space exploration and aviation among them—than girls."

I'm skeptical. Most *Jeopardy!* clues strike me as gender-neutral because the knowledge they test is just simple factual recall about the world we all live in, men or women. The world's highest tides are in the same place,[5] the same author wrote *Vanity Fair*,[6] and the Magna Carta was signed in the same year,[7] whether you have two X chromosomes or two X boxes. The odd clue may favor a male perspective once in a while, but I don't think it's prevalent enough to cause the show's gender gap. What does lead to the disparity, then?

After all, it's not just *Jeopardy!* Women are underrepresented in nearly all competitive quiz games, from quiz bowl to pub trivia. You see the same imbalance in a lot of other brain games as well: chess, Scrabble, competitive math, and crosswords are all dominated, at the highest levels of play, by men.

And everybody has a different notion of what causes it. At Northwestern State, in Louisiana, where Trivial Pursuit is a popular campus pastime and dorms even hold tournaments, I meet student body president Mindy McConnell. Yes, her parents named the poor thing in honor of 1970s TV.[8] And yes, she notices a gender disparity when she plays Trivial Pursuit with classmates. "I think men are just better at trivia than women are" is her simple explanation, delivered in a meandering New Orleans accent.

Few I talk to would agree with that contention, that men are somehow just better biologically wired for trivia knowledge. Emily Pike, Carleton's former quiz bowl captain, thinks girls tune out of trivia in high school for social reasons. "Girls at that age are more aware of the social ramifications of the activities they choose than boys are. They understand there will be a stigma if they participate in the same activities the geeks do. Like quiz bowl." Other women players have said that it was instances of poor hygiene, sexual crudeness, or awkward propositioning that soured them on quiz bowl.

As for *Jeopardy!*, hard-core game show fans on the Internet often argue that the gap springs from specific elements of the *Jeopardy!* game that have nothing to do with trivia. Depending on who you ask, this could include buzzer speed, gutsy wagering, or educated guessing at answers, "skills" at which men supposedly excel.

My guess is that women in trivia competition are disadvantaged more by the "competition" part than by the "trivia." Researchers studying gender gaps in math and science often find that men learn best in competitive learning environments, while women prefer a cooperative learning style. For men, trivia achievement can become a macho thing—

confidently hammering on your phallic signaling device, demoralizing the enemy with your superior knowledge. *Booyah!* Women, on the other hand, might be just as knowledgeable, but might not be as able—or as eager—to show off their skills in situations where the competition is so cutthroat.

Bryan Quinn runs the Sacramento-based company The Ultimate Game Show, which rents game show equipment and puts on quiz games for corporate training and events. He's very familiar with "trivia anxiety"—contestants who refuse to "come on down" and risk failure in the quiz show pressure cooker, even at the lighthearted events he hosts. At one corporate mixer in Lake Tahoe, he remembers, he drew the name of an attendee who refused to take the stage, even when he explained to her that the questions were easy and that all the players would win between $250 and $2,500 for participating. After the round was over, he tracked her down in the crowd.

"Did you know any of those answers?" he asked amiably.

She said that she knew almost every answer in all nine game rounds.

"And you still didn't want to play?"

She was mortified by the idea of having to play, she said. "I almost got physically ill when you called my name. No amount of money would have got me up on that stage."

Bryan agrees that, while both men and women suffer from "trivia anxiety," it seems to afflict women disproportionately. I saw this difference in confidence, or at least in preference, at many a BYU quiz bowl tryout or intramural game. Male players unfamiliar with the game would still want to give it a shot, and when it turned out that they *didn't* know the only U.S. state with a non-rectangular flag[9] or the more familiar name for "Arrangement in Gray and Black, No. 1,"[10] it only motivated them to improve. Women players, on the other hand, would hear about the game and assume it wasn't for them. If they tried it anyway and didn't know the answers, they felt vindicated in their skepticism and didn't come back. It's a shame, because the boys'-club environment of trivia games then becomes an even bigger deterrent to more women taking up the game.

Despite what studies show, I guess I haven't been gifted with the traditionally male advantage of better spatial perception. I've just won another $150,000 or so on America's toughest quiz show, and yet here I am wandering through the Sony parking garage, schlepping five heavy suits of clothes over my shoulder, unable to find my rental car. I'm not a smart person. I just play one on TV.

In fairness to me, the Sony garage *is* some kind of impossible topological oddity, like a Möbius strip or a Klein bottle. Depending on where you start, you can follow a path all the way through it and somehow miss every other floor. Finally I decide to start from the roof down instead of from the basement up, and five minutes later, I find my Dodge Neon. I must have passed through a dimensional wormhole or something.

Cell phones backstage are a *Jeopardy!* security violation, but as soon as I'm in the car, I call Mindy with an update, as per our standing agreement.

"Tonight, Mindy, our little project, our company, had a *very big night.*" It's something Tom Cruise tells Renée Zellweger in *Jerry Maguire,* and it's the first thing I always tell Mindy after a successful taping day. "I have to come back next Tuesday."

"'Have to'?" she teases. "How much did you win?"

"I'm not sure," I say truthfully, fumbling in my jacket pocket for my sheaf of yellow carbons of the *Jeopardy!* Prize Description form. "I'll have to add all these up on the plane."

After hanging up, I can't help studying the prize forms and doing a little back-of-the-envelope math. Eighteen wins, well over half a million dollars. I sit in the silent parked car for a moment, numbly shaking my head in bemusement. When I decided to reconnect with trivia, I never expected anything like this.

Suddenly remembering that I have a plane to catch, I toss the forms down beside me on the seat and dig through five pairs of pants until I find the pocket with my car keys.

Now: How do I get out of this garage?

ANSWERS

1. An island off **Crete** is Europe's
southernmost point.

2. **The Little Prince** is the character that
lived on Asteroid B-612.

3. The mascot of the Duke basketball team
is the **Blue Devil.**

4. Winston Churchill told inquiring reporters,
"I think **'no comment'** is a splendid expression."

5. **The Bay of Fundy,** between New Brunswick and
Nova Scotia, has the world's highest tides.

6. **William Makepeace Thackeray**
wrote *Vanity Fair.*

7. The Magna Carta was signed in **1215.**

8. Mindy McConnell was **Pam Dawber's character
on** *Mork & Mindy.*

9. **Ohio** is the only U.S. state with
a non-rectangular flag.

10. *Whistler's Mother* is the more familiar name for
Arrangement in Gray and Black, No. 1.

CHAPTER 9

What is TRANSITION?

Bechuanaland became Botswana. Bob Dylan went electric. Cape Canaveral became Cape Kennedy (and then, quickly, Cape Canaveral again). A young María Martinez Molina Baeza became "Charo." Dick Sargent replaced Dick York on *Bewitched*. Yes, the 1960s were a portentous time of upheaval and change. And trivia was in for a sea change as well.

The idea that general-knowledge questions and answers could be fun had been around for forty years, but there still was no trivia phenomenon as such—in fact, the word "trivia" to describe recreational quizzing didn't even exist yet. A "question-and-answer game" was a book you read, or something that Ivy Leaguers in horn-rimmed glasses did on TV quiz shows. Trivia still wasn't something America *played*.

That all changed in 1965. Dan Carlinsky and Ed Goodgold met during freshman week when both were entering Columbia University in the fall of 1962. By junior year, they were collaborating on humor pieces for the student paper, the *Spectator*, where Ed was the features editor.

Ed grew up in Brooklyn, but his parents had moved to the United States from Tel Aviv when he was six years old. An outsider at first, he learned to speak English by listening to radio and television: the Shadow, Captain Video, and Hopalong Cassidy were his tutors. "I'm a total product of American culture," Ed tells me. I've tracked him down forty-odd years later; he's now a dean's assistant at the NYU School of Education.

The formative American pop culture of his early years stuck with Ed. When he and his friends were back at home from school, they'd spend summer nights sitting out on the stoops of their buildings reminiscing about the radio, TV, movie, comic, and sports heroes of their childhood. Remember the Hardy Boys and Buster Brown and Green Hornet? Remember Davy Crockett? Remember Haystacks Calhoun? Over time, the boys developed a kind of question-answering parlor game based on their childhood nostalgia. "What was the name of the eccentric Duckburg inventor in *Uncle Scrooge* comics?"[1] "Oh, yeah? Where did Paladin live on *Have Gun—Will Travel*?"[2]

Ed's friend Dan Carlinsky, now an author, agent, and freelance journalist living in Connecticut, remembers that this game continued at Columbia. Students would gather in the Gehrig Room, a common room in the dorms, under a large portrait of the "Iron Horse" himself (Gehrig was a Columbia alum) and lob nostalgia questions back and forth. The game was such a hit that, in February 1965, Ed Goodgold wrote about "trivia," as he had taken to calling it, in his *Spectator* column, and proposed that Columbia should hold a trivia contest. The reaction was enthusiastic and immediate. "It was clear that this wasn't just my experience," Ed realized. "It was a phenomenon shared by many people growing up. That's why it took off so quickly, because it wasn't anything you had to teach people. They were already doing it! They just didn't codify it."

There was no shortage of applicants for the trivia contest that Dan and Ed threw together in the spring of 1965. So many students showed up to Ferris Booth Hall that they were hanging out of doorways. In a format borrowed from *G.E. College Bowl*, panels of players faced questions about the bread-and-butter of their childhoods: old-time TV and radio and comic books. The enterprising Carlinsky and Goodgold wrote up the contest in the *Spectator* the next day, whetting Columbia's appetite for an even bigger and better follow-up: 1966's "First Annual Ivy League–Seven Sisters Trivia Contest."

This interschool contest and the one that followed in 1967 were held in huge Columbia auditoriums and drew over a thousand students eager to demonstrate their encyclopedic knowledge of Fearless Fosdick, Ma and Pa Kettle, and Dale Evans's horse.[3] These World Series of trivia ended not long after Dan and Ed's graduation, but, in their short lifespan, they changed the way people thought about quiz games. The questions were light and breezy rather than academic, the prize was a green forty-nine-cent mixing bowl from Woolworth's, and instead of the staid library silence of a quiz show, the contests featured musical interludes, with doo-wop classics and TV themes and ad jingles sung by the King's Men, Columbia's all-male a capella ensemble. "There he goes, / Think of all the crap he knows," the King's Men would sing, celebrating the winner in mock Miss America fashion.

The King's Men had never sung doo-wop before, says Dan Carlinsky. "We asked them to sing the Diamonds' 'Little Darlin',' so they went out and tracked down an old 45." The group enjoyed the fifties style so much that it came to dominate their act. Not wanting to be confused with those *other* Kingsmen, who had recorded the biggest garage-band hit of 1963,[4] the boys renamed themselves Sha Na Na, and, not knowing where else to turn, asked Ed Goodgold to manage them. "I was the closest thing to show business that they knew," explains Ed, who was becoming well known as trivia's inventor and foremost guru. Sha Na Na went on to play Woodstock, and became forerunners of the 1950s nostalgia boom of the next decade. We might never have had *Grease, American Graffiti,* "Crocodile Rock," or *Happy Days* if not for Sha Na Na, and we never would have had Sha Na Na, God bless 'em, if not for trivia.

Fortunately, preppies pretending to be greasers were not Ed and Dan's only legacy. The Associated Press wrote a paragraph about their first contest, and the story was put on the wire and ran nationally. "Other college kids found out about it, so it started spreading, and we started getting phone calls from campuses all across the country," Dan tells me. The University of Colorado's copycat contest, Trivia Bowl, began in 1968 and still runs today. For much of the 1970s and 1980s, it was a de facto "national championship" for buffs who would drive from both coasts all the way to Boulder just to play trivia.

In the wake of the campus fad, Dan also shopped around the notion of a trivia book. When Dell Publishing bought off, Dan and Ed asked their professors for extensions on their coursework and scurried to get enough trivia questions together to fill a slim paperback. *Trivia* and its follow-up *More Trivial Trivia* were smash hits, together selling over half a million copies. Dan had his tongue only partially in cheek that fall when he called trivia "the nation's number three pastime!" *Time* maga-zine even ran a story on the 1967 Ivy League Trivia Contest.

Trivia had gone national. "Our biggest mistake was on national tel-evision," remembers Ed. "We thought we'd come up with a great ques-tion: What was Dracula's first name?"[5] The only problem was, they didn't know the answer, so they dove into the stacks at Columbia's But-ler Library. "We go into the ancient Romanian history, and we come up with Voivode." They later watched as Johnny Carson and Woody Allen discussed the trivia fad on *The Tonight Show*, and Woody, apparently fa-miliar with Dan and Ed's trivia questions, asked Johnny for Dracula's first name. "Well, we find out two weeks later, 'Voivode' in Romanian just means 'Count'!"

Nostalgia trivia spread so far, so fast, that it's clear that Dan and Ed had tapped into something in the national mood of the midsixties. What's most interesting to me is that the first people to pick up on the fad weren't wistful, middle-aged man-in-the-gray-flannel-suit types, yearn-ing for the decoder rings and yellowing baseball box scores of their youth as they caught the 5:48 to New Rochelle. No, instead it was *college kids*, of all people, already nostalgic for their innocent childhoods.

"We were teenagers!" says Ed Goodgold. "So when you'd reminisce about your childhood, you didn't have far to reminisce."

"Maybe that's part of the late-twentieth-century speed thing," Dan suggests, "where everything moves very quickly." Instant nostalgia: just add water and yearn.

I also think it's odd that, on sixties college campuses, which were quickly becoming hotbeds of protest, thousands of students were taking a break from burning their draft cards in order to celebrate, of all things, the good old buttoned-down days of *Ozzie and Harriet* crew cuts and the Lone Ranger. "Do you think people started obsessing about a sim-pler time because of all the tumultuous changes going on around them?" I ask.

Dan and Ed pooh-pooh the idea. "People were looking back fondly on an era in their own lives: childhood. Not the Eisenhower years specifically," says Dan. Still, I have to wonder. The innocent black-and-white adventures of Flash Gordon or Joe Friday must have seemed pretty appealing from the comparatively complicated, disillusioned viewpoint of 1967.

Susan Sontag, of all people, also helped lay the foundations for Goodgold and Carlinsky's brand of trivia. She was teaching at Columbia's religious studies department in 1964 when she published her influential essay "Notes on 'Camp,'" which helped legitimize the academic study of so-bad-it's-good pop-cultural ephemera. As Sontag wrote, "The sensibility of high culture has no monopoly upon refinement. . . . The man who insists on high and serious pleasures is depriving himself of pleasure." Surely it's not entirely coincidental that just months later two Columbia students trotted out a quiz game that, for the first time, privileged Sid Caesar over Julius Caesar, and *Doctor Kildare* over *Doctor Faustus*.

In fact, that very idea—that quiz games should test popular knowledge as well as academic knowledge—is the single longest-lasting legacy of Dan and Ed's conception of trivia. They rescued trivia from the lonely isolation booths of the TV quiz shows and brought it into the dorm room, the neighborhood bar, the barbershop, anywhere arguments can be had and bets settled. For the first time you could enjoy trivia just by leading a normal American life. You didn't have to know a single king of Belgium or Beethoven's only opera[6] or the softest mineral on geology's Mohs Scale.[7]

Goodgold and Carlinsky insisted that all trivia questions had to be nostalgic—otherwise, they were just "little-known facts," Ed says dismissively. The nostalgia hook resonated with so many people that it helped keep trivia-the-idea alive long after trivia-the-campus-fad had died down. When Trivial Pursuit ignited the next trivia boom, in 1983, one of its first supplementary editions was the Baby Boomer box, full of nostalgic Carlinsky/Goodgold-style questions. Even the Alexander Pope quote on the old Trivial Pursuit boxes (the first lines of a mock epic about a girl named Belinda and her hair)[8] reveals the game's debt to Ed and Dan, who used the same quote in their introduction to *More Trivial Trivia:* "What dire offence from am'rous causes springs, / What mighty contests rise from trivial things."

Today's trivia games—*Jeopardy!*, bar trivia, and subsequent Trivial Pursuit releases alike—still look to nostalgia for a big part of their question inventory. The eras may vary—for demographic reasons, you want to appeal to players whether their idea of nostalgia is the Mickey Mouse Club, *The Breakfast Club*, or "In Da Club"—but the pleasure is the same. Dredging up facts is more fun when those facts conjure up cherished memories.

"When we started," says Ed, "I would ask questions about *Sergeant Preston of the Yukon*. But it's not just the great wonder dog, Yukon King, or the ending when he caught the bad guy: 'Well, King, this case is closed.' It's not just the question itself, but when you remember the answer, it's the environment in which you first *learned* the answer. I remember having pea soup at my parents' home as a kid, and the way it smelled, the way that late afternoon felt. I think that's the most powerful part.

"And that's the difference between that and 'What state consumes the most Jell-O?'[9] or 'What's the capital of Illinois?'[10] Those are questions, in the response to which, you have limited satisfaction possible. But with nostalgia, you know, this is like Marcel Proust, where you dunk a cookie into something and you have a hundred pages worth of memories. There's this great multiplier effect in the listeners. And that I like. The personal memories, but also the camaraderie between those who remember. That's a wonderful feeling."

Neither Ed nor Dan thinks their style of nostalgic trivia will ever really unite "those who remember" in the same way again. "These students came from all over the country, and maybe didn't share the same upbringing or geography or major," says Dan. "But they all watched the same movies. They all listened to the same pop music. That's much less true today."

Ed agrees. "This happened in a world that was much simpler. The world was really divided into three choices, best exemplified by Sunday night television: Ed Sullivan, Steve Allen, or Maverick. Three networks. Three choices. And basically one person could take it all in.

"What makes us Americans, in a certain way, is the centrality of popular culture. It ties us together." But the explosion of TV channels and fragmentation of popular music genres have changed all that. "There's so much more out there, that there's less that people share. As a result, we have less of a strong, unifying cultural force in society in general. Things that used to be very, very deep cultural reference points don't mean anything at all nowadays. How flimsy the connective tissue was.

"Nostalgia isn't what it used to be anymore," Ed adds with a rueful laugh.

I'm still thinking about Ed's words—the "flimsy connective tissue" of modern life—on my next plane flight back from *Jeopardy!* It's my fourth time making this same trip in the last month. I'm starting to recognize all the flight attendants.

I'm also getting good at chatting with my fellow passengers without ever explaining the real reason for my California commute. For all I know, there are *Jeopardy!* spies seated in the next row back.

"Oh, I have a sort of part-time job in L.A. this month," I demure to the middle-manager type sitting next to me. "What do you do?"

He looks up from his laptop. "I'm visiting some clients in Park City. I sell wine."

"Oh, really?" That's pretty much the end of my small talk right there. Trying to talk wine with a Mormon is usually a conversational dead end. We're not much better on "women" and "song," for that matter. And my "Potent Potables" flash cards only covered mixed drinks.

"Yeah, I work for Niebaum-Coppola."

"Wait, is that Francis Coppola's winery?" Suddenly I'm interested— I may be no oenophile, but I'm a screenophile, and some of my favorite movies were directed by Francis Ford Coppola. Even if I have nothing to say about Pinot Noir, I could quote big chunks of *The Godfather* verbatim to this guy, if the ninety-minute flight got boring enough.

I start to pepper him with questions. Does he know Francis? What's he like? Is he prepping a new movie? Has this guy ever met Sofia? Talia Shire? Nic Cage?

The wine salesman narrows his eyes and looks at me appraisingly. "Okay, if you're such a Coppola fan, answer me this."

I suddenly realize what's going to happen. There's going to be a trivia question. The trivia question will determine how the conversation goes. If I know the answer, I'm obviously a True Fan, and therefore qualified; I'll get to hear all the cool stories and get the insider dirt. If I get it wrong, I expose myself as a dilettante, and I'll be politely shut out and spend the rest of the flight enjoying Southwest's fine in-flight magazine.

"What did Francis Coppola win his first Oscar for?"

Luckily, I've heard this before, and I remember the trick: Coppola's first Oscar wasn't for directing.

"Best Screenplay, *Patton*, 1970."

The wine guy nods, impressed. "Very good. You *are* a fan." It turns out he's been with the winery a long time and knows the whole family, and their movies, very well. For the rest of the flight, I bask in Coppola anecdotes. The hour and a half flies by.

I've been noticing it more and more lately. It's not usually so overt as this, but there's no getting around it: at a time when, as Ed Goodgold pointed out, fewer common things connect us, trivia represents everything that can still bring people together.

We live in an age of specialization, in which our educational and career choices force us into increasingly narrow niches. People ask me what I do in my day job as a software engineer, but their eyes glaze over if I actually try to answer. It's not just that it's a terribly nerdy, abstruse profession (though it is) or that I'm doing an especially boring job of explaining it to them (though perhaps I am). It's just that they would need to take a handful of introductory college-level computer courses to grasp even the basic mechanics of what a programmer does all day. The same would be true if I tried to learn their jobs.

Time was, you knew and understood what everyone on your street did for a living. Next door was the bus driver, next to him the English teacher, next to her the pet-food salesman. Nowadays, half the time, Johnny Gilbert will announce the occupation of the contestant standing next to me and I'll have no idea what it even means. "An information security analyst from Fishers, Indiana!" "A senior production controller from Brooklyn, New York!" "A consulting program manager from Watertown, Massachusetts!" These are narrow niches—each, I'm sure, with its own specialized vocabulary and set of procedures. When we speak to one another, we might as well be speaking entirely different languages.

Trivia, as I've said before, shouldn't really be called "trivia." Facts about history, geography, books, movies, music—this is the stuff that used to be called good old-fashioned "general knowledge," the stuff that *everybody* was supposed to remember from school, regardless of their career niche. We lost something the more we specialized—it started to drain away this vast pool of information that everybody knew. Knowledge was what connected us, and now it distinguishes us.

And so there's an immediate sense of camaraderie, of a created bond, that results when two people realize they own some piece of knowledge in common. It doesn't take much. If a stranger in an airport tells me that she's from Fargo, North Dakota—well, if I know nothing whatsoever about Fargo, North Dakota, that could be the end of the conversation right there. But trivia can come to the rescue. If I remember that Yankees great Roger Maris hailed from Fargo, I can ask her if she's ever been to the Roger Maris Museum. If I remember that Fargo sits on the Red River of the North, I can ask her if she's ever fished the Red River. Heck, if I've even seen the movie *Fargo*—of which only the first scene is actually set in Fargo, by the way—that's at least an ice-breaker. People are flattered that you know something about them: their profession, their hobby, their hometown. It's as if you took the time to get to know them before you ever met.

The thing that always worried me most about trivia expertise was that it seemed like something that divided people, the swaggering know-it-alls from the proud know-nothings. Sure, there are always going to be people who see trivia as a dueling sword, a means to intellectual show-offery or one-upmanship. But trivia can bring people together too. It sounds Coke-jingle naïve, but maybe if we shared more of the same general knowledge, the way we used to, then we wouldn't have so many of the communication breakdowns we see today—between individuals, between nations, between races or religions. If more of us enjoyed "trivia"—that is, knowing a little bit about everything—we would know more about one another, and therefore might all get along better.

That's one thing I'm starting to see about trivia. It's rewarding to know a lot of great facts, but that knowledge is almost pointless if those facts don't help you get to know a lot of great people as well.

———

Dan and Ed understood the camaraderie that comes from shared knowledge. At Columbia's McMillin Theater, their trivia contests would always end with the participants partying like it was 1949, all linking arms and singing "Happy Trails." "And if you don't think seeing a thousand Ivy Leaguers link arms and sing 'Happy Trails' is a hoot," chuckles Ed, "it *is* a hoot."

During the brief heyday of their nostalgic brand of trivia, Ed Goodgold and Dan Carlinsky changed the face of question-and-answer games. For the first time, quizzing was more than just a series of isolated ivory-tower books or TV shows. Instead it was a community, a subculture, a way of life. And that way of life finally had a name: trivia.

ANSWERS

1. **Gyro Gearloose** is the name of the eccentric Duckburg inventor in *Uncle Scrooge* comics.

2. Paladin lived in **San Francisco's Hotel Carlton** on *Have Gun—Will Travel.*

3. Dale Evans's horse was named **Buttermilk.**

4. The Kingsmen's big hit of 1964 was **"Louie Louie."**

5. Count Dracula has no first name, but his likely historical inspiration was the fifteenth-century prince Vlad III Dracula, so **"Vlad"** is probably the best answer.

6. *Fidelio* is Beethoven's only opera.

7. **Talc** is the softest mineral on geology's Mohs Scale.

8. The quote on the Trivial Pursuit box comes from Pope's *The Rape of the Lock.*

9. **California** consumes more Jell-O than any other state.

10. **Springfield** is the capital of Illinois.

CHAPTER 10

What is COGNITION?

I've already lucked into the first two Daily Doubles of the game, and, doubly lucky, I knew both answers, so the score is not particularly close when I find the third Daily Double as well. I have $28,000 on my scoreboard. Bill Carter, the vaguely Billy Blanks–esque fitness trainer at the third podium, is in second right now, but it's a distant second. There are no more Daily Doubles hidden on the board to guard against, and the category is a strong one for me: "Literary Pairs." I have a little room to maneuver.

My typical Daily Double wager is only a couple thousand or so. I believe the technical *Jeopardy!* term for that kind of wager is "wussy bet." Some of that is strategic—why risk a lead when you don't need to?—but much of it is just cowardice. I'm the kind of gambler who gets antsy when the casino doesn't have a one-dollar-minimum blackjack table, so I don't much like the idea of blowing tens of thousands of dollars on a single trivia question, even if it's "found money" that I'm risking, even if I'll have more big scores than crippling losses.

Often I'll bet an amount that will give me a nice, round score if I answer correctly. This too is partially strategic—it tends to make the math easier—but it's mostly anal-retentiveness and superstition. I do the same thing at restaurants, making sure the tip neatly "evens out" the total tab. Right now, I have $28,000. I *could* bet $2,000 to make a nice clean thirty grand. But that's way too low, given the category. What's the next round number?

"I'll bet $12,000 of it, Alex," I hear myself saying.

This is the biggest wager of my young *Jeopardy!* career. There's an immediate hush in the already quiet auditorium. Alex's voice seems even more sober than usual as he reads the question:

"The film title *Eternal Sunshine of the Spotless Mind* comes from a poem about these ill-fated medieval lovers."

I grimace and my tongue probes an upper molar. I'd read the question in a flash, trying to give my brain a head start while Alex finished reading out loud, but precious seconds are ticking away and the answer's still not coming. I nervously lean my chin on one hand. Soon Alex will sternly prompt me for a response. What do I say?

Mindy and I both loved *Eternal Sunshine of the Spotless Mind* when we saw it a few months back. I remember the title quote is from Alexander Pope, because, in the movie, Kirsten Dunst's character is embarrassed when she mistakenly attributes it to "Pope Alexander." But I don't remember the movie ever naming the poem in question.

Okay, the category is "Literary Pairs," so you're probably meant to remember the answer from its literary source, not from a Jim Carrey movie. Did Pope write about any famous lovers? Nothing leaps to mind. Is there a clue in the quote? Sunshine. Spotless mind. Forgetfulness. Amnesia. No, I'm drawing a blank. *I* might as well have amnesia.

Well, what about the answer space? What ill-fated lovers make up a "literary pair"? Romeo and Juliet—too easy for a $1,600 clue. Let's see, title lovers. Antony and Cleopatra? Troilus and Cressida? Nope, there's already been a "Rosencrantz and Guildenstern" question in the category, so Shakespeare is out altogether. Hero and Leander? They're classical, not medieval. Plus, I think that's Marlowe, not Pope. "Medieval" is starting to bother me. Who are the great star-crossed lovers of medieval romances, anyway? Medieval. Middle Ages. King Arthur. Hmmm. Arthur and Guinevere? Lancelot and Guinevere? They were "ill-fated," sure, but I don't remember anyone of Pope's day writing too much poetry about Arthurian romance. That came back in with the Victorians. "Tristan and Isolde" is another Arthurian possibility, but it seems a little too *hard* an answer for the $1,600 space.

Alex is looking fixedly at me. All this internal monologue has taken seven or eight seconds, though it feels like hours. "Whhhhhooooo . . . aaaaaaarrrrrre . . ." I begin as slowly as I can, hoping inspiration will strike while I stall. Another long pause. $24,000 is at stake here: six months' take-home wages at my day job, the price of, say, a new Toyota Camry. I don't even have a good guess, so I'm on the verge of saying "Tristan and Isolde."

Wait. "Medieval lovers." You wouldn't really say that about fictional characters, would you, even if their lives were set in medieval times? Something about the wording almost makes the clue sound historical, like the answer is a pair of real people who lived during the Middle Ages. Then what makes them a "literary" pair? Either because their story became popular fodder for poets, or—

Or one was an author.

Something accelerates in my head, and suddenly I can sense the answer tantalizingly out of reach. Dante and Beatrice. Petrarch and Laura. Wait! I know who it is! Love letters, castration. The Alexander Pope clue jibes as well. What were their names?

Alex is about to rule against me for taking too much time. "Uh, er, Heloise," I blurt out. "Uh, and Abelard." Peter Abelard, the famous French theologian who fell in love with Heloise, the gifted teenaged girl he tutored, got her pregnant, and then lost his "little Peter" Abelard in violent fashion when her angry uncle found out.

"Yep!" says Alex, to my great relief. Only then do I realize that I've been holding my breath for the whole twenty-five-second ordeal, and forcefully exhale.

Back in my motel room that night, I replay the Daily Double in my head. The clue wasn't what I would call a Puzzler, like a Final Jeopardy that requires some special "Aha!" leap of insight. But at least for me, it wasn't just a Plain Vanilla you-know-it-or-you-don't clue either, as evidenced by the internal agonies I went through to unearth the right answer. This was hard, brain-straining *work*.

I've always been skeptical that trivia prowess is the same thing as intelligence. No one likes trivia more than I do, but the idea that having memorized a lot of facts is synonymous with intelligence strikes me as unlikely. Memorizing a lot of trivia could just mean that you're interested in a particular subject, or have a lot of spare time on your hands, or a good memory, or OCD, or that you're Rain Man. It doesn't necessarily mean that you're also a Nobel Prize–worthy genius, working to cure cancer or end world hunger or design shopping-cart wheels that won't squeak.

When I ask former *Jeopardy!* and quiz bowl champ Craig Barker about the relationship between trivia and brains, he's dismissive as well. "Being a great quiz bowl player only proves that you're a great quiz bowl player. It doesn't prove you're smarter." I remember Rob Hentzel's theory about "quiz bowl disease," that trivia skills often seem to distract people from real intellectual achievement, instead of contributing to it.

Psychometricians—experts in psychological measurements—gauge intelligence by breaking it down into two categories. The first category is one's innate learning and reasoning ability, and the second is one's acquired knowledge. They call these two factors "fluid g" and "crystallized g," possibly because it makes psychometrics papers seem cooler when the constructs sound like street drugs. A person's ability to look at a sheet of paper and memorize a list of South American capital cities is determined by fluid g. But once the capital cities are stored in one's head, they're part of crystallized g.

I had always assumed that trivia, therefore, was nothing but crystallized intelligence. Facts are stored somewhere in the dusty attic of your head. You dislodge the right one from its hiding place somewhere behind an artificial Christmas tree or old armoire, and, voila, produce it on command. The process seems so prosaic that the real mental work must happen elsewhere. But this Abelard and Heloise question has made me realize that trivia often requires a complex interplay of both fluid *and* crystallized intelligence. I started out with a set of crystallized facts—a line of Kirsten Dunst dialogue, my sketchy knowledge about Alexander Pope, vague memories of medieval literature—but those just became fuel in the fluid-g fire when the real problem-solving began. I also needed a separate set of rule-based "meta-knowledge" to solve the problem. Which possible answers are eligible for the category? Which seem too easy or too hard? Which words in the clue are meant to be helpful hints and which are just distracting? Sometimes the reasoning is even subconscious—does this answer seem intuitively "righter" somehow than that other one?

Not every trivia question, in other words, is an open-and-shut case, a simple act of recall, like remembering your multiplication tables. The mental wrangling I went through to get to "Abelard and Heloise" was really more like trying to solve a puzzle on some kind of test—an IQ test, for example. That familiar IQ-test headache of trying to make six squares wrap up in your mind, so you can picture how the faces are oriented on the finished cube, or testing dozens of math operations on a set of numbers, trying to deduce the pattern so you can calculate the next number in the series—that's exactly how I felt, pursuing all angles on the Daily Double.

This little realization startles me. If the solving of trivia feels a lot like the solving of an intelligence test (and this coming from someone who's weird enough to sort of enjoy both), does that mean that I was wrong all this time? Could trivia acumen actually be related to, well, intelligence?

The casual *Jeopardy!* viewer would probably be surprised that I'm even asking the question. Of course *Jeopardy!* players are smart—to the person on the street, "smart" and "*Jeopardy!*" are practically synonymous. If you looked up "smart" in the dictionary, most people would probably expect to see a nerd in a sweater standing behind an electric-blue podium and holding a buzzer, end of story.

No less a luminary than Thomas Edison would have agreed. In the early years of the twentieth century, decades before *Ask Me Another!* kicked off the first nationwide quiz fad, Edison graded all his job applicants with a 150-question trivia "questionnaire" so tough that only 10 percent passed it. Disappointed by these results, Edison called America's college graduates "amazingly ignorant" in the pages of *The New York Times*. In the resulting public outcry, newspaper editorials huffed and puffed about the evils of equating intelligence with trivial knowledge, and chuckled when Albert Einstein himself took a shot at Edison's test and failed miserably. Edison grumpily maintained that his questions were "exceedingly simple," and that they helped him measure "alertness of mind, power of observation, and interest in life and the world." He wanted the kind of factory workers who would know what country, besides Australia, has native kangaroos,[1] where Napoleon was born,[2] and the principal acid in vinegar.[3] Unfortunately, those were the *easy* questions—applicants also needed to know "exceedingly simple" facts like the voltage used by electric streetcars, the population of Japan, the weight of the air in a twenty-by-thirty-by-ten-foot room, and the places where the most prunes are grown.

The Wizard of Menlo Park would go on to tailor his tests to specific kinds of craftsmen, with odd results. Cabinetmakers were asked, "Who was the Roman Emperor when Christ was born?"[4] Masons were asked, "Who assassinated Abraham Lincoln?"[5] Carpenters had to know "What are the ingredients in a martini cocktail?"[6] I encourage you to try these questions out the next time you're calling around for an electrician or a plumber. Well, maybe not the martini one.

The idea that trivia people are necessarily smart people has even been endorsed by the United States government—yes, the same organization that vouched for Santa Claus's existence in *Miracle on 34th Street*. In this case, it's not the U.S. Post Office giving trivia the stamp of approval, but the State Department. One of the most demanding of government jobs (assuming that "demanding government job" isn't an oxymoron) is a spot with the U.S. Foreign Service, the cadre of diplomatic officers in charge of staffing embassies, analyzing developments overseas, and representing America to the world. It's a weighty responsibility. And how does the government fill these posts? With a trivia test.

Well, they call it a "Job Knowledge" test. I first heard about the test from Mindy's dad, a longtime Foreign Service officer who has, in the past, even administered the test as part of his Commerce Department duties. "Oh, it's absolutely a trivia test," he tells me after dinner one night, looking at me over his glasses in his slightly distracted way. "One hundred percent *Jeopardy!* material. You should take it; you'd do very well."

I order a study guide, and, sure enough, the bulk of the test is a series of general-knowledge questions on history, geography, and culture, both American and international. If diplomats are going to represent America and report on the world, I suppose it makes sense that they should be well versed on both. But it still seems odd to me that we're staffing our embassies based on which trivia buffs knew what the grasslands of Argentina are called[7] or which jazz saxophonist helped create bebop while playing with Dizzy Gillespie.[8]

One purveyor who has stayed in business by shrewdly finessing the difference between "smart" and "trivia-savvy" is *mental_floss* magazine. The oddly punctuated trivia mag has been dispensing bite-sized factoids since 2000, when Duke University juniors Will Pearson and Mangesh Hattikudur, along with some friends, started printing a flimsy campus newsletter by that name. Their mission statement, then as now, was to make learning fun. Rather than just spewing facts, the magazine would dress up trivia with humor or novel themes to make the medicine go down smoother.

They had no experience in running a magazine—Will was a history major, Mangesh studied anthropology—but their newsletter was successful enough to reveal a niche. Together, they worked part-time and summer jobs to save up money and print a few pilot issues, sort of a trivia version of a Mickey Rooney/Judy Garland musical. ("Say, kids, we can put on the magazine right here!") Mangesh waited tables. Will nannied. With the twenty thousand dollars they cobbled together and a name borrowed from an Ontario improv troupe, *mental_floss* premiered in 2001, selling six thousand five hundred copies of its first issue.

A big corporate publisher, a Condé Nast, wouldn't launch a magazine without a reader base in the hundreds of thousands, and would lose millions on low-cost subscriptions just to build up that reader base and attract advertising. The success rates in starting a magazine are worse than starting a restaurant—it's more like trying to start a successful *bad* restaurant. Fully 80 percent of magazines fail before making it to their fourth year. And yet, four years later, *mental_floss* is alive and well, with thirty-five thousand subscribers and ninety thousand copies on national newsstands bimonthly.

mental_floss got a burst of publicity from a coffee-table appearance on a 2003 episode of *Friends* (fan David Arquette had given a copy to his wife, Courteney Cox), but its real success has come from the magazine's three secret weapons. First, there's the format: *mental_floss* pessimistically and accurately judges the attention span of the modern American reader. "We're reaching busy professionals that may have only ten or fifteen minutes of time every day," Will tells me. A topic that would be a laborious ten-page slog in *Smithsonian* becomes a single factoid or bullet point. Item! The Guatemalan highlands are home to thirty-three volcanoes! Item! Vampire bats share blood with each other by "kissing" it from mouth to mouth! Yellow highlighter marks further distill already brief blurbs for the super-impatient. High and low culture blend seamlessly—betcha didn't know that one obscure Mayan dialect has an *N* character with an umlaut over it, just like the faux metal band Spiñal Tap! Betcha didn't know that Groucho Marx memorized parts of *The Waste Land* so he could quote it when he invited poet T. S. Eliot over for dinner! The result is a magazine that's compulsively easy to pick up and enjoy for ninety seconds in a guest bathroom or dentist's office. It reminds us that trivia can be, as Hitchcock once said about drama, "Life with the dull bits cut out."

mental_floss also benefits from the surprising business savvy of its founders. Will Pearson may have been a wide-eyed college junior five years ago, but he's now a relentlessly on-message CEO. He uses *mental_floss* core-competency buzzwords like "quirky" and "factoid" a half dozen times each during our brief conversation. He's already re-making the magazine into the flagship of a vast *mental_floss* media empire, complete with pop reference books, a board game, and Will's own weekly appearances talking trivia on CNN Headline News. The Discovery Channel is developing TV projects. *mental_floss* is well on its way to becoming the most successful all-media branding for trivia since Ripley's Believe It or Not.

When I track Will down, he's in Philadelphia meeting with a company that wants to release a *mental_floss* "Genius Kit" or maybe "Cocktail Party Cheat Sheet Flash Cards." These marketing ideas point up the third and most interesting jewel in the *mental_floss* crown: its implicit promise to the reader that the ten-megaton trivia payload in each issue isn't just going to entertain you, it's actually going to make you feel better about yourself. "Feel smart again!" every cover crows. With this goal in mind, one article in each issue is a sort of CliffsNotes summary of a great novel, symphony, or other work of art. Travel blurbs on exotic lands allow you to keep up when your brother-in-law whips out the vacation slides.

"We didn't want it to just be a magazine of pop-culture information. We wanted to cover all the things people feel like they should have learned in school," says Will, and that "should have" speaks volumes. In this age of information overload, we all feel woefully ignorant in more fields than we care to mention. The *mental_floss* brain trust sees trivia the same way I've come to: as the cure for modern overspecialization, a way for us to recapture the kind of well-rounded mind boasted by the great Renaissance men of the past. They're not just selling a moment's amusement during a dull commute. They're selling broad intellectual competence. Or, at least, the conversational illusion thereof.

Is *mental_floss* right? Is trivia really some good-for-you substance that you need to ingest a Recommended Dietary Allowance of, the mental equivalent of omega-3 fatty acids or betacarotene?

If nothing else, trivia does help keep the brain limber. The famous "Nun Study" conducted by the National Institute on Aging, among other research, has shown that mental activity late in life can help stave off Alzheimer's and dementia. Most of these studies looked at pastimes such as reading, solving crosswords, or playing board and card games. Trivia exercises the same mental muscles that all of those do.

And, unlike a game of pinochle or an issue of *Easy Crosswords* magazine, trivia often delivers content that's far from trivial. Look again at Edison's test, or the State Department's: knowing about Lincoln's assassination or South American geography isn't "trivial" in the same sense that it's trivial to know the last name of Mattel's "Barbie"[9] or which *Brady Bunch* cast member was written out of the show's very last episode.[10] As I stand behind a *Jeopardy!* podium and answer question after question on cancer drugs and the civil rights movement and the lives of Einstein and Gandhi and Mozart, I realize why the word "trivia" is so inappropriate. It's actually *important* to know who history's great geniuses were, that some cancer is treatable, or that the civil rights movement happened. Educator E. D. Hirsch coined the term "cultural literacy" to describe the set of core knowledge that all of us need in order to navigate in society. When you describe trivia as "random general knowledge about life," you realize that trivia knowledge *is* nothing but good, sound cultural literacy, though it may be dressed up in game show neon.

Sometimes even the most bizarre trivia can end up having real-world effects. Snapple Beverage Group marketing VP Steve Jarmon oversees the "Real Facts" campaign that puts trivia under the lid of every Snapple bottle. He still remembers an ecstatic phone call from a research scientist who had been inspired by a Snapple cap that read, "Camel milk doesn't curdle." This single unexpected fact, so-called trivia, had launched her onto a new avenue of research in her work with liquids and spoilage.

Even when it deals with less weighty matters, then, trivia can serve as a gateway drug to more substantive learning. Trivia is the marijuana of knowledge (and, as pub quiz players well know, can just as often lead to a case of the munchies). Life is full of subjects too intimidating to dive into headlong, from quantum physics to Russian cinema. But trivia can provide an easy, intriguing introduction to any topic you feared might bore you silly.

Let's take someone like me, who strongly suspects that ballet is boring, despite Mr. Rogers's many attempts, during my childhood, to convince me that ballet was cool because football players like Lynn Swann took lessons. If you corner me at a party even today and try to give me a speech on the beauty and wonder of ballet, you're wasting your time. My eyes will glaze before you even get to second position. But give me a good trivia fact about ballet—for example, that at the 1913 premiere of Stravinsky's *Rite of Spring*, the crowd *rioted* because the music and choreography were so shockingly modern—and you've got my attention. I'm suddenly curious about ballet, of all things. Similarly, baseball bores Mindy silly, but I nursed her through the 2004 World Series on a steady diet of Red Sox lore and "Curse of the Bambino" trivia. Maybe she was faking it, but she almost managed to seem interested at times. That's the power of trivia: it ignites our curiosity about things we didn't think we were interested in.

Trivia, in other words, is bait on the fishing rod of education. By the time you realize what you've swallowed, you're hooked. I wonder if there's a historian who studies the Civil War today because, as a kid, he was amazed by the remarkable story of Wilmer McLean, the man who was so upset when the first major battle of the Civil War, the Battle of Bull Run, began on his farm, that he moved his family to a quiet town called Appomattox and, four years later, saw the war end with an armistice signed in his front parlor. Or maybe there's a marine biologist somewhere who got into her field because, in elementary school, she read that the Atlantic giant squid has the largest eye found in nature—

about the size of a volleyball—and was fascinated. The right trivia fact at the right time can do more than answer a Daily Double for you. It can change the way you think. It can change your life.

Even though Rob Hentzel was the one who described "quiz bowl disease" to me, he was quick to point out that even if trivia ability and intelligence are by no means the same thing, the two certainly seem to be correlated. *Jeopardy!* champs and quiz bowl team members and kings of the Trivial Pursuit board are almost always the very model of a modern intellectual. They read voraciously. They are articulate conversationalists with large vocabularies—walking thesauri as well as walking encyclopedias. They succeeded in school. They correct you if you say "imply" when you mean "infer," or "i.e." when you mean "e.g."

Obviously the State Department isn't expecting Foreign Service officers to spend all their time at cocktail parties discussing Argentine terrain and bebop (though what a party that would be!). Thomas Edison knew his craftsmen would rarely need to consult Roman history in order to build a cabinet. But I realize, Uncle Sam and Thomas Edison weren't equating trivia smarts with general aptitude when they drew up their tests. They had just determined, like Rob, that there was often a correlation between the two, and that the former was an easy-to-grade indicator of the latter.

Even if being smart isn't the same thing as being full of facts, it's easy to see why the two might go hand in hand. If you're an intelligent person, you probably have a knack for quick learning and a sponge-like memory. You'll be curious about the world around you, and more likely to remember the trivia that you learn. Conversely, as quiz bowl coach Eric Hillemann pointed out to me, the more facts you accumulate, the easier it becomes to learn new things, because you have a web of knowledge to fit those new facts into. Facts and intelligence form a vicious circle.

Esquire editor A. J. Jacobs explored the relationship between intelligence and knowledge accumulation in his 2004 bestseller *The Know-It-All*. A.J. wanted to "feel smart again," in the words of *mental_floss*, but instead of treating himself to a magazine subscription, the poor guy decided to read the entire *Encyclopaedia Britannica*, A to Z, all forty-four million words of it. This leads, in his book, to lots of rumination on the nature and definition of intelligence, but mainly—spoiler warning!—it makes A.J., by his own admission, a really annoying guy at cocktail parties. His shoehorned-in *Britannica* facts ("Well, speaking of Jesus and Tolstoy . . .") are so superfluous that, at one point, his friends nickname him "The Great Conversation Stopper."

"So I assume that was all pretty well exaggerated, right?" I ask A.J. when I meet him at a midtown Manhattan hotel. In person he's a sweetheart of a guy with arched eyebrows and a goofy grin. He looks almost nothing like gangly Australian actor Noah Taylor, the celebrity whom, for a magazine piece, he successfully impersonated at the 1997 Oscars. "You weren't really that annoying, right?"

"Oh, you'd be surprised how little I had to exaggerate," he says.

Oops. I try to recover by asking him what his very favorite fact was. A.J. could have volunteered any of the loftiest, weightiest Deep Thoughts from thirty-three thousand pages of *Britannica*-approved wisdom, but instead he proves himself a man after my own heart with these two gems:

1. Opossums have thirteen nipples.
2. René Descartes had a fetish for cross-eyed women.

Since I doubt A.J. has ever tried to milk an opossum, or set his cross-eyed cousin up on a blind date with a dead seventeenth-century French philosopher, I have to assume he's not measuring these facts by their utility. He seems to love trivia facts like these for the same reason I do—they remind us that truth is stranger than fiction, that the universe really is a brilliant and mysterious place. In the midst of our humdrum daily routine, trivia can be a bolt out of the blue, reminding us how weirdly wonderful life really is.

A.J. reminds me even more of myself when he describes childhood bookshelves full of trivia books. "When I was growing up, I had all sorts of collections—a drink stirrer collection, an airsickness bag collection, and then the trivia collection. The rarer the fact, the better—like you're looking for the rare silver dollar coin or the stamp with two imprints or whatever. The René Descartes fact, that's a wonderful rare coin." He's nailed the almost addictive nature of accumulating trivia, which, for many acolytes, is more of an acquisitive pursuit than an inquisitive one.

As we talk, I can tell that A.J. wasn't exaggerating in the book—he really does pepper a conversation with odd facts whenever possible, almost compulsively. There's even something a little bit competitive about trivia for him, as I learn when I tell him that I work as a computer programmer.

"Hey, I know a computer programming fact!" It's like a switch has flipped in his head, the one labeled IRRITATE. "Did you know that the first computer programmer was a woman, and she was the daughter of poet Lord Byron?"

"Hey, yeah, it's funny you should mention that. The first computer language I ever learned was named Ada, in honor of that very woman. Ada Lovelace."

I thought we'd shared a friendly little knowledge-bonding moment, but A.J. doesn't look gratified. He looks chagrined. "You got me," he says in a subdued voice, evidently feeling one-upped. "I didn't know that one."

He traces his hypercompetitive view of trivia back to childhood. "I don't know about you, but I could barely catch a baseball or throw a football. So this was something I could excel at; I could excel at presidents' middle names. So that always stays with me."

I nod. "I've seen that in quiz bowl matches. People who can't get that competitive aggression out on the basketball court, for example, get it out by knowing the mating cycle of a penguin."

"I do know they have a high rate of homosexuality."

This throws me for a second. "What? Oh! Penguins! I thought you meant trivia geeks."

When you talk to A.J., be prepared for abrupt conversational left turns like this one as you carom through the encyclopedia from "a-ak" to "zywiec." But what comes through more than anything else, in the book as well as in person, is a sweet, almost childlike love of learning. His thirty-two-volume adventure reveals that memorizing thousands of facts may not be the *best* way to get smarter, but you could do a lot worse. "Knowledge and intelligence are not the same thing," he concludes, "but they do live in the same neighborhood."

I have to agree. Simple facts, even trivial ones, are the building blocks that can be stacked and combined to form substantive knowledge, and even wisdom. A trivia obsession might turn some people into bores, and others, like poor John Timbs or Albert Southwick, into unfocused failures, but I'm willing to bet it turns thousands more into engaged, curious, successful adults. The list of self-confessed trivia fans who have also excelled in their "day job" includes William Rehnquist, Tom Hanks, Bill Clinton, the aforementioned Thomas Edison, and Maya Angelou. All learning starts with facts, after all, and trivia games reveal—perhaps better than any other arena—how inseparably facts and intelligence are bound up with each other. You're going to need a good supply of both if you're going to puzzle through the really tough questions, in trivia just as in life. That's the main lesson of the Abelard and Heloise question for me—apart, of course, from the obvious "Don't knock up the sixteen-year-old French girl you're tutoring, or her crazy uncle might track you down and castrate you."

Not all trivia facts are trivial, and even the trivial ones might come in handy someday, I think to myself as I leave the hotel and walk out into the afternoon sunlight on Seventh Avenue. Even trivia like "Opossums have thirteen nipples" might mean something to *somebody*. If nothing else, it's a matter of life and death to the thirteenth baby opossum.

ANSWERS

1. **Papua New Guinea** (then known as New Guinea) is the only country, besides Australia, with native kangaroos.

2. Napoleon was born on **Corsica** (in the city of Ajaccio, to be precise).

3. **Acetic, or ethanoic, acid** is the principal acid in vinegar.

4. **Caesar Augustus** was emperor of Rome when Christ was born.

5. **John Wilkes Booth** assassinated Abraham Lincoln.

6. A martini contains **gin and dry vermouth.**

7. The grasslands of Argentina are called **the Pampas.**

8. Jazz saxophonist **Charlie Parker** was one of the founding fathers of bebop.

9. Barbie's full name is Barbie Millicent **Roberts.** (*Millicent?*)

10. Robert Reed's father character, **Mike Brady,** was written out of *The Brady Bunch*'s very last episode.

CHAPTER 11

What is JUXTAPOSITION?

My twentieth *Jeopardy!* game gets a lot closer down the homestretch when the contestant to my left, Alan Paul, a ramrod-straight L.A. economist with tinted glasses, finds a late Daily Double in the category "The Roaring '20s." He adds $4,000 to his score for knowing what event was planned by Machine Gun Jack McGurn, with the help of his girlfriend's alibi.[1] When the Double Jeopardy round ends, Alan has just over half my score. If he knows the final answer and I don't, he'll win.

"'Children's Lit'!" announces Alex. "Will that help our champion or the challengers?" Whether the game is close or not, Alex always serves up his patter with the same offhand equanimity; you get the impression that, after twenty years, he could do this in his sleep. He is, after all, the guy who told *The Washington Post* that he even affirmed his wedding vows in *Jeopardy!* form: "The answer is . . . yes!" I wonder if they played the *Jeopardy!* think music after "Speak now or forever hold your peace."

"'This title character's full name is Oscar Zoroaster Phadrig Isaac Norman Henkle Emmannuel Ambroise Diggs.'[2] You have thirty seconds to identify him. Good luck."

There are two ways to answer this question correctly. You could stare at the name long enough to realize why Oscar had to have nine names, and why those particular names, and what joke might be contained therein. Or you could arrange to have spent your entire childhood poring over the collected works of a former air traffic controller from Sacramento named Fred L. Worth.

Luckily, I'm in the second group. I can still picture the entry for "Oscar Zoroaster Phadrig Isaac Norman Henkle Emmannuel Ambroise Diggs" atop page 514 of Worth's 1977 opus *The Complete Un-*

abridged Super Trivia Encyclopedia, right in between an entry reminding you that Oscar the Grouch's birthday is June 1 and one informing you that Osgood Conklin, played by Gale Gordon, was the name of the high school principal on *Our Miss Brooks.*

Fred Worth was the closest thing to a trivia icon that the 1970s produced, and I'm one of the tens of thousands of fans who owned his bestselling eight-hundred-page *Encyclopedia* and its two sequels. I spent hours thumbing through these untidy alphabetical grab bags, gratified for some reason to absorb facts on things I'd never even heard of, many from thirty years or more before I was born. The Dempsey-Tunney "Long Count," *Little Nemo in Slumberland,* "Garbo Laughs," the opening narration to *Ben Casey*—decades worth of cultural flotsam and jetsam that I never would have heard of, if not for the fertile memory and prolific pen of Fred Worth. Thanks to Fred, I successfully identify Oscar Zoroaster Phadrig Isaac Norman Henkle Emmannuel Ambroise Diggs's secret identity, end the game $40,000 richer, and live to fight another day.

The phone book helps me track Fred down to the Sacramento bungalow where he lives today. When he opens his front door, the omniscient trivia guru of my childhood is revealed to be a cheerful, slightly gnome-like sixty-year-old suburbanite with a newsprint-gray beard. He could be Kenny Rogers playing the lead in the TV-movie version of *The Orson Welles Story,* or, even more horrifically, the other way around. I didn't know what to expect, but he looks, I realize, exactly *right.*

"Come in!" He welcomes me into the house.

As the door closes behind me, blocking out the bright California sunshine, my eyes struggle to adjust to the dark living room. Even before I can see anything, I smell a familiar odor, something old and musty from my childhood. As walls of floor-to-ceiling shelves coalesce out of the darkness, I recognize the smell: old books, thousands of them. Fred's house smells like a used bookstore—not the patchouli-and-kitty-litter smell of your typical mom-and-pop used bookstore, but the ancient aroma of someplace like Portland's Powell's City of Books or New

York's Strand. This is the stale, hallowed smell of the sheer weight of millions upon millions of *words*.

Except for the antique Wurlitzer jukebox on the north wall and a few movie posters, every available space has been covered with books. Even the sofa has been backed by three-foot shelving facing the entry-way. The books are mostly biographies and memoirs of Old Holly-wood, alphabetically arranged, the fuel that feeds Fred's love of movie trivia. "From these eight books on Elizabeth Taylor," he says, gesturing to the *T*s, "I might pick up one new fact each." One prominent but narrow shelf features various printings of all of Fred's books—not just his three trivia encyclopedias, but also quiz and fact books on U.S. presidents, on movies, on World War II, on Elvis. A spare bedroom is full of more nonfiction, and fiction's in the garage. Fred's office is reserved for trivia books, which fill every shelf. I see pop reference titles that I remember from the dog-eared, endlessly reread copies piled beside my childhood bed. *The Dictionary of Misinformation. Not-So-Great Moments in Sports. Big, Bigger,* and *Biggest Secrets. Extraordinary Origins of Everyday Things.* Row upon row of *Ripley's Believe It or Not!* paperbacks.

And yet Fred wasn't always a bookworm, much less a trivia fan. He grew up in a poor Irish family, he tells me. When his mother, a divorced waitress, needed to settle a dinner-table argument between the boys, she might call the newsroom of the *San Francisco Chronicle* for an authoritative answer, but that was as far as the trivia went. After graduating from high school, Fred joined the air force and shipped off to England for three years. The whole time, he says, "I only read one book. And it was a porno book."

But while stationed overseas, Fred noticed something about British LPs that would change his life. The sleeves of the rock and roll records he bought were full of information—they'd list every session musician who played on every track, something you'd never see on American albums of the time. The jackets intrigued him, awakening in him the defining characteristic of every trivia fanatic: an insatiable compulsion for detail. After returning to the States and enrolling in college, Fred wandered through the campus bookstore for the first time, looking at shelves full of titles he'd heard about but never read. *The Invisible Man. The Grapes of Wrath.* "I'm going to explore what that's all about," he told himself, and began keeping a journal of every book he read. By the time he quit keeping track, decades later, the journal held over six thousand titles.

Those British rock albums awoke Fred to a wider world, where there was joy to be had in unearthing baroque, recondite knowledge about your pop-culture hobbies. We live in an age where entertainment trivia has been mainstreamed, a time of exhaustive DVD special features, of Internet fan sites, of specialized magazines for filmophiles and rock snobs of every persuasion, and so it's easy to forget that the world didn't used to be this way. Fred argues that it simply wasn't *possible* to be an American trivia fan in the 1950s and early 1960s. The resources didn't exist. "Did you know that it took fourteen years from the time Elvis became popular for a single book to be written on him?" laments Fred. "In this country, we were not into detail. *Europe* developed detail."

"Why do you think that is?"

"Weather. The whole history of England consists of finding things to do out of the weather. Which tells you why Russia was even worse. That's why Russian novels have 182 characters: bad weather."

That our country's culture has now been "trivialized," that we all know bushels of behind-the-scenes lore about our favorite people and places and movies and music, is part of Fred Worth's legacy. In the wake of the campus trivia boom of the 1960s, Fred dreamed of a book where all manner of trivial oddments would be easily at hand, for the browser or researcher alike, anyone who wanted to find out what "Hoss" Cartwright's real first name was[3] or who appeared on the first *People* magazine cover.[4] "There was a need," he says. So he began wandering through toy stores and libraries and late night TV, assembling little-known facts on three-by-five cards. In 1974, the year I was born, he published *The Trivia Encyclopedia*, indexing trivia from A (the first initial of A. Mutt, of *Mutt and Jeff* fame) to ZVBXRPL (the encoded horse racing tip from the Marx Brothers flick *A Day at the Races*).

In the years that followed, Fred kept his day job as an FAA air traffic controller, while simultaneously becoming a one-man trivia industry. He produced an updated version of his *Trivia Encyclopedia*, brimming with reader additions and corrections, and then two sequels and a smattering of other quiz books. For five years, he edited *Trivia Unlimited,* his own trivia newsletter. He wrote questions for the short-lived Mark Goodson game show *Trivia Trap,* an episode of which included one of his favorite trivia questions of all time: "Robert Stroud raised canaries in what United States penitentiary?"[5]

Fred peppers me with questions like this one the whole time I'm with him—he's a seething, bubbling cauldron of trivia. Who's the only TV lead character with the initials F.U.?[6] Where was the Caesar salad invented?[7] What subject did "Mr. Chips" teach in *Goodbye, Mr. Chips*?[8] What actor was a member of both *The Dirty Dozen* and *The Magnificent Seven*?[9] But he's not dueling for intellectual supremacy the way some trivia fans do. He seems to have a genuine, eye-twinkling interest in sharing the answer with me, whether I'm wrong or right.

"A lot of people are intimidated by trivia," he says. "They just don't feel like participants. You can always tell these people—their first response is always 'Who cares?' "

"Are they right?" I ask him. "Does trivia have some function, or is 'Who cares?' a valid response?"

Fred thinks for a minute. "The steam engine," he finally says. "Let's use that as an example. The Greeks had a little toy that they would put water in, and it would roll across the floor. It was really the first steam engine. They didn't know how to apply it, but they knew how to make it. Every great invention, when it first started out, it was created like a toy. So just like science fiction is a blueprint for science, trivia is a blueprint for information. You've got to remember when trivia came along: right before the computer age. Read the writing on the wall—trivia was trying to tell us something. Trivia knew there was going to be a big influx of information coming."

There's something to that. Whether trivia was a harbinger or a gentle nudge or just an early symptom, it certainly epitomizes the information-rich (and information-obsessed) age we live in today. You can bet fourteen years wouldn't go by today between an Elvis-sized musical phenomenon and the first book examining it. Today, there'd be hundreds of websites dissecting leaked tracks and analyzing lyrics and fashion trends ("wtf is with those sideburns? lol!!!") months before Elvis's first album even hit stores. Maybe that's why trivia as we know it didn't exist until the twentieth century. Human beings just hadn't accumulated enough pointless information to start annoying one another with it yet.

Fred Worth's pop reference books are still known to today's trivia fans for their founding importance to the genre, but they're just as well known for some of their quirks. For example, turn to the page of any of his encyclopedias where a number would fall alphabetically—at the beginning of the Os for "one," for example. Here the entries reach a new high of triviality, with page after page of numerical data: addresses, phone numbers, sports statistics, serial numbers, and license plates. Does anybody really care that Klinger's army serial number, on *M*A*S*H*, was 19571782? Or that 1313 Pleasant Avenue was Don Knotts's home address in *The Incredible Mr. Limpet*? Or that Slim Pickens's Social Security number in the Spielberg bomb *1941* was 106-43-2185? Is this the kind of stuff that comes up at *your* pickup trivia games?

"I'm not proud of the license plates and things, because knowing that doesn't make you a better person," says Fred, looking back. "That, I would call minutiae." Even Fred Worth draws the "trivial" line somewhere.

Other readers have carped about the books', shall we say, somewhat *leisurely* approach to fact-checking. "Fred Worthless," says Ray Hamel bluntly. "His books have so many mistakes that they're not even accepted as references anymore" at local trivia contests. It's true that his encyclopedias have their fair share of urban legends and apocrypha, but you have to remember that Fred was writing this stuff off the top of his head, in a time before there were shelves full of books by scholars of pop culture. Settled areas of trivia inquiry today—did a young Andy Williams *really* dub Lauren Bacall's singing voice in *To Have and Have Not*? Was "crying Indian" TV actor Iron Eyes Cody *really* Cherokee?—were still open questions in the 1970s, when a generation of trivia fans was discovering them for the first time.

"I worry about accuracy a lot," says Fred. "I don't have the time or the resources to go back and check everything, but if you read enough, you will know what the bogus stuff is."

"So when you tell me that"—I glance down at the top page of a manuscript of food facts sitting on Fred's office desk—"that Henry David Thoreau invented raisin bread, for example, you have a pretty good sense that that's so?"

"Yeah. And if you read enough, you'll run across it again in another book and then again in another book. And you have to basically, in an introduction, confess that you're trusting the word of other people."

A newspaper feature, if its author gets nailed for making stuff up, as has happened in some recent scandals, might at least have some *literary* value, even if it's out to lunch factually. But trivia, unique among the lively arts, is worthless if it's not always, 100 percent, mathematically, epistemologically, verifiably true. The point of trivia is to amaze people with facts that sound unbelievable but are nevertheless authentic. If trivia doesn't have to be true anymore, you can wow your friends with whatever made-up facts you want. The sky's the limit. "Did you know that Martin Van Buren used to attend Cabinet meetings stark naked and slathered in strawberry preserves?" "Did you know that a giraffe's neck is made entirely of tin?"

Phony trivia devalues the currency of facts just like forged money can devalue the currency of a nation. And sadly, most people today get their trivia from the widely disseminated lists of "facts" on the Internet. Some of it is just poorly researched, some may be invented from the whole cloth, but the end result is the same: much of it isn't true. No matter what your e-mail in-box tells you, the name "Wendy" did *not* appear first in James M. Barrie's *Peter Pan*, babies are *not* born without kneecaps, Donald Duck was never banned in Finland for his lack of pants, and Winston Churchill was born quietly at home, not in a ladies' room during a dance. The invention of ersatz trivia is so widespread nowadays that debunking it has become a cottage industry. The cable TV show *Mythbusters* often devotes itself to disproving trivia "facts" such as "The daddy longlegs is the world's most poisonous animal" and "A duck's quack does not echo." Columnists like Cecil Adams and websites like Snopes.com shoot down a different trivia legend practically weekly.

But accuracy in trivia can be a funny thing. Take the item about Thoreau inventing raisin bread. That story is presented as fact in the scholarly, definitive biography of Henry David Thoreau published in 1965 by professor Walter Harding, the world's leading Thoreau scholar.

What source could be more authoritative? Surely this fact, at least, is one I can annoy all my friends with via e-mail.

There's only one hitch: Henry David Thoreau may have had many great qualities (unfailing moral compass, lucid prose style, always chopped his own firewood), but innovative baking skill wasn't one of them. In fact, cookbooks with raisin bread recipes date back to at least 1671. It seems the eminent Professor Harding was taken in by, of all things, a story in a 1943 *Ladies' Home Journal* article, which got its delicious, raisiny facts from a longstanding legend in Thoreau's hometown of Concord, Massachusetts. The *Walden* author *was* fond of dried fruit, it turns out, but he was far from the first to bake it into bread. Ultimately Harding recanted his claims in a 1990 *Thoreau Society Bulletin* article titled "Thoreau and Raisin Bread." You probably remember the resulting shock and outcry in the Thoreau-baked-goods community.

And thus does a great trivia fact die. But not all trivia can be discredited so definitively. Was Bugs Bunny voice actor Mel Blanc *really* allergic to carrots, as many of his obituaries claimed, or did he merely dislike the taste, as he himself wrote in his autobiography? Did Sir Isaac Newton really invent the cat flap, as many references insist, or does this come down to us from an old "absent-minded professor" joke told around 1802? You could spend a lifetime trying to pinpoint puzzlers like these, and still never be 100 percent sure.

Sometimes a trivia fact seems to recede indefinitely from us, the closer we examine it—you might call this the Heisenberg Trivia Principle. Take "the Windy City," for example. Even trivia rookies probably know that "the Windy City" is a popular nickname for Chicago, from the winds off Lake Michigan, right? But more experienced buffs will tell you that the expression actually comes from 1890s newspaper columnist Charles Dana, who used it to refer to the city's talkative ("windy") blowhards, and not to the weather at all. But then a decade passes and an amateur etymologist named Barry Popik, looking even *closer*, now thinks the meteorological explanation was right all along—he's found the phrase "the Windy City" in an 1876 *Cincinnati Enquirer* article about a Chicago tornado. Truth in trivia isn't always as straightforward as it seems. Give a fact a few years, and the wind might change yet again.

"Have you had lunch?" Fred asks suddenly, interrupting my thoughts. "I thought we'd hit the Black Angus up in Roseville. Do you mind driving?"

At lunch, I learn that Fred is a movie trivia buff even when flirting with waitresses. "You have remarkable eyes," he tells our jaded server. "You remind me of Virginia Madsen in *Sideways*. Doesn't she look like Virginia Madsen in *Sideways*?"

The waitress eyes him suspiciously. "I don't know who that is," she says.

In 1983, everything changed for trivia, and Fred Worth tells me over a steak sandwich and fries the sad story of how, as a result, everything changed for him as well. That parallel story begins in December 1979, just as Fred was starting to assemble the first *Trivia Encyclopedia* sequel. In Montreal, two journalists named Chris Haney and Scott Abbott were passing a long Saturday afternoon with a beer-fueled kitchen-table game of Scrabble. Their hearts weren't in the game. Instead, they were talking about a way to earn a little extra money, just as they had the previous year, when they'd dreamed up a chain-letter scheme that had brought in a couple thousand dollars. Neither man was a blazing career success at the time. Haney, a high school dropout, and his wife, Sarah, had recently taken in Abbott as a housemate because they couldn't afford their mortgage payments alone.

A mere forty-five minutes into the Scrabble game, as the story goes, Haney and Abbott had their new get-rich-quick scheme mapped out. They envisioned a board game that, like Scrabble, would actually be *for adults*. It's hard to see it as such today, but this was a revolutionary idea in 1979, when board games were boring rainy-day pastimes for seven-year-olds, not adult party staples. But this game would involve no hungry hippos, no Lord Licorice and Mr. Mint, nary a chute nor a ladder to be seen. Instead, it would be based around trivia questions, like the ones that the two men liked to bat around while shooting pool in local bars.

Haney and Abbott recruited two slightly more respectable friends to their idea: Haney's brother John, a washed-up hockey player, and a lawyer named Ed Werner. All four were children of the sixties—in pictures from the time, with their receding hairlines and droopy handlebar mustaches, they look like the finalists in a David Crosby look-alike contest. And so this unlikely quartet set about creating a board game in characteristically unorthodox fashion: drinking lots of beer, badgering friends to donate a thousand dollars or so each, and sailing to the burnout-crowded shores of southern Spain to bum around on the beach and make up the six thousand questions they figured their game would need.

The final product, dubbed "Trivial Pursuit," was nothing like any board game anyone had ever seen before. Its unusual, upscale packaging—a square, somber, midnight-blue box with classy Scotch-bottle gold script lettering—made it look more like chocolates or cologne than a fun party game. The guys sold out their first run of eleven hundred games to Canadian retailers, but their production costs meant they were losing sixty dollars per game. Even in Canadian dollars, that adds up quick.

A hoped-for spike in publicity never happened. Orders at toy fairs were almost nonexistent (1982 was the heyday of Pac-Man, and it was generally believed that board games were as dead as winter grass). Milton Bradley and Parker Brothers both turned the game down. It just broke too many rules. "We were the world's largest game publisher," said one Milton Bradley executive. "We knew it all. First, we knew adults didn't play games. We also knew no one would pay $29.95 to $39.99 retail."

Things looked bleak for Horn Abbot Ltd., the quartet's little start-up company. Sarah Haney was paying for groceries by returning bottles for deposits. Scott Abbott was living in a perpetual state of hungover trivia burnout. Chris Haney had a nervous breakdown from all the stress, and was hospitalized. At the last minute, U.S. game company Selchow & Righter (makers of Scrabble and Parcheesi) swooped in and decided to take a chance on the game, granting the inventors a whopping 15 percent royalty—triple the industry average.

The guys were momentarily safe from bankruptcy, but the game didn't sell immediately. So Selchow & Righter began a very smart viral marketing campaign, sending Trivial Pursuit cards in weekly mailings to top toy buyers, and even mailing the game cards to celebrities whose names were mentioned in questions—Gregory Peck, Larry Hagman, and James Mason were among those who responded with endorsements. The watershed moment, though, was Glenn Close's introduction of the game to the cast of *The Big Chill,* then filming in South Carolina. They all went nuts for it. When this was widely reported in the press, the game gained not only Hollywood cred but also a link to the eventual hit film, which was *the* baby boomer phenomenon of the time.

Trivial Pursuit took off, selling twenty-two million copies in 1984 alone, a board game record by an order of magnitude. The game was everywhere, unless it was sold out—smart-set parties on both coasts, family vacations, neighborhood bars, college dorms, a national tournament—and my grandparents' dining room table in Eugene, Oregon, where I first played the game. I was twenty years too young for most of the trivia, but I wanted to compete anyway, at least until it got too late and I was sent to bed. At ten years old, it seemed like a badge of adulthood to be able to answer questions about grown-up Trivial Pursuit standbys like *M*A*S*H* and golf and Watergate.

Trivial Pursuit was king, *Jeopardy!* had just returned to the airwaves after a decade's absence, and for a couple years, just as during the salad days of *Ask Me Another!* or *The $64,000 Question,* America couldn't get enough trivia. By Christmas of 1984, there were over fifty copycat trivia board games on toy store shelves. The crossword collections in bookstore Puzzles and Games sections had to grumpily scoot aside for dozens of quickie trivia books in 1985, just as they had for backgammon in 1975, just as they would for headache-inducing "Magic Eye" pictures of 3-D dolphins in 1995 and for poker and sudoku in 2005.

You'd think Fred Worth would be ecstatic—his oddball hobby was suddenly a national obsession. But that was before Philip Columbo broke his heart.

Fred explains over lunch. "There's an old thing that goes back to the days when New York had to have, like, four daily papers. If you wanted to know where information was coming from and you thought that the *Globe* might be stealing from the *Post,* you'd put a ringer bit of information in the *Post,* and you'd watch where it went." This is a surprisingly common tactic among editors of reference works as well. Road atlases add fake towns, dictionaries invent words, encyclopedias create fictional famous people, all so that they can later trace who's stealing their material. Don't believe the *New Columbia Encyclopedia* when it tells you about the life of noted mailbox photographer Lillian Mountweazel, and don't start using the word "esquivalience" just because the *New Oxford American Dictionary* tells you it means "the willful avoidance of one's official responsibilities." Both entries are utter fakes designed to trap plagiarists who take the bait. "It's like tagging and releasing giant turtles," says one dictionary editor.

Fred cleverly did the same thing. His *Trivia Encyclopedia* entry for "Columbo" includes this fact: "First name: Philip." In fact, Columbo, like his TV brethren Quincy and Gilligan, never had an official first name; Fred invented "Philip" as a snare for trivia thieves. (Today, fans with the *Columbo: The Complete First Season* DVD and a pause button can see that Peter Falk's badge clearly says "Frank Columbo" in one early episode.) When Fred read through the trivia in the first edition of Trivial Pursuit, he immediately knew that a lot, maybe a third, of the questions had come straight from his encyclopedias, almost unchanged. And there, on one of the cards, was his smoking gun, next to the little pink oval of the Entertainment category. "What's Columbo's first name?" Answer: Philip.

Fred sued Trivial Pursuit for $300 million in damages, and appealed his case, *Worth v. Selchow & Righter,* all the way to the U.S. Supreme Court (which declined to hear it). Ultimately, though, the original district court ruling stood, affirming summary judgment in favor of the Trivial Pursuit creators. No one disputed that over a thousand questions (Fred's lawyers put the count at 1,675, or 27.9 percent of the game's material) had been borrowed from *The Trivia Encyclopedia* and its sequel. The problem was one of copyright—unfortunately for Fred, you can't copyright a fact. You can't copyright 1,675 facts, even if you spent years tracking them down and separating the wheat from the chaff, only to have four semi-employed Canucks steal the wheat and bake billion-dollar bread out of it. "The discovery of a fact, regardless of the quantum of labor and expense, is simply not the work of an author," wrote the Ninth Circuit Court of Appeals in their opinion. For their part, Scott Abbott and Chris Haney freely admitted using Fred's works as references, but they'd used a host of other books as well. They thought encyclopedias were *supposed* to be for general reference. The court agreed.

Fred had mortgaged his house to pay for the lawsuit. His ex-wife, from whom he had recently been divorced, filed a separate suit claiming her share of any cash Fred got from the Trivial Pursuit case, so he was fighting two legal battles at once. His first *Trivia Encyclopedia* publisher had gone bankrupt, owing him fifty thousand dollars in royalties. Not long after that, Fred was one of the air traffic controllers involved in the PATCO strike of 1981, all of whom were fired and permanently banned from federal service by President Ronald Reagan. "So I was on quite a roll," he says dolefully.

Fred was out of work, out of money, and bitter every time he turned around to see Trivial Pursuit selling another million copies of *his trivia*! When I ask him if the Trivial Pursuit–fueled trivia boom of the 1980s helped his career at all, he scoffs. "You know, you're right. I should put this in perspective. Let's see, the copy of the book they bought to take the questions from would have given me twenty cents in royalties. So out of their success, I made twenty cents."

Trivial Pursuit couldn't sustain its meteoric market penetration—after only a single year of sales, a Trivial Pursuit game could be found in one in five American game closets. There was nowhere to go but down. The abrupt sales plunge—from twenty-two million games in 1984 to 5.5 million in 1985—was disastrous for Selchow & Righter, which was acquired in 1986 by video game giant Coleco, still flush with Cabbage Patch Kid money. Trivial Pursuit finally ended up with Hasbro after Coleco's 1989 bankruptcy.

To get out of his financial hole, Fred took a dreary job administering medical benefits for the county Department of Social Services, where he spent the next fourteen years. Dealing with the county bureaucracy even soured him on his one true love: information. "Trivia is the fun side of information. But working for the county, I saw the downside, the nega-

tive part of information. The evil side. It's the people who write regulations! You and I love detail, sure, but these people, when they're writing
regulations, they can't be detailed enough."

Fred knows about my *Jeopardy!* success, but he still won't let me pay
for lunch. "That would be too obvious." He smiles as he grabs for the
check. "This way I get to say that I bought *you* lunch."

Fred retired a year ago. At long last, he has time for trivia, and he hasn't
wasted any time, judging by the binders, folders, and card boxes squir-
reled away in every cranny of his office. By my count, he's working on at
least five perpetually unfinished books. There's the manuscript of food
trivia where I spied the raisin bread fact. There's a box full of index cards
dividing semifamous people into unusual categories: Cosmetologists,
Home Owners, Eaters, Lexicographers. ("Look at this: 'Contestants,'"
says Fred. "Your name's going to go in here someday.") There's a book
about celebrities and World War II. There's an idea for a Guinness
Book of World Records–style trivia annual, with rotating information
in ten different categories.

"But this is what takes up most of my day," says Fred, pointing to
his desk. "This is going to be huge." "This" is Fred's comprehensive bi-
ographical encyclopedia of film, which he's been compiling for decades.
It's *already* huge. Big binders line the shelves above his desk and mean-
der over to the bookshelves, enough binders to open your own DMV or
county courthouse. They're neatly alphabetized, like everything else in
the house, beginning with volume one: "Aaliyah–Albertson." Aaliyah to
Jack Albertson: a slain R&B ingénue and the grandpa from *Willy
Wonka* mix freely in Fred's century-spanning Hollywood history.

"One hundred and thirty binders, three folders each," says Fred
proudly. "Six thousand pages. Go ahead, give me somebody. Some
actor."

I don't want to be too obvious. "Joel McCrea," I finally say. McCrea
is one of my personal screen faves, the underappreciated leading man of
Hitchcock's *Foreign Correspondent*, some of Preston Sturges's best
comedies, and a corral full of westerns.

Fred is already paging through binder number seventy-something.

"Interesting choice. Let's see. Ewan McGregor, Malcolm McDowell, Hattie McDaniel . . . aha! Joel McCrea."

He hands me the binder, which is full of newspaper and magazine clippings, in addition to pages of neatly typed data on a fairly obscure Hollywood cowboy star. The hospital where he was born. His measurements. Addresses of homes he lived in. Starlets with whom he was romantically linked. The name of every horse he rode on-screen. His official time and cause of death.

I'm flabbergasted at the level of detail—it would be stalker-like if the good Mr. McCrea hadn't died on October 20, 1990 (at 4:50 A.M., apparently). "So this is why you have all the Hollywood biographies? You've been condensing them into this?"

"That's the service I'm providing. I've done the work for twenty years so you don't have to."

"And you're going to publish all this?"

"Oh, someday," says Fred vaguely.

Today, Trivial Pursuit is in its umpteenth edition, having sold over eighty million units, and having earned well over a billion dollars retail. The game is played in thirty-odd countries in twenty-odd languages. The four original creators all made untold millions, and live quietly today in Ontario as landed gentlemen of leisure, or at least the nearest Canadian equivalent thereof. Scott Abbott and Chris Haney created the Devil's Pulpit, a world-ranked thirty-six-hole golf course north of Toronto. Abbott also owns a minor league hockey team, the Brampton Battalion. John Haney and Scott raced horses for a time, most notably Charlie Barley, Canada's 1990 turf champion and proud offspring of the last horse to win the Triple Crown.[10] Ed Werner, now a gentleman farmer, grows grapes.

And meanwhile, Fred L. Worth lives on a county pension, barely visible behind stacked binders in a dusty office, carefully entering movie trivia into an ancient IBM personal computer that looks like it was bought around the height of Trivial Pursuit mania in 1984. His books are canonical trivia classics for thousands of buffs, the essential missing link between the campus trivia fad of the 1960s and the board game trivia fad of the 1980s, but how many know his name today? He's trivia's forgotten man.

"It did make me kind of bitter, watching their success, and even knowing . . ." He doesn't finish the sentence. "All those years I thought, nobody knows. I watched *Who Wants to Be a Millionaire*, and nobody ever called me as a lifeline."

But his face brightens almost immediately. "That's why I was so tickled when you contacted me! What fun today was."

Before I leave, I ask Fred to sign my own worn copies of his encyclopedias, and tell him that I can't wait to buy copies of his new books as well, if they're ever finished.

"Well, I've got the same 24/7 Stephen King does. It's nice having all that time now." Fred may not have a share in the hundreds of millions he helped earn for Trivial Pursuit, but at least, and perhaps for the first time in decades, he seems content. We say good-bye, and Fred L. Worth closes the door and goes back inside his dark house full of books.

ANSWERS

1. **The St. Valentine's Day Massacre** was planned by Machine Gun Jack McGurn.

2. **The Wizard of Oz's** full name is Oscar Zoroaster Phadrig Isaac Norman Henkle Emmannuel Ambroise Diggs. (The initials spell out "O.Z.P.I.N.H.E.A.D.")

3. "Hoss" Cartwright's real first name was **Eric.**

4. **Mia Farrow** appeared on the very first *People* magazine cover.

5. Trick question: Robert Stroud raised birds in **Leavenworth.** By the time the famous "Birdman" had moved to Alcatraz, his canary privileges had been revoked.

6. **Felix Unger,** from *The Odd Couple,* is the only TV lead character with the initials F.U.

7. The Caesar salad was invented in **Tijuana, Mexico,** in the kitchen of chef Caesar Cardini.

8. "Mr. Chips" taught **Classics**—Latin and Greek—in *Goodbye, Mr. Chips.*

9. **Charles Bronson** was a member of both *The Dirty Dozen* and *The Magnificent Seven.*

10. **Affirmed** was the last horse to win the Triple Crown.

CHAPTER 12

What is REPETITION?

Late one night, Mindy and I catch a cable TV showing of *Champagne for Caesar*. This little-known 1950 screwball comedy is a hilarious riff on the game show craze of the time, and specifically on *Take It or Leave It*, the money-doubling radio quiz that later spawned *The $64,000 Question*.

Ronald Colman, the ultimate in sexless, sophisticated 1940s leading men, plays his last starring role as the unfortunately named Beauregard Bottomley. Bottomley is described by the narrator as America's "last scholar. . . . His cornflakes in the morning are well-sprinkled with Schopenhauer. His blue plate at lunch is balanced with a generous helping of the latest developments in atomic research."

In short, Beauregard is an insufferable intellectual snob. When his sister drags him in front of a department store window to watch her favorite TV quiz, *Masquerade for Money* (hosted by one "Happy Hogan," played by real-life TV host Art Linkletter, in his only movie-acting role), he lectures snottily to the storefront crowd about the evils of game shows. "How can you stand such drivel? I can't let this go on without a word of warning. This man is the forerunner of intellectual destruction in America. If it is noteworthy and rewarding to know that two and two makes four to the accompaniment of deafening applause and prizes, then two and two making four will become the top level of learning!" It's the familiar argument against trivia: that it dumbs society down by offering the illusion of intellectual mastery while only providing a smattering of shallow, frivolous facts.

Beauregard changes his tune, however, when he is turned down for a job by the Milady soap company. Remembering that Milady is the sponsor of *Masquerade for Money*, he decides to take the company for all it's worth by winning big on the show. *Masquerade,* you see, doesn't limit its contestants' doubled winnings to $64, like the real-life *Take It or Leave It*. On *Masquerade,* you can keep on doubling forever.

As even grade-school math students might guess, this turns out to be a spectacularly bad idea, arithmetically speaking. Beauregard appears on the show week after week, soon inflating his winnings into the millions, and becomes a nationwide sensation. Soap exec Vincent Price, with his company facing bankruptcy at Colman's well-manicured hands, is apoplectic. "I now believe that we have a Frankenstein on our hands—a very well-informed Frankenstein! He must be stopped!" Even congenial Art Linkletter is pissed. "I don't like it any better than you do! What do you expect me to do, go out and shoot him?"

In the movie, the "trivia" questions are the typical impossibilities that Hollywood screenwriters always paint as easy pickings for their nerd character. "How many plates are there on the molar of an Asiatic elephant?" "What is the frequency of a bat's shriek?" "How does Professor Einstein regard the space-time continuum?" Fiction writers never write believable trivia. I once read an old Donald Duck comic where Donald's final question on a big-money radio quiz is, "How many drops of water pass over Niagara Falls in a week?" Amazingly, Donald knows the exact answer!

When the stakes rise to $40 million, *Masquerade for Money* broadcasts a special show live from the Hollywood Bowl, and all of America tunes in to watch Beauregard face the final question: "What is your Social Security Number?" And against all odds, the erudite champion is stumped! Oh, the irony!

It's a strange feeling to watch an old screwball comedy and realize that the zany goings-on, written decades before I was even born, have somehow predicted the current state of my life. I've never prowled through a Connecticut estate by night looking for a dinosaur bone and a lost leopard, like Cary Grant does in *Bringing Up Baby,* but I know *exactly* how it feels to be, suddenly, improbably, in Ronald Colman's wingtip shoes. I know how it feels to change an entire TV game show paradigm by simply refusing to go away for weeks on end. (As the inventor of the flexible urinary catheter[1] once said, "Fish and game show contestants stink after three days.") I know the mounting tension and attention. I've imagined the panicked conferences backstage, the confused producer, the annoyed host. I may not have a plummy British accent and a trim little mustache, but *I am Beauregard Bottomley*.

After squeaking by the Children's Lit clue in my twentieth game, I take the last twenty-eight shows of *Jeopardy!*'s season in decisive fashion, locking each game up before Final Jeopardy. As with the ill-planned cash-doubling on *Masquerade for Money*, my ever-lengthening streak seems mostly due to a miscalculation by the *Jeopardy!* producers. When they removed the five-day limit, they underestimated the advantages that a long-running champion would have: well-honed buzzer timing, comfort behind the podium, intimidation of the two challengers. By the law of averages, I'm sure that over the last few months I've defeated quite a few players who knew more answers than I did, but just lacked game-day experience.

The *Jeopardy!* format was never designed with a long-running champion in mind. Every day I sit through the same contestant orientation, hearing the exact same rules phrased the exact same way. The fun, seemingly spontaneous jokes in the patter always fall in the exact same places, with the exact same beats. Everyone always laughs politely when Susanne Thurber mimes buzzing in with her forehead, as an example of What Not To Do. One lucky contestant is chosen every day to be the butt of Maggie's "eighties porno" joke. The whole spiel has, by this time, been pounded into my head like a catechism.

Likewise, the mini-interview segment in the middle of the show was *certainly* not designed with the fifty-game champion in mind. I've run out of witty, charming things to say about myself after three shows, much less forty-three of them. And at the end of every fifth taping, Maggie swoops down on me like the anecdote vulture. "I'll e-mail you this week. We're going to need ten more stories out of you for next week's taping." My "stories" are getting duller and duller every day, especially compared with everyone else's first-string material.

"So, Darcy, you spent a year flying bush planes in the Sudan for the U.N. humanitarian effort there? Amazing. And now our returning champion, Ken Jennings. It says here, Ken, that you sorta like airline food?"

"That's true, Alex. I sorta like airline food."

My stories dwindle away until they're not really stories at all. A few times, desperate for material, I even make something up. Lying to Alex Trebek feels a little like lying to a priest, but I soon get over it. It gets to where Alex and I just shoot the breeze a little.

"So, Ken, is there anything you'd like to ask *me*? I've run out of stuff."

"Uh . . . what did you have for breakfast this morning, Alex?"

Despite all the quality time Alex and I have been spending together lately, he still seems a little chilly, as if he's rooting against me. Is this just part of his constant saltine-dry impartiality? Does he think I'm bad for the show? Does he dislike sharing the spotlight with a sidekick? Or is he just plain sick of me? I feel like passing a junior-high mash note up to his podium. "Dear Alex. Do you like me? Check one. Yes/No."

I may be uncomfortable with my sudden *Jeopardy!* success, but that's nothing compared to the way the *other* contestants feel. Remember that none of my shows have aired yet. There is no joy in Mudville every morning when Maggie reveals, in an offhand way, that a twenty- or thirty- or forty-day champion is sitting in their midst. Smiles freeze. Someone usually laughs nervously and says, "No, really, how many games?" I, in turn, become suddenly interested in brushing lint off my pants or adjusting my collar while every eye in the room turns to inspect me sourly.

I understand the resentment. I felt the same way about Anne Boyd during my first day. I try to smile and hold doors for everyone and wish every contestant good luck before every game, hoping to be hated as little as possible. When they demand explanations for my good fortune, I just say that I'm as bewildered by it as they are. This doesn't take much pretending.

Sometimes I do hit it off with a fellow contestant backstage. Nick Aretakis (game twenty-four) is a New Haven bookseller who shares my love for the 1940s British movie-making team of Michael Powell and Emeric Pressburger, and knows a lot about rare books from Mormon history. Kollin Min (game forty-three) not only practices law in Seattle, where my dad used to practice, but he even attended my elementary school in South Korea for a year. But there's a strange dynamic to these brief friendships. We bond backstage before the game, whether from nervousness or Stockholm syndrome or genuine affinity, I don't know. But after the game doesn't go their way, some turn cold and distant. Most get out of Dodge as quickly as possible. A few leave muttering in frustration, either kicking themselves or cursing me, or both. I can't say I blame them.

Some contestants actually seem relieved to find out they'll be playing me, as if it lessens the unbelievable pressure of appearing on *Jeopardy!* After all, there's no shame in losing to Goliath, and everything to gain if David actually manages to beat him. A cheerful Canadian man named Brian Shipley, rather than shunning me in the greenroom, asks eagerly for my autograph. I have a sudden mental picture of the excited Angolan basketball team seeking autographs from Jordan, Bird, Magic, and the rest of the Dream Team during pregame warm-ups at the Barcelona Olympics. Another contestant, a self-described "pothead" for thirty years, confides to me that he smoked two bowls of weed before boarding the Radisson hotel shuttle the morning of his *Jeopardy!* appearance, trying to relax himself. It must have worked—during our game, he seems *very* relaxed.

But one by one, confident or not, stoned or not, they all go down. The orchid specialist, the telephone psychic, the nice old Welshman who survived the Blitz, the daughter of actor Brian Dennehy, the geologist, the belly dancer, the guitarist from nineties lounge-pop band Combustible Edison—they all head home with runner-up prizes and parting gifts. I feel guilty about each and every one. I'm not being glib— I really do. We might have been friends, if the *Jeopardy!* gods hadn't pitted us against one another. After all, they're all trivia junkies just like me, hoping to fulfill longtime dreams of *Jeopardy!* glory. And then they get blindsided by the guy with the unfair advantage of forty games under his belt. It eats at me. Not badly enough for me to actually, you know, drop a game on purpose or anything, but still . . .

I have another advantage that never would have occurred to me. Nobody on *Jeopardy!* is giving me the Charles Van Doren treatment and feeding me the answers, of course. Except when, sometimes, they do.

Trivia is finite. There are only so many facts out there, especially if you limit yourself to those factoids that might be fun, interesting, and accessible to a broad audience. Fred Worth told me he's read so much trivia that he almost never sees a great new fact that surprises him anymore. "I call them four-stars, and they're a treat. I would rather find a four-star trivia fact than a twenty-dollar bill."

Trivia, according to Fred, is a beach that's been so picked over by years of combers that most of the good shells are long gone. So it should come as no surprise that I'm not on *Jeopardy!* long before facts and questions start to repeat. Not word for word, and certainly not intentionally, but enough to nab me a few answers that I might have missed otherwise. It's a lot easier to remember which political party held their 1968 convention in Miami when a question just last week reminded me that the Dems were in Chicago that year. It's a lot easier to identify the kind of antibiotic drugs replaced by penicillin during World War II[2] when I'd lost $4,200 botching that same question on a Daily Double a few weeks back. (I don't know if you've ever blown a couple house payments on a single trivia question, but it tends to indelibly engrave the right answer in your mind.) Ditto for the clue about the country singer who did time in San Quentin before Ronald Reagan pardoned him,[3] which I remember from my very first game when it shows up again months later.

This kind of repetition is inevitable, given the fact that *Jeopardy!* airs such a vast amount of trivia—almost fifteen thousand questions every year. But in general, I don't agree with Fred that trivia is so easily exhausted. Collectors of all kinds run the risk of eventually—horror of horrors!—*completing* their collection. They find they now have a complete set of Dale Earnhardt commemorative plates or Ant-Man comic books or *Joanie Loves Chachi* collector's cups, and there's nothing left to scour flea markets or eBay for. (At this point you can either start "upgrading" all your *Joanie Loves Chachi* merchandise to "mint condition," or decide life is now empty and meaningless and put your head in the oven.) Trivia fans are collectors as well, as A. J. Jacobs pointed out, only they're a lot luckier—their chosen object of pursuit is practically endless. "Four-star" trivia questions may be few and far between, but you'll never run out of new trivia. The sum of human knowledge, assuming you could somehow measure it in megabytes, grows astronomically every day. In fact, computer scientist Dr. Jacques Vallee (one of the founding fathers of the Internet, and also the UFO expert on whom the François Truffaut character in *Close Encounters of the Third Kind* was based) estimates that it now *doubles* every eighteen months.

New trivia, in other words, is being produced all the time. It wasn't possible ten years ago to ask "Who's the only person to win an Oscar for portraying another Oscar winner?"[4] or "What's the only middle name to be shared by two different U.S. presidents?"[5] because the events referenced hadn't even happened yet. The beach might be picked over, but the waves are always washing new shells onto the sand.

Forty-odd games of *Jeopardy!* have taught me something else about knowledge—namely, that it's everywhere. I had always assumed that the brains lined up behind the *Jeopardy!* podiums got all their knowledge from books, from a lifetime of voracious reading. Their sensitive, pallid complexions certainly support that theory. But in my case—and other contestants I talk to have backed me up—reading is secondary (don't tell your kids). Sure, I like to read. I recognize many answers from things I read in books. But many, many more clues I just remember from a lifetime of general curiosity, of keeping an eye open for what's going on in the world around me.

It's almost embarrassing how many *Jeopardy!* answers I give that come not from some highbrow leather-bound reference book but from somewhere a little more plebeian. Should I admit how many mythology questions I knew only because of the *Thor* comic books I read as a kid, or how many geography questions from globe-trotting reality shows? Almost all my knowledge of stars and constellations comes from bad sci-fi movies. All my national flags come from NBC Olympic coverage. All my aquatic birds come from crossword puzzle clues.

It's encouraging, I guess, to realize how much information we wade through every day, stuff we could absorb if we were engaged enough to notice it. Back at home between tapings, I'm aware for the first time of just how easy it is to learn something new every hour of every day. If I'm watching a few minutes of an old war movie on late-night TV, I'm probably learning something about World War II that I didn't know before—the only D-Day beach that shares its name with a chemical element,[6] for example. If I'm flipping through a magazine at the dentist's office, I might be learning about something new on every page: global warming, or the NBA play-offs, or health-care reform. If I'm cooking dinner with Mindy, I might learn some new word of French or Italian that shows up in the recipe, since those are languages that I don't speak —the kind of pasta whose name means "little turnips," for example.[7] Even the mindless *Thomas the Tank Engine* videos that Dylan makes me watch with him, when I pay attention to them, turn out to be a treasure trove of information on trains and railroads. Dozens of times every day, the "Hey, that could come up on *Jeopardy!*" alarm will go off in my head. It's not a panicky feeling anymore. Now I sort of enjoy it.

Without a doubt, the most surreal part of the whole streak is the secrecy. Before my first taping, I signed a form swearing that I wouldn't reveal the events or outcome of my game until the night it aired, and I had decided even before then that I wasn't going to tell anyone back at home what had happened. Nobody likes to hear the final score of the football game they have on their TiVo, right? I decided I'd let my family and friends enjoy the suspense of watching my game without knowing if I'd won or lost.

This plan was hatched when I assumed I would appear on only one game, of course, with an outside chance of two or three at the most. The *Jeopardy!* record, at that point, was seven wins. I had never considered that my appearance on the show could long outlast the week—that it could turn, in effect, into a summer job.

Ever since I learned that I'd have to return to L.A. to tape a third week, Glenda, my boss, has been covering for me at work. She's had to come up with a seemingly inexhaustible supply of cover stories, explaining why I've been out every other Tuesday and Wednesday all spring.

"Ken has the flu." "Ken's painting his basement." "Ken's watching a sick kid." If you have the idea that computer programmers are all impossibly brilliant, I'm sorry to tell you that no one at the office ever caught on.

The whole charade starts to seem unnecessarily complicated around my fifth or sixth trip to California, and I start to wish I'd just told everyone the secret to begin with. There are the practical considerations of having a secret identity. Why do the people at work think I was out yesterday? Do we have enough in the bank to cover the travel expenses of three more trips to California this month? Once I run out of ties and jackets to wear on-air (I'm a computer programmer, after all—"dressed up" for me is wearing the shorts *without* the ketchup stain), how do I borrow some more from Dad without telling him what I need them for?

Lying to everyone I know for months on end is taking a *psychological* toll as well. The secret starts to make me feel a little schizophrenic. A couple days a month, I'm the Ken Jennings who's shattered game show records, whose ever-growing daily winnings total is starting to look like a life-changing amount of money. But nobody knows about him yet. I still have to come home and be Ken Jennings the boring suburban dad, in his same old mundane treadmill of an office job, pretending nothing has happened.

I start to feel a little like Clark Kent at the *Daily Planet*, keeping up bland appearances to all his friends, who of course have no idea about the bullet-stopping adventures in his double life. I spend my days quietly at my desk, cranking out a parade of nearly identical Internet applications, and then it's secretly "Up, up, and away!" to Culver City. The psychological jet lag is killing me.

The adrenaline rush of playing *Jeopardy!* is great, but the thing I miss most when I'm back at home is the confidence and competence I feel with that buzzer in my hand. It's probably the same charge a marine gets holding his rifle. "This is my buzzer. There are three like it, but this one is mine. My buzzer, without me, is useless. Without my buzzer, I am useless. I must buzz my buzzer true. I must buzz faster than my competitor who is trying to outbuzz me. . . ."

I've never felt confident *or* competent sitting in front of a computer monitor. I've been working in computers for five years now, and almost every day of that half decade has been another reminder that, whether due to aptitude or attitude or both, I'm a lousy programmer. It's just not my thing.

I've been a trivia buff since infancy, seemingly, but there didn't seem to be a way to make a living at it, and it sure wasn't a plus with girls to know the northernmost world capital,[8] Cap'n Crunch's first name,[9] or the only publicly owned team in U.S. sports,[10] so I forgot about it. Trivia just didn't seem like a practical adult vocation. I was an English major in college, but that didn't seem like a very marketable skill either ("What's the difference between an English major and a large pepperoni pizza?" "The pepperoni pizza can feed a family of four"), so I switched to computer science. I knew it would be less fun but, again, it seemed like the safe, responsible thing to do. The year I finished college, I applied to some graduate programs, but I was getting married soon, and we decided it might be nicer to pay the rent from time to time. So I gave up on going back to school and took the first job I could find as a programmer. I always liked my job environment, but the work itself ranged from merely unexciting to soul-crushingly tedious. The bills got paid, but I was never really happy.

Jeopardy! is the first time in my life I ever dreamed an improbable dream and did something about it. It's out of character for me. And yet somehow, the fourth-down gamble paid off. Here I stand, doing something I'm good at for a change—and the rewards have been hundreds of times greater than those for any of the safe, practical, responsible choices I'd spent the rest of my life making.

The magic bullet was, of all things, trivia, that seemingly most frivolous and least marketable of all possible pursuits. Who knew?

ANSWERS

1. **Benjamin Franklin** invented the flexible urinary catheter (and gave the famous quote about "fish and visitors," not game show contestants, stinking after three days).

2. **Sulfa** drugs were replaced by penicillin during World War II.

3. **Merle Haggard** did time in San Quentin before Ronald Reagan pardoned him.

4. **Cate Blanchett** is the only actress to win an Oscar for portraying another Oscar winner, for playing Kate Hepburn in *The Aviator*.

5. **Walker** is the only middle name shared by two different U.S. presidents (George H. W. Bush and George W. Bush).

6. Of the five code names for D-Day beaches, **"Gold"** was the only one borrowed from a chemical element.

7. **Ravioli** is the pasta whose name means "little turnips."

8. **Reykjavik, Iceland,** is the northernmost world capital.

9. Cap'n Crunch's full name is **Horatio** Magellan Crunch. (*Magellan?*)

10. **The Green Bay Packers** are the only publicly owned team in U.S. sports.

CHAPTER 13

What is TRADITION?

The town of Stevens Point sits smack-dab in the center of Wisconsin, about a hundred miles north of Madison on Highway 39. It's the central-casting version of a small midwestern town. There are shady tree-lined avenues and a quaintly nineteenth-century Main Street. There's great pan-fishing in nearby McDill Pond. There's even a medium-sized state college, the kind of sweetly generic campus where Kurt Russell might get up to laboratory mischief in a 1970s Disney flick.

The calendar in Stevens Point is punctuated by a series of yearly events, each as predictable and unremarkable in its way as almost everything else here. Riverfront band concerts begin every June. Deer season opens in November. Every March, lines go out the door when Belt's Soft Serve, a beloved ice cream place on the south side of town, first opens for the summer. But one annual event stands out above all the rest to residents and outsiders alike, one proud eccentricity in the regular yearly orbit of peaceful central Wisconsin life.

For fifty-four hours every April, tiny Stevens Point, Wisconsin, is the trivia capital of the world.

"It's the biggest thing in town," Mayor Gary Wescott tells me, shouting to be heard over the car engine and the applause of onlookers. "It's bigger than anything at the university. It's bigger than homecoming."

I'm standing with His Honor the mayor in the open back of a Jeep Wrangler, winding through the streets around the campus of UWSP—University of Wisconsin, Stevens Point—at about ten miles per hour. He's waving and throwing miniature Almond Joy candy bars to the crowds lining the streets. Ahead of us crawls a black-and-white driven by one of Portage County's finest, red and blue lights flashing. Behind us a motley assortment of vehicles trails for well over a block. The bizarre procession includes a flatbed truck full of dancing eggrolls, a zombie-filled cemetery, a Viking ship, a hotwired 1979 Chevy Beauville that looks like it could rust apart any second, and a guy dressed like Batman, riding a moped and dragging a wheelchair holding another guy dressed as Spider-Man. This is the Trivia Parade, the event that always kicks off America's biggest trivia contest, held every April for the past thirty-six years in Stevens Point.

Mayor Wescott himself is an alumnus of 90FM WWSP, the campus radio station that organizes and broadcasts the yearly triviapalooza. He was a member of the news department and an on-air DJ during his college days. "We were, what, thirty watts back then?" he asks a fellow station veteran. "So, actually, right here"—we're just a few blocks off campus—"you couldn't get the station."

Times have changed. The station now transmits at 11,500 watts, and is the Midwest's largest student-run radio station. They plan to go to 50,000 watts as soon as they can fund a new transmitter and antenna, and their biggest fund-raiser of the year is, of course, the trivia contest. Between the advertising sold, the entry fees for the four-hundred-plus participating teams, and the merchandising (the registration/T-shirt table back at the station brought in over twenty thousand dollars on the first day alone), the contest can gross over sixty thousand dollars every year.

We pull into the parking lot of a local junior high school, the parade's end point. Each of the floats was built and manned by one of the teams that assemble every year to play in the contest, and there are prizes to be awarded for the best floats. The parade winner this year is the Viking ship, which, it turns out, belongs to a team that calls themselves "Norwigan Studs," ten-year veterans of the contest. In addition to their dominance of the parade prizes, the Studs routinely finish in the top one hundred of the contest proper, so I assume their trivia is a little sharper than their spelling.

The Viking ship is certainly impressive, every bit the equal of the Norwigan Studs submarine and the Norwigan Studs space shuttle that have won the parade prize in years past. But I strongly suspect that the judges' decision this year may have had something to do with the flotilla of pubescent girls in halter tops and short shorts that roller-skated around the longship throughout its voyage. It's the first really warm Friday afternoon of spring, and ogling the sun-worshipping UWSP student body—or bodies—seems to be a big component of the parade. "That's my four-year-old daughter's dance instructor," one of the judges remarks absently to me as a Viking-ette skates by. "She's certainly . . . well proportioned."

With the prizes awarded, the mayor passes his megaphone to a stocky grinning fifty-something man whose spectacles and unruly salt-and-pepper beard remind me a little of Jerry Garcia, circa "Touch of Gray." This is Jim Oliva, who has been on his own long, strange trip for the past twenty-five years. He's been writing and organizing this trivia contest every spring since 1979. In the process, he's earned himself the nickname "the Oz" for his wizardly omniscience. He's been rubbing his hands together all afternoon, gleefully and unconsciously, impatient for the contest to begin. "Are you ready to trivia?" Jim bellows into the megaphone. The crowd, even the dancing guys in the eyehole-free eggroll suits, goes wild.

"The World's Largest Trivia Contest," as the now-defunct U.S. Trivia Association once billed the Stevens Point event, predates Jim Oliva's involvement, though today it's hard to imagine the contest without him. It began in 1969 as a simple one-day affair: sixteen hours, eighty questions, and just a handful of teams. It was inspired by a radio trivia event that Lawrence University had been running in nearby Appleton since 1966. (The first Lawrence question ever: "Who was Superman's father?")[1] The Appleton event had been inspired by an *even earlier* contest at Beloit College. Wisconsin is nothing if not a hotbed for campus radio trivia.

By 1975, the contest had achieved its current dimensions: a fifty-four-hour event, with eight trivia questions every hour. Play goes as follows: a 90FM DJ reads a question over the air. Teams then have the span of two songs to phone an answer into the radio station, where results for each question are fed into a computer. Each team can phone in only once per question and can give only one guess. At the end of the second song, the DJ announces, "Phones down! Phones down in the back!" and time is up. The correct answer is then read on the air, but there's no time for teams to indulge in much celebration or recrimination ("I *told* you it was Alex Karras!") because the next question begins immediately. This cycle repeats 428 times, from 6 P.M. Friday night until midnight Sunday, with scoring updates broadcast every hour on the hour.

The blistering pace of the contest, one question every seven minutes or so, never lets up. But that's not all teams have to worry about. There are also the twenty-odd visual questions in the *New Trivia Times* newsletter that 90FM releases the week before the contest. There are the three audio questions—a *Name That Tune* game of twenty-four short song snippets played on the air during the contest. There are the "running questions," a quick scavenger hunt played on Stevens Point's Main Street early Saturday and Sunday mornings. ("Something to get people out into the fresh air at least once a day during the contest," explains Jim.) There are the "trivia stone" clues, a car-based treasure hunt whose cryptic directions are read out on the air every so often during the weekend. And this year, on top of all that, there are *also* eight ultra-difficult questions that will be read out intermittently during the contest. Teams will have the whole weekend to try to crack them. In short, there's never a dull moment over the contest's fifty-four hours. Trivia players must multitask.

There is no shortage of players willing to take the daunting fifty-four-hour challenge. In a town of under twenty-five thousand folks, enrollment for the contest hovers at a remarkable twelve thousand year after year. And that's just the people officially registered. You can't quite say that half the town takes part, because many contest regulars are former residents or out-of-towners who make a yearly pilgrimage. But even so, there's no way around it: this town goes radio gaga for its radio trivia. The prize for their efforts? Well, there really isn't one. The top ten teams each get a little trophy, and that's about it.

I drove into Stevens Point in a rented Nissan Altima right before the parade's start a few hours earlier. I'd wanted to rent a compact, but the larger Altima is a concession to the long legs of Earl Cahill, who's decided to come with me to check out the contest. "Are you going to register to play?" I ask him.

"Nah, I just want to see what it looks like when a whole city goes trivia crazy. Would you look at that?"

We're driving down Division Street, the commercial strip that runs through the center of Stevens Point. It's completely familiar in its commercialized anonymity: we could see these same convenience stores, muffler shops, and Burger Kings anywhere in America—but here there's one difference. Every single signboard on the street is trivia-themed. WELCOME TRIVIA PLAYERS! TRIVIA 36 KEEP ON TRUCKIN! TRIVIA SPECIAL—DORITOS $1.59! Earl and I stop at Taco Bell for a late lunch, and even though the place is set to be gutted and remodeled in less than a week, they're hawking trivia too: CLOSING MONDAY FOR DEMOLITION / WELCOME TRIVIA FANS!

"Stevens Point is a small town," says Jim Oliva, "but it really kicks it up for the trivia weekend." Trivia has put Stevens Point on the map nationally, garnering mentions on CNN, in national newspapers, in Leno and Letterman monologues. The contest was even the subject of a *Jeopardy!* clue once, though all three contestants were stumped on the correct response. ("What is Stevens Point?") And trivia has shaped the town as well. As recently as the late 1970s, the old-style phone circuits in the Stevens Point exchange meant that only seventy-two callers could be connected by phone at any given time. Most of the year, this wasn't a problem. During trivia weekend, though, hundreds of callers might be trying to call in answers at once. "You could go ten minutes without getting a dial tone," recalls John Eckendorf, who has been Jim's co-writer since 1989. That ten-minute delay might be annoying if you're calling in a trivia answer, but local officials worried more about the potential for ten-minute delays on 911 calls and other emergencies. The contest forced AT&T to update the phone equipment with new digital technology about a decade ahead of schedule.

Despite all the hoopla, I have a confession to make. As Earl and I head to our hotel to drop off our bags, and as I watch the parade later, I'm skeptical. I have a problem with the Stevens Point format: in my head, I'm putting air quotes around the word "trivia" every time I see or hear it. To me, this isn't trivia. I've always associated trivia with the unexpected joy, the epiphany, the ego stroke, of mentally dredging up answers you didn't even know you knew. But Stevens Point players aren't standing on a stage holding buzzers. There's one thing wrong with a contest where the players are sitting at home with seven minutes to come up with each answer, and you've probably spotted it already.

Google.

Even before Google, apparently, there were Notes. Notes with a capital *N*, to Stevens Point trivia diehards. These aren't just notes, these are Notes—not just a study aid but a way of life.

Cribbing is frowned upon at *Jeopardy!* Writing African capital cities on your hand for a quiz show is morally equivalent to when you did it for a test in junior high: it's cheating. You could probably show up wearing a tie with the periodic table on it, or print a list of U.S. vice presidents on your shirtsleeve, but they wouldn't let you wear that stuff on the show.

In Stevens Point, on the other hand, Notes are the only way to play. It didn't take too many years before players realized that it's a lot easier to answer the question "What's the burger-inspired name of the military supercomputer in the movie *WarGames*?"[2] if you actually have a notebook in your files labeled "Movie Notes: 1982–1983." If you don't know the answer off the top of your head, have books and magazines handy so you can find it before the second song ends. If it's a piece of information not likely to be in any of your books and magazines, you'd better have it in a notebook.

It takes the observer a little while to realize that Stevens Point isn't just a quaint, normal little town that saves its craziness for one weekend a year, à la Shirley Jackson's "The Lottery." To stay competitive, these folks live their nutty trivia-centric lifestyle *year-round*. Players will tape TV commercials so they can watch them frame-by-frame, taking notes on likely-looking details. What's the visitors' score on the scoreboard behind LeBron James in that Nike ad? Can you read the T-shirt on that teenager ordering Little Caesar's? To stay on top of network TV shows, some teams assign each player a TV weeknight. Every week, you might have to spend all week watching every Tuesday night show, via VCR or

TiVo, and taking exhaustive notes. After all, you don't want to be the one who lets the team down when there's an *According to Jim* question on an episode you missed.

"It's an obsession," says Ray Hamel, who drives up from Madison every year for the contest. "I can't watch a movie and *not* take notes. I had a rule when I was dating: the first date, I wouldn't take notes. Second date, you had to get used to the notebook coming to the movie theater." In his thirty-one notebooks, Ray has detailed notes on over eight thousand movies.

Jim Oliva likes to ask consumerist questions—snack ingredients, packaging details, you name it. As a result, the basements of Stevens Point are overflowing with decades of neatly filed candy wrappers, cereal boxes, and Happy Meals. I stop by one such basement in the house where the team known as "YAARGH!: Two Porta Potties, No Wading" will be playing this year. The team name is a reference to last year's trivia weekend, when the septic tank in "team headquarters" backed up, necessitating emergency portable toilets. I thumb through a file of carefully collapsed food packaging marked "N-Z": Scooby Doo dog treats, Shrek breakfast cereal, SpongeBob SquarePants macaroni and cheese. The collection seems to have survived last year's plumbing mishap. "Do you ever worry that this is a little Howard Hughes, keeping all this stuff?" I hesitantly ask team member Gavin Scott.

"If we ever start wearing Kleenex boxes on our feet, we'll start to worry," he breezily answers. A junior member of YAARGH!, not more than ten years old, appears underfoot. "Mom bought some popcorn and some Fruit Roll-Ups and all this stuff that we didn't even eat, but it's got trivia on it!" he chimes in.

I'm a little weirded out by the idea of a trivia contest that, instead of rewarding trivia knowledge, seems to reward excellent note-taking skills. I had high school teachers who would probably approve. But even if Jim's contest was creating a town of stenographers back in the 1980s, players were at least looking at *their own notes*. They had to put in the time and the effort. Fast-forward a decade to the early 1990s: Al Gore, tinkering in his barn, produces an amazing invention, a loosely connected group of university and government computer networks. A few tech-savvy teams start to realize that lots of pop-cultural information is starting to be archived and searchable on this so-called Internet.

The subsequent explosion of the World Wide Web and one-click search engines represented a huge paradigm shift for the contest. Remember that file cabinet where you and your trivia team painstakingly collected film credits for every movie ever released back to 1916? Remember the thousands of hours you spent organizing it and keeping it up-to-date? Well, now everyone has it, and it's called www.imdb.com. That six-thousand-page cross-referenced concordance of rock lyrics you're nearly done with? Good news, you can throw it away. Suddenly every team, experienced veterans or tyro first-timers, had exactly the same set of notes, and it was the most exhaustive set imaginable. With no time or effort expended whatsoever. In the era of Notes, Stevens Point trivia success was at least a measure of preparation and attention to detail, if not knowledge. Now the contest measures—what? Google prowess?

I want to ask Jim Oliva how the Internet has changed his approach to trivia, but when I get to the radio station, a low brick building on the edge of campus, the contest is just minutes away from starting. Eighteen volunteer operators sit at eighteen telephones, eating free pizza provided by the local Domino's. The contest will require thirteen four-hour shifts of eighteen volunteers each, and take-out food for all of them, and there's never a shortage of either, even in the wee hours of the morning. The local public-access TV station is setting up cameras in the phone room. They'll be broadcasting all fifty-four hours of the contest this year. Jim's aide-de-camp, John Eckendorf, is dressing down one TV staffer, whose roving camera just caught—and aired!—the whiteboard on which the answer to each trivia question will be written during the contest.

Jim will take the first DJ shift, as he does every year. He's already in the booth, hamming it up for the public-access cameras, shimmying to "Born to Be Wild" by Steppenwolf, which always heralds the beginning of the contest. My Google questions will have to wait.

All over Portage County, in hundreds of "team headquarters," radios are being tuned to 90FM. No one, upon pain of death, will be changing the station for the next fifty-four hours. The day has been spent greeting out-of-town friends and family, stockpiling groceries, networking computers, unpacking boxes of reference books and file cabinets full of Notes. Now children are being shushed, web browsers opened, caffeinated soda stocked into fridges. I can feel the tension. The biggest event of the year for these people, Christmas and summer vacation and the Super Bowl all rolled up into one, is just moments away.

A prerecorded Mr. Voice announces this year's contest: "Trivia 36: Keep On Trivia!" with appropriate fanfare and hyperbole, and then Jim leans his scraggly beard into the mike. "Are you ready to play trivia, Fast Eddie?" he asks, paraphrasing Jackie Gleason in *The Hustler*. "Here we go. Question 1 of Hour 1." We are under way.

The questions will get mind-numbingly tough, but the first question of the contest is, by long-standing tradition, impossibly easy. In fact, it has the same answer every year: "Robert Redford."

The tradition dates back to 1980 (Question 7, Hour 42, to be precise) and the question "Who is the newly appointed sewer commissioner of Provo, Utah?" Jim was confident that the answer, as he had recently read in a magazine, was Robert Redford. But controversy ensued when enterprising players placed calls to Utah and got a different answer from some poor Provo civil servant, no doubt surprised at the sudden outpouring of out-of-state interest in the city's sewer commissioner. Jim called Redford's publicist to settle the dispute, only to find that the Leathery One had actually been appointed sewer commissioner of nearby Provo *Canyon*. The question was tossed out, and every contest since has begun with a Robert Redford question, "out of humility," as John Eckendorf says.

90FM is normally an alt-rock station—"The Only Alternative!" according to a banner at the station. On trivia weekend, though, it turns into a whatever-the-hell-the-DJ-feels-like station. Jim, I'm not shocked to discover, is spinning oldies: "California Girls" by the Beach Boys (his favorite band), "Elenore" by the Turtles. Then Question 7 of Hour 1: What movie poster was visible behind John McEnroe's head on the second night of his short-lived talk show? (*Live and Let Die*, apparently. What, you didn't know that?) Then the Rolling Stones and

Vanilla Fudge. Question 8: What secret U.S. military base was named for a processed food in 1942?[3]

Any hopes I had of playing along with the contest start to melt away. This stuff borders on the impossible-to-answer—without Google, anyway. There's at least the occasional question with some kind of real-world appeal, the kind that doesn't require you to have extensive Notes on the exact right episode of *Crossing Jordan*. They're still brutally hard, though. Hour 2, Question 5: What is Jimmy Neutron's middle name?[4] Hour 3, Question 1: What has Evelyn Mulwray been doing that makes her hot and sweaty the first time she meets J. J. Gittes?[5] My head snaps up—this is the first question I've known cold. That's *Chinatown*, Jake. I wonder if two songs is enough time for teams to cue up the scene on a DVD. DVD, quicker and more flexible than videotape, must have changed the contest almost as much as the Internet has. Jim has already started the second song, and it's a short one: "Last Train to Clarksville." Only two minutes and forty-seven seconds to get the DVD in the player and skip to the right scene, trivia fans!

A Chicago native, Jim Oliva came to Stevens Point in 1974 to teach math at Ben Franklin Junior High, and a decade of the town's ninth-graders learned to factor polynomials under his tutelage. He's spent the last twenty years as the proprietor of a local computer store. He'd already been volunteering at 90FM for two years in 1979 when then-trivia-writer Steve Hamilton left the station. Jim inherited the mantle by default. "I was the old guy," he explains.

Jim Oliva is a personable, thoughtful man, a real softie. But "the Oz" is another story. Come trivia time, Jim Oliva turns into Oz the Great and Powerful, ruling the Emerald City in full-on flaming-green-giant-head mode. Oz administers the contest with a will of iron. He brooks no quibbling over his rulings on contested questions. Soft-spoken, sentimental Jim Oliva hides in his little booth while Oz bellows to onlookers, "Pay no attention to the little man behind the curtain!"

The players eat it up. When Jim has to crack down and rule against a complaining player, "The hard-core teams love it, because he's being the Oz," says Eckendorf. And plenty of teams see the contest as an adversarial match—not between themselves and their fellow teams, not even between themselves and the questions, but between themselves and the Oz. "I think a lot of people go, 'Let's beat the Oz,' because he can be quite cocky," confides one team captain.

I can tell that, in the years since he took over trivia, Jim has become much more than a head writer for the contest: he's guru, cheerleader, mascot, and chief inquisitor, all in one. When I talk with him between shifts in the booth, his enthusiasm and even sentimentality for trivia are evident. He's the heart and soul of the contest. "It's hard to not be somewhat of a father figure, at fifty-nine years old," he says. "It's kind of tough to avoid that." I get the impression he wants me to think he might *like* to avoid it, but I'm not buying it.

He takes his responsibility seriously. Trivia season begins with the Rose Parade every year. Starting the first Saturday night in January, he and John Eckendorf lock themselves in their writing room every night of every weekend until the contest starts in April. "Everything in my basement, all the garbage we generate, I have to hold on to until after the contest," says Jim. He knows that, otherwise, teams would be going through his trash. After all, this is a guy who gets stalked every time he goes to the supermarket. "I'll grab something off a shelf, and people will stop dead at both ends of the aisle, just staring at my cart." One player tells me she spent weeks trying to track down a tube of the same toothpaste she heard Jim used.

All told, one hundred fifty hours of work go into the questions. During the contest, he's adept at surviving on just a couple hours of sleep, which he grabs early Sunday morning. The other fifty-odd hours, there's just too much to do.

It's clear he has a vision for the contest that transcends the mere asking and answering of questions. He's forged a tradition that unites over ten thousand people every April, year after year, and he's justifiably proud of it—proud of the popularity and size of the event, proud of the money the contest raises for student scholarships, but mostly proud of the way it brings the town together. Every year the contest begins with a list remembering those players who have passed away since the previous April. And Jim has had to interrupt the contest before to announce to trivia-playing husbands that their wives have just given birth. The audience is, in a very real sense, a family of twelve thousand strong.

Has Google changed the way he has to run the contest for his big trivia family? Jim pooh-poohs the idea, claiming he's always one step ahead of the Internet searchers. You can ask about more visual information, he says, the kind of thing that's not really text-searchable. You can phrase the questions more descriptively, so there's really no frame of reference, no proper nouns to type into a search engine text box. I remember the way he asked the *Chinatown* question without ever using the word "Chinatown," for example. But I wonder if he's not being a little naïve, especially when he tells me, "We typed every question into Google, word for word, and often we wouldn't get a single hit." For a computer store owner, that shows a remarkable lack of Internet savvy. Players have told me that Jim drastically underestimates the number of his questions that the Internet can answer for you, that it actually hovers somewhere north of 60 percent.

I think Jim can sense my skepticism. "There was this reporter one time from the Minneapolis *Star Tribune*, came to do a little story about the contest," he tells me. "The guy got the fever, and he ended up staying here all weekend. He called the paper, he said, 'I won't be in on Sunday, this is too big!' It's one of those things where you have to experience it." He looks at me meaningfully.

So I too head out to experience it.

Perhaps no team exemplifies the spirit of Stevens Point trivia better than the Franklin Street Burnouts. If nothing else, they're the bizarrely long-lived giant sea tortoise of the contest. "I think we're the longest-running single intact team. We've never merged with anybody, or split up," says Burnout captain Mike Wiza. They're playing in their thirty-first trivia contest this year. This team is older than I am.

Mike is a jovial, laid-back family man in his late thirties. If you expect a computer engineer and city alderman to look at all buttoned-down, you'll be surprised by his wavy foot-long ponytail, retina-searing tie-dyed T-shirt, and fondness for dirty jokes. He and his wife, Chris, welcome Earl and me into an upstairs room in a tall, ramshackle house on—where else?—Franklin Street. Team headquarters is notable for (a) its peaked ceiling, completely papered with decades of yellowing newspaper clippings, but mostly (b) the perhaps two dozen people crammed into every nook and cranny of the smallish room. A smaller, older group is downstairs in the kitchen, provisioning the team and chatting around the table. I will learn that this is a common trivia weekend pattern: for many teams, the contest looks like a huge three-day family reunion, with one room full of hard-core types who just happen to be playing trivia. "A lot of these people, this is the only time we ever see them, once a year," explains Chris Wiza.

The house belongs to Mike's aunt and uncle, the Grulkowskis— "for just seventy-two more hours!" says Mike. The Wizas, it turns out, have decided to buy their longtime trivia headquarters. They close Monday.

"You're not buying it just so you can keep playing trivia here, are you?" I jokingly ask.

"Well, yeah," admits Mike. My disbelieving look speaks for itself. I'm an alien here, a resident of a strange outside world where no one would ever *buy a house* just because of an annual radio contest. "You have to understand: the Franklin Street Burnouts have been playing in this house for thirty-one years. What are we going to do, go to Oak Street? We can't do that!"

The Burnouts span perhaps sixty years in age. Mike and Chris's daughter Madison is among the youngest members. She used to get shipped off to Grandma's in Green Bay every trivia weekend until she was five, when she insisted on playing for the first time. "I want to do this for real now," she told her parents. She still remembers the first question she ever answered: the name of the warthog in Disney's *The Lion King*.[6] Jim Oliva has told me he keeps the contest multigenerational on purpose: he'll drop in cartoon questions to keep the kids listening, and add some nostalgic radio-era questions for the older folks.

The team is obviously loose and having fun, but every seven minutes, a new trivia question causes a rush of activity. A question on Fred Sanford's high school graduation produces a flurry of searching on Internet TV message boards. A question about what message was printed on the back of Annika Sorenstam's cap at a recent golf tournament brings out a pile of *Sports Illustrated*s and a magnifying glass. (An adjoining room is a veritable magazine of magazines. "We have every *TV Guide* going back to 1974," says Chris proudly.) A question about the pumpkin grower whose statue stands in downtown Windsor, Ontario, leads to an international phone call.

"We've called all over the States trying to get answers," says Chris. "Mike actually got on a live radio show once doing that. Because what's open in the middle of the night? You call the DJ at the radio station."

The energy in the room is contagious. Despite ourselves, Earl and I find ourselves looking over the shoulders of Burnouts as they race the clock in reference books or online. We may not own every *TV Guide* back to 1974, but at least we're both computer programmers, professional nerds. The least we can do is offer our backseat Googling abilities.

Mike seems like the most relaxed Burnout of them all, but don't think for a second he's not serious about the contest. He's down at the radio station turning in the answers to a set of audio questions when the DJ asks us what song Katie Morosky and Frankie McVeigh once danced to. The Internet quickly informs us that these are the names of Barbra Streisand's and James Woods's characters in *The Way We Were*, but we're at a dead end there. Suddenly the phone rings. It's Mike, calling from his car. "I remember this scene. It's 'The Sunny Side of the Street.'" This turns out to be a 285-point question—only six other teams got it right, and it moves the Burnouts up into fifteenth place. "That's my man!" says Chris, beaming.

Mike can be equally intense when there's a dustup over a judgment call. Robert Redford's sewage-related duties aren't the only fact that Jim Oliva has gotten wrong, and the players never let him forget it. Wounds are still raw from the infamous Hamilton/Horowitz Incident of 1997, in which Jim asked for the last name of Cher, Alicia Silverstone's character in the movie *Clueless*. Apparently an attendance roll call in the movie calls her Cher Horowitz, but her report card is addressed to her biological dad, Mel Hamilton. Jim, in his Ozzian infallibility, decreed that "Hamilton" was the right answer, and teams complained loudly, no one louder than Mike Wiza.

"Jim kept saying, 'No, the report card's a legal document.' Well, I sent Jim a legal document addressed to 'Fugnuts.' And he got it," says Mike proudly.

The evening wears away question by question. I'm amazed when I realize it's eleven o'clock—I've been here over four hours. There's no such thing as "o'clock" during the contest, apparently. We're caught in a timeless void, as if floating at the event horizon of a black hole, only there's more kids running around, and the promise of nachos later. "You measure time by if the sun's out and whether it's top-of-the-hour. That's it," says Mike.

Earl and I have been gradually ceding our spectator status with each question. Soon we're even talking the talk. A question asks what design skier Bode Miller wore on his suit at a recent competition, and within seconds, I'm in the group paging through *Sports Illustrated*s while Earl looks for images online.

"Is it B-O-D-H-I?" someone asks.

"B-O-D-E," says Earl, typing furiously on a laptop he's snagged from someone.

I've found the right week in the *SI* pile. "I can almost see it here in the table of contents. They're dark blue. Let me go to the main article. Whoa, got it. They're spiderwebs."

"I've got a few photos on images.google.com. If I blow them up . . . yeah, we got spiderwebs here."

"Is this still first song?"

"Second song!"

"Call it in."

Earl makes the call to the radio station—a rare privilege. We are honorary Burnouts.

We stumble back to the hotel. The contest is only seven hours old, and I already feel like my brain is full, like I've ingested the trivia equivalent of Thanksgiving dinner. Hundreds of teams will be doing this for almost fifty more hours, I realize. How do they do it? I just started and I'm already ready for bed.

Back in my room, I flip on the TV. It doesn't take long to find the public-access channel airing the contest. A weekend-long static shot of a dozen people answering telephones, to a *Big Chill* soundtrack of late-sixties favorites. I can't believe they actually air this, I think to myself.

I watch it until 3 A.M.

"It's addictive," I blearily explain to Kris Oliva, Jim's wife of almost a decade, early the next morning, as she drives us over to see the "running questions" on Main Street. And it is. A. J. Jacobs told me about the addictive properties of trivia, but this is no garden-variety trivia. This is a cunningly refined, lab-engineered breed of trivia, with a new hit pumped straight into your cerebral cortex every seven minutes, just as the last blast is wearing off. This is the trivia equivalent of crack cocaine.

Kris has been a trivia player longer than she's been Mrs. "the Oz." She's the co-captain of Dyslexics of the World Untie, which has played in the contest every year since 1989. For most of the spring, while Jim writes the questions for the contest, she can barely talk to him, for fear that something might slip. "January through April is the hardest part of our relationship," she says. "I used to have to hide in the bedroom and warn Jim and John when I was coming out."

This year, for a variety of personal reasons, the Dyslexics have decided to take a year off from trivia, which may take some strain off the Olivas' marriage, but is turning out to be hard on the rest of the team. When the contest started last night, "We bawled for an hour," says Kris's teammate and old college roommate, Laura Winge. I'm surprised and a little touched at how close to the surface all the emotional connections are here: among teammates, between teams, between teammates and the contest.

Dyslexics co-captain Diane Knaust felt the compulsion to play so strongly that she raced off to the phone to call in the answer to the first question, the one that's been "Robert Redford" every year since 1981.

"Paul Newman!" she breathlessly told the operator, to the great amusement of her teammates.

Earl suddenly jerks awake in the front seat. "Did you hear that? They just asked the name of the cat that gets caught in the tree at the start of *The Incredibles*. It's Squeaker. I know this, it's Squeaker. 'Officers. Ma'am. Squeaker.' That's what Mr. Incredible says. I should call the Burnouts. Do you have their number?" If I am in the early I-can-quit-anytime-I-want stages of trivia addiction, Earl is more of a strung-out ready-for-the-methadone-clinic kind of trivia junkie.

We meet up with Jim in the parking lot of a local Shopko, where teams are assembling for the scavenger hunt.

"Get some sleep!" Jim tells his wife, who's been up all night listening to the contest.

"Then stop asking questions!"

Earl and I decide to spend the day visiting as many trivia players as possible, and so we pore over a list of all 435 registered teams. "Shall we just go by team name?" asks Earl. "I want to visit K-Y Jelly Doughnuts and Drain Bamage."

"Some of these names are pretty dirty," I notice. "Let's just visit every team where the name is an oral sex reference."

"I don't think we have that kind of time."

Many of the teams we meet remind us of our friends the Burnouts: multigenerational family reunions with food, folks, and fun—and a room in the back stuffed with almanacs and old *People* magazines. Dad's Computers play in a basement rec room that's been made over into a middle school BASIC programming class: thirty oldish PCs manned by thirty youngish players. The Choirboys, mostly law enforcement types, play in a hosed-down towing garage, while brats and sauerkraut are served cafeteria-style and tow-headed children play outside in the sun. It feels more like a church picnic than a cutthroat trivia contest. I'm enjoying myself even more unapologetically every team like this that we visit. I can't help liking people who get this stoked about trivia.

Many teams may be variations on the Burnouts, but many *more* teams, apparently, are variations on Team Diesel. Team Diesel plays out of a deafeningly loud apartment above a local pub, crammed with a few dorms' worth of UWSP students. This looks like a standard Wisconsin collegiate drinkathon, but with a few partygoers occasionally trying to hear trivia above the din.

"Did you get the question right?" I overhear someone ask.

"What question?"

Team Diesel goes on to finish a respectable 162nd place in Trivia 36. *Someone* must have been calling in answers.

Sunday morning, Kris and her Dyslexics co-captain, Diane, meet up with us again. For a team that's pointedly *not* playing in the contest this year, the Dyslexics sure seem to be following it pretty closely. Diane seems annoyed that her daughter Allyson, who has played with the team in the past, has missed most of the morning's questions. "She's still at church? Since when is Jesus more important than trivia?"

The Dyslexics and I catch up with the leaderboard at the top of the hour: the Burnouts are still flirting with the top ten, but they're thousands of points behind the contest's Darth Vader, the trivia behemoth known as Network. Network's trivia domination—seven wins in a row in the early 1990s, as well as three of the last four contests—defies explanation. This is a contest where hundreds of teams compete, where a single question can swing scores as much as five hundred points, where every single team has access to the terabytes of pop-cultural effluvia available on the Internet. And yet Network keeps winning, with sixteen trophies spanning three decades.

Needless to say, this doesn't make them the most popular nerds in Stevens Point. "Network may win, but at least *we've* all had sex," begins the "Quotes" section in the "media guide" produced every year by the hard-drinking team called the Cakers. The team called Occupation: Foole, perpetual Network runners-up, are among the most vocal haters. The rivalry dates back to high school, where Foole were apparently the older and slightly cooler kids (still "trivia-contest cool," I hasten to add, which must be the Stevens Point version of "band-camp cool" or "drama-club cool"). The bitterest run-in came in the late 1970s. According to Network, Occupation: Foole wandered uninvited into Network headquarters after the contest that year, gloated over Foole's top ten finish, egged a Network car, and then peeled out to collect their trophy. Typical high school hijinks, maybe, but Network still feels the sting.

Other teams speak of Network in hushed tones and concoct conspiracy theories to explain their success. Network uses computers to communicate with thousands of experts nationwide, who answer the questions for them. Network enforces military-like discipline during the contest to keep players on strict sleep and duty schedules. Network gets the answers fed to them straight from the Oz, who (this part is true) first hooked the Network guys on trivia while he was their ninth-grade algebra teacher.

Earl and I visit Network in the nearby town of Plover, where they play in the basement of a team member's parents (yes, his parents' basement: make your own joke here). Other teams—and even Kris Oliva—have warned us that Network keeps their team headquarters off-limits to outsiders. But as it turns out, there is no such security. We wander downstairs into a semi-finished basement that looks quite a bit like a dozen other team headquarters we've seen. A handful of tired-looking players, including, evidently, a few married couples, are chatting and snacking between questions. They greet us cheerfully and offer us homemade doughnuts. Ray Hamel is there—he's been a "ringer," as he says, for Network for almost two decades. When a question comes over the air, players wearily hit books, Notes, and Google, just like 430 other teams are probably doing at exactly the same time.

This is the vaunted Network? As I look around the basement, I do notice a few competitive advantages. Shelves groan under the largest library I've seen in any team headquarters. There are literally thousands of trivia volumes, evidently assembled by completists. I see every annual pro sports register back to the 1960s. Decades of *World Almanac*s are lined up on a jury-rigged shelf that runs above a doorway at ceiling level. If, as one survey recently found, half of all American households don't buy a single book in any given year, Network is taking up the slack for a medium-sized city.

An unoccupied computer displays a file that appears to hold the complete dialogue from a 1959 episode of *Leave It to Beaver*. It takes me a while to realize what I'm seeing: Network has somehow been pulling the closed-captions from TV broadcasts into text files, so they have a computer-searchable index of dialogue from fifty years of American television.

Much of one wall is taken up by a gigantic library card catalog, cast off from the university years ago when they went digital. The little square drawers are now full of alphabetized trivia facts on three-by-five cards. I open one drawer at random and thumb through. Flea Roast. Flintstones, The. Flood Control Siphons, Longest. Flowertown, USA. I try to imagine a library where the card catalog actually looked like this. I'd definitely want a library card there.

Computer programmer Barry Heck wanders down the stairs to join me. Barry is the soul of Network—it's his parents' basement. This morning, he's been catching a few hours' sleep, and his blue terry-cloth bathrobe and silly Bill Gates hair are the perfect complement for his soft-spoken, pensive demeanor.

I tell him that I feel very much at home, even nostalgic, among these rows of dusty reference books, obsolete everywhere but in this one little town. Barry is nostalgic as well. "This basement is a picture of trivia history as it was," he says. In the Google era, these books are apparently the trivia equivalent of a butter churn or a hand-cranked washing machine.

The longer I talk to Barry, the more elegiac he becomes, unruly black eyebrows rising and lowering emphatically as he tries to convey to me how much the contest has meant to him and his team. "We count the years from trivia to trivia, not from Christmas to Christmas or birthday to birthday." It's the landmark event of each year, the one constant thing that marks the passing of the time of their lives. But in spite of that, he predicts, "The team may be toward the end of its life span."

It's a confluence of things. Some players, like Barry, have wives who vaguely disapprove of trivia. Some players, like Ray, are disappointed that, because of the Internet, there is less genuinely interesting or surprising trivia every year. "I've become less and less interested in the questions. Especially candy wrappers. What's the third ingredient on a Milky Way candy bar wrapper? Who cares, you know?"

Team member Jim Newman has flown up from L.A., where he directs a live stage version of the old *What's My Line?* game show. He doesn't have the trivia endurance he used to. "It's pretty addictive for about fifty-four hours, and then you're done for a year."

After more than twenty-five years and sixteen trophies, "We're a relic in some ways," says Barry sadly. "But it's a hard passion to give up, even if the game doesn't match your memory of it."

I'm glad I met these guys. They're genuine lovers of trivia—we compare notes on recent trivia reference books we liked, all agreeing, for example, that a new compilation of fictional rock bands is indispensable. Even better, they see all the contest's warts—the gnat-straining questions, the screwy obsessiveness of its players—and they love it anyway. After all, the contest built this little team family, steeped in traditions like homemade Sunday morning doughnuts. It gets them coming back to central Wisconsin every April, year after year, often with new books or new babies in tow. It's home.

While I've been talking with Barry, Earl has commandeered a computer. In fact, he's just endeared himself to Network by finding a list of episodes of the old movie serial *Tailspin Tommy*, landing them the tough question that kicks off Hour 47. "'Death at the Controls!' Call it in!" It appears Earl is now an honorary Network teammate as well.

"Look at you. You should carry a sign: will Google for food," I say.

"I'm a trivia whore," he agrees, his eyes never leaving the screen. "Are you taking off? Car keys are on the table. I'll catch up with you later."

I'm pretty sure I know the way back to the radio station from Plover, but it takes me a few wrong turns before I find my way. The waning hours of the trivia contest play on the radio of the rental car, and I've given up pretending to myself that I'll turn it off "after just one more question." The previous day, Chris Wiza tried to explain to me the widespread appeal of the contest. "We're all sick and wrong. If you haven't figured it out yet, we're all weirdos." Maybe so, but I've decided they're definitely my kind of weirdos.

Sure, trivia is a different kind of game when you add in Google and DVDs and a filing cabinet full of Notes. But criticizing it for its different rules now seems wrong somehow, like I've been criticizing the game of basketball because it lacks an outfield. I have an elitist idea of trivia, I'm ashamed to admit. In Stevens Point, Jim Oliva has forged the ultimate populist trivia game, where whole families, whole neighborhoods, can play together, even folks (kids, women, oldsters) who get left out or underrepresented in other trivia arenas. Some things are still tantalizingly familiar to me as I watch these teams play: the camaraderie of shared knowledge, the occasional "I didn't know that!" moment of learning something new, the vertiginous thrill of producing the right answer at the last second.

The windows of the Altima are rolled down to the warm night. More than once, I pass a brightly lit house where I can hear the contest playing, and then again at the neighbors' house, and then again from the car next to me at the light. Everyone in town, it seems, is playing trivia.

"What chain of stores markets Craftsman tools?"[7]

"What baseball player's signature is on the baseball bat Wendy Torrance uses in *The Shining*?"[8]

"What game show featured a segment called the Golden Medley?"[9]

"What candy invites you to 'taste the rainbow'?"[10]

The thrice-repeated questions and the constant refrain of "Phones down! Phones down in the back!" become a kind of litany, soothing in its familiar rhythm, and I relax into it. Network has a comfortable lead going into Hour 51, and it's starting to look like they'll be taking home their seventeenth title. Come Monday, Stevens Point will effectively shut down, as thousands of trivia-playing locals catch up on their sleep and cause a yearly spike in absenteeism. But for now, the contest goes on, eight questions an hour, on and on and on, sent out into the gathering night.

ANSWERS

1. Superman's father was named **Jor-El.**

2. **WOPR** (War Operations Plan and Response) is the burger-inspired name of the military supercomputer in the movie *WarGames*.

3. **Spamville** is the secret U.S. military base named for a processed food in 1942.

4. Jimmy Neutron's middle name is **Isaac.**

5. Evelyn Mulwray was **horseback riding** (and thus hot and sweaty) right before she meets J. J. Gittes for the first time in *Chinatown*.

6. **Pumbaa** is the name of the warthog in Disney's *The Lion King*.

7. **Sears** is the chain of stores that markets Craftsman tools.

8. The baseball bat Wendy Torrance uses in *The Shining* bears **Carl Yastrzemski**'s signature.

9. *Name That Tune* featured a segment called "The Golden Medley."

10. **Skittles** is the candy that invites you to "taste the rainbow."

CHAPTER 14

What is RECOGNITION?

At my final *Jeopardy!* taping before the summer hiatus, I spot a familiar face in the studio parking garage. Nick Meyer, a perpetual math grad student at Berkeley, used to be a fixture at West Coast quiz bowl tournaments back in my playing days. His savage pom-pom of a hairstyle has been neatly mowed for TV, so I barely recognize him. As it turns out, our past acquaintance means the show won't let us play each other, so Nick goes into Matt Bruce's lonely world of *Jeopardy!* limbo.

As the contestants take their midday break for lunch in the dreary Sony cafeteria, I tell Nick how surreal my "secret identity" has made my life lately.

"That's a great story," he says. "You need to save that for Letterman."

"Letterman? Are you kidding me? Nobody ever gets famous in America just for winning on a game show. Not since gum was two for a penny, anyway."

Nick looks at me with a strange, crooked smile, like he knows something I don't. "Wait and see" is all he says.

A month later, my first show finally airs. We have a big shindig in the lobby of my office building, so I get to watch friends and family teeter on the edge of their seats during the exciting "Who is Jones?" finish. I also experience, for the first time, the biting-down-on-a-Popsicle-stick shudder of having to see my own goofy face and hear my own squawky voice on a big-screen TV. My media career is only twelve minutes old, and I'm already the first victim of Ken Jennings backlash.

It's a relief, after four months, to finally be able to talk about my experience—the first game out of forty-eight, anyway. As the next few weeks of shows air, the phone calls begin—at first, local newspapers and TV stations, then national magazines and TV shows. *Jeopardy!*, not wanting to overdose on publicity too soon, has barred me from talking to the media at all, so there isn't really much I can say to placate the desperate Jimmy Kimmel bookers, no matter how many times a day they call.

I pay Earl back for his share of the expenses from our *Jeopardy!* audition trip, as we'd agreed at that gas station over a year ago. "You know," he says, "I told some people at work that you and I had tried out together, and everyone says, 'Then he should split the money with you!'"

We both laugh, but there's probably some truth behind the joke. In my view, Earl's tryout had been better than mine. He should have been the one getting The Call and reaping game show glory, not me. Like Pete Best and the Beatles, like Buddy Ebsen getting fired from *The Wizard of Oz* because he was allergic to the shiny Tin Man makeup, like astronaut Michael Collins buffing his nails in lunar orbit while Neil and Buzz walked on the moon, Earl quite rightly feels that he was tantalizingly close to a headline-making success story—and barely missed out.

For the next month, I'm amazed to watch my *Jeopardy!* streak build into a national watercooler phenomenon, simply through word of mouth. Suddenly every office, blog, and coffee klatch in America is talking about—of all things—last night's *Jeopardy!* It's just like my sixth-grade classroom all over again. A month ago, the same people's response might have been, "*Jeopardy?* Is that still on the air?" But now the show's ratings are up 25 percent. Dylan, always a big *Jeopardy!* fan, is now watching so religiously that he's taken to calling me "Ken Jennings!" around the house instead of "Daddy."

When I break the million-dollar mark in mid-July, *Jeopardy!* finally quits winking coquettishly at the media and indulges in the full PR orgy. I'm on every morning show I've ever heard of and some I haven't, not to mention the front page of *USA Today* and the last-page essay in *Time*. In the snarky *New York Times*, I'm "the most annoying man in game show history." (Worse than Charles Nelson Reilly? I silently wonder, as I cry into my pillow that night.) Nick Meyer's prediction is quickly fulfilled: within a ten-day period, I guest on both Leno and Letterman.

It doesn't let up. As the year goes on, I'm Peter Jennings's *World News Tonight* Person of the Week and one of Barbara Walters's Ten Most Fascinating People of 2004 (it must have been a slow year). I fulfill a childhood dream when I'm asked to appear on *Sesame Street*—Grover and I dutifully extol the virtues of eating fresh fruit. I'm the punchline of a *Mad* "fold-in." The novelty of Googling my own name, initially a new favorite pastime, wears off when the hit count passes fifty thousand (also when my wife discovers how many Ken Jennings fan sites seem to be run by giggly teenage girls).

Some of the attention is pretty weird. I'm flattered but mostly bewildered when Jennings/Trebek "slash" fiction (stories fantasizing about same-sex genre characters finally throwing caution to the winds and getting it on—you know, Kirk-slash-Spock, Frodo-slash-Sam, Sylvester-slash-Tweety) appears on the Internet. The more politically minded settle for JENNINGS/TREBEK '04 stickers on their car bumpers. Leading members of Congress must have spotted these, because a couple of them call me up and ask, quite seriously, if I'd contemplate running for the Senate. A Salt Lake City sign painter named Ken R. Jennings, no relation, who made the mistake of having a listed phone number, starts to tire of the boxes of crank letters and all the middle-of-the-night phone calls.

"Is Ken Jennings there?"

"No! He ran off with Vanna White!" he finally answers one late-night caller, slamming the phone down.

The whirlwind of this new, wholly unexpected notoriety leaves me befuddled. I've underestimated once again the monstrous appeal of trivia, which is making one of its periodic, faddish resurgences, and this time taking me with it. As a fairly quiet, private person by nature, I'm slow to get used to the onslaught of stares, elbow-nudges-with-pointing, photo and autograph requests, and total strangers yelling my name (es-

pecially if you count "*Jeopardy!* guy!" or "Hey! *Jeopardy!*" as my name).
Jeopardy!'s traditional early-evening time slot means that its most loyal
viewers are the people who aren't coming home from work at that hour:
under-seventeens and over-seventies, mostly. The latter half of that
demographic duo probably comes as no surprise to anyone who's noticed
the AARP-friendly ads that run in the show's commercial breaks, plug-
ging denture adhesive, adult diapers, prescription drugs, and the like. As
a result, many of my supermarket encounters feature adorable grandmas,
along with plenty of cheek- and arm-pinching and long, meandering anecdotes. The kids are more fun, gazing shyly upward while some boastful
mom assures me that her little genius wants to study harder in school
now, so that he/she too can be a big strong *Jeopardy!* champ someday. I'm
genuinely touched to see that my own juvenile *Jeopardy!* obsession is alive
and well among the tube-sock-wearing, non-gym-rope-climbing math-
letes of the rising generation. The future of trivia is in good hands.

Apart from the fascinating behind-the-scenes look at big media and
the occasional hero worship from children, the third highlight of my
temporary Z-list celebrity is getting to meet other long-running game
show champs of the past. I was a six-year-old fan, for example, when
Thom McKee won a record-setting forty-three games on *Tic Tac Dough*
in 1980. Thom was a contestant coordinator's dream: a handsome navy
pilot with thick blond hair and piercing blue eyes, newly married to a
pretty young wife. He was also an insanely good trivia player, taking
home over three hundred thousand dollars in cash and prizes during his
two months on the show. Thom is now a Maryland real estate developer,
a little grayer, and shorn of his studly early-eighties mustache, as I learn
when he and his wife, Jenny, invite me and Mindy out to dinner in
Washington, D.C., one night. But at heart, he's still the clean-cut sailor
America fell in love with. His speech is peppered with squeaky-clean in-
tensifiers like "Jiminy Christmas!" and he dutifully says grace over dinner, even in the midst of a boisterous power-player crowd at The Palm
steakhouse. Thom and I bond easily, each nodding in amazed recognition as the other describes some curve of the emotional roller coaster of
a record-breaking quiz show appearance, some subtlety that few other
people would understand. Most comforting of all, he reassures me that
no one has recognized him on the street for over a decade.

Ruth Horowitz is another member of our little club. Her uncanny rebus-solving abilities won her twenty straight games of *Concentration* back in 1966, before the show retired her, undefeated. She e-mails me from Florida with grandmotherly affection and congratulations, still full of forty-year-old *Concentration* war stories—how Hugh Downs would scold her for solving puzzles *too* quickly, before the high-ticket prizes could be revealed; how being on TV made her so nervous that she lost ten pounds during her two weeks of taping; how an FCC attorney showed up at her front door and tested her on rebuses to ensure for himself that her shows hadn't been rigged. Besides Thom and Ruth, past *Jeopardy!* all-stars whom I'd idolized since childhood come out of the woodwork as well. I like the feeling of having joined a noble fraternity that stretches back to the days of kinescope—it's pure wish fulfillment to be in the same pantheon as all my game show heroes. I keep expecting the reclusive Charles Van Doren to appear beneath a street lamp one night and silently teach me the secret game-show-celeb handshake. Sadly, Chaz never shows.

My new inability to go out in public unrecognized is why I'm currently in the parking lot of a bar in Weymouth, Massachusetts, just south of Boston, trying on various disguises as the sun sinks behind the trees.

"We brought you a Red Sox hat," says Cherie Martorana. "And these!" She hands me a bundle of funny-nose-and-glasses options. "Too much?"

The novelty combo on top is something called "Chop Suey Specs," which would probably violate federal antidiscrimination laws were I to put them on. "Wow, they still make these?" I ask, a little shocked. "Yeah, too much. I'll just pull down this Red Sox cap real low."

"If anyone asks, you're Sully from Southie."

The bar is Hajjar's, a semi-dive that still boasts the dated décor marking its 1983 conversion from a roller-skating rink. The walls, alternately and unaccountably bright red and kelly green, are decorated sparsely with gaudy bar mirrors: Miller, Bud, Heineken. On a TV in the corner, the Sox are down by one run to the last-place Devil Rays. We—

Cherie, her parents, and I—slide into a burgundy padded booth near the tiny corner stage. "This is the Trolls' lucky booth," says Cherie happily. The Trolls are Cherie, her dad, Albert, and mom, Sarah, her brother, Al Jr., and his fiancée, Danielle—and me, Sully from Southie, hunched low in the booth, hoping no one notices the *Jeopardy!* ringer filling out the Trolls' roster tonight. Tuesday is pub quiz night at Hajjar's, and the large crowd filtering in is here for the trivia.

Pub trivia, like 1960s rock and roll, is a British invasion, and just like the Beatles, it can be traced back to Liverpool, circa 1959. Inspired by the vogue for quiz shows that had swept across the Atlantic, Britain's first quiz league formed in the Merseyside town of Bootle that year, and spread quietly across the north. The fad didn't reach London, however, until the late 1980s, when live quiz nights began to replace the pub trivia machines spawned by the Trivial Pursuit craze. Pub owners quickly saw that trivia was a surefire way to draw crowds on otherwise slow weeknights.

During the next decade, quiz nights gradually began to pop up in the States as well, mostly in urban areas with a thriving Irish pub scene. To this day, Boston and San Francisco are the beachheads in the pub trivia invasion, but nudged along by *Millionaire* mania in 1999 and 2000, the pastime has spread to red-state college towns as well. Belfast-born Bay Area native Liam McAtasney, whose company, Brainstormer, provides trivia questions to bars all over America, counts bars from Morgantown, West Virginia, to Missoula, Montana, among his clients. Boston's Bob Carney, who writes the questions for Stump!—the trivia game we'll be playing tonight at Hajjar's—compares the phenomenon to karaoke: he foresees that after a faddish, meteoric rise in bars, it'll be omnipresent. "It's going to plateau eventually, but it's still on the rise right now."

Cherie started playing Friday night pub trivia five years ago while working for a game-publishing company in San Francisco, where she also earned family disapproval for starting to say "car" instead of the Bostonian "cah." After moving back to Boston, she organized the Trolls as an excuse to get the family together once a week. Albert swears that Cherie is the tomboy of the family—"She thinks she's a guy!"—since, as the fourth girl out of six kids, he'd given up hope of ever having a son and took her with him to Bruins games and softball practice. She doesn't look like a tomboy tonight, in a black "Wicked" T-shirt—commemorating the Broadway musical, not the Boston slang term—with a short denim skirt and coral pink nail polish. Her Irish American mom, Sarah, is even more fabulous, in a puffy denim newsboy cap dripping, like her jeans, with faux pearls, beads, and rhinestones. There's an uppercase *S* engraved on one lens of her big hexagonal glasses. She may look relaxed, as she sips a raspberry Stoli, but everyone swears that she can be the Trolls' most competitive member.

"Don't ever play shuffleboard with her," Cherie warns, winking at her dad.

Albert fills me in. "I told her she was cheating. She didn't like it. She stabbed me with a pole."

"That's the only way to shut him up," Sarah explains.

The wisecracking, faux-grouchy Albert (the Trolls are named in honor of his famously grumpy behavior) owned a chain of men's-wear mall stores until he closed shop a decade ago. His face betrays his Sicilian descent (gray hair, archly angled dark eyebrows, and a handsome aquiline nose) just as his clothes betray his retiree status (a pale green silk shirt over white walking shorts). He's a loud talker, but Cherie explains that's only because his hearing aid doesn't work. "We don't drink much, but people always think we're trashed because Dad talks so loud."

Longtime rival team Tiger is seated at the bar, watching the Sox. Its own loudmouth anchor is Dave Blowers (a.k.a. Blowhole, a.k.a. Blowhard), a wild-eyed guy with shaggy gray hair and an appalling beige polo shirt with scarlet sleeves and belly. "He can get pretty loud after a few cups of 'the creature,'" says Albert at full volume.

Al Jr. and his fiancée, Danielle Justo, arrive just minutes before the eight o'clock kickoff, as score sheets and scratch paper are being passed around. My bacon cheddar burger arrives then too, with Swiss cheese and no bacon. Al Jr. is immediately glued to the baseball game, but Danielle is serious about trivia, having grown up trading *Jeopardy!* answers with her dad. She and Sarah spend a few minutes comparing notes on seat coverings and dress fittings for the upcoming wedding, but when the game begins, Danielle clams up and ties her hair back into a businesslike ponytail for the first question.

The "Stump!" trivia game is four four-question rounds, each followed by a specialty round using a different gimmick. After the first question is read ("In 1981, the cable channel known as Pinwheel, named for one of the channel's original programs, changed its name to what?"[1]), we have four minutes of Rob Thomas singing "Lonely No More" to decide our answer. The emcee alternates as quizmaster and DJ, switching off questions and songs until each round is over.

After nailing each of the first four questions, we confidently enter the first specialty round: picture identification. This is a favorite of the Trolls, who have in the past excelled at identifying dog breeds, vice presidents, celebrity mug shots, and the like. Tonight, we have the span of two songs to identify pictures of ten actors playing devilish characters (Al Pacino in *The Devil's Advocate*, Max von Sydow in *Needful Things*, and so on).

Writing good trivia is no picnic, but I like the questions here— they're breezy yet challenging. Teams can choose how many points they want to wager on each question, so everyone can minimize their losses on the stuff they don't know. And the clues in this visual round include clever twists like an animated movie (James Woods as Hades in Disney's *Hercules*) and even a never-released one (Jennifer Love Hewitt as Satan in an abortive remake of *The Devil and Daniel Webster*).

We thought we'd nailed the devils and the details, so it comes as a shock when the emcee announces the scores and we realize we're down two points to a team called the Intact Toads. None of the Trolls know the Toads, but their score tells us they only missed two points on the tricky visual round. Clearly a trivia force to be reckoned with.

We know all four questions in the next round as well—the founder of Parliament and Funkadelic,[2] the pH number of a neutral solution,[3] the kind of bird that makes its summer home at San Juan de Capistrano.[4] The oldsters both know this last one and beam proudly as Cherie fills out the answer. This time, the bonus round asks us to name a famous person, based on five separate clues. The clues are read one at a time, and graduate from very hard to very easy, quiz-bowl-style. You're awarded points based on how early you can identify the subject . . . but you only get one chance at it, so guessing too early can be suicide.

The first clue is totally unhelpful to me—our guy is a Rochester-born actor who graduated magna cum laude from Harvard in 1967 and then landed a Fulbright to study in London. That's the whole clue.

Cherie suggests Tommy Lee Jones, but then has a brainstorm and scribbles "John Lithgow" down on her scratch paper. We all peer at it skeptically. "Well, I *think* he went to Harvard," she says.

"I think I read once that he had a Fulbright," agrees Al Jr., his attention diverted now from the Sox. Al was slow to let Danielle convert him to trivia. "I never thought I'd get some of the answers," he says, but he now counts himself among the "diehahds." In the end, we're not certain enough about Lithgow to risk falling behind ten points. We decide to wait for the next clue.

"His roles have included that of a judge in the 1998 real-life legal drama *A Civil Action,* a newspaper editor in the 1993 thriller *The Pelican Brief,* and an international terrorist in the 1993 thriller *Cliffhanger.*"

"Holy cow, that *is* Lithgow!" I whisper, impressed.

We saw only one team hand in their answer ahead of us, on the impossible first clue. But when the scores are read, the Intact Toads have widened their lead over us to 60–56. They must have been that team. We all crane our necks to glare at the players that must, therefore, be the Toads: five flabby, crabby-looking people sitting three booths back.

We fumble the next question, not knowing that Andre the Giant was the pro wrestler on the stickers that artist Shepard Fairey hung all over the world, and scowl when a blond Toad in pink turns in her team's answer immediately. But we do know the name of the only American-born Monty Python member,[5] and the name of the German baroque composer who was largely forgotten until his Canon in D became a twentieth-century hit.[6] I come through for the Trolls for the first time by remembering the name of Don Quixote's horse—Rocinante—which no one else on the team knew. Then we go seven-for-seven on the specialty round, identifying the last words of famous people. (None of us knows the answer to Cherie's follow-up question: Whose last words were reportedly, "Great game of golf, fellas"?)[7]

The Toads must have stumbled on some of the famous last words.

When the scores are next read—Trolls 90, Intact Toads 85, Tiger 85—there is much rejoicing and backslapping from our booth.

"Tiger, we lead!" Albert yells jubilantly to his archrival.

"Watch out or Tiger will lift his leg!" responds Blowers. The dethroned Intact Toads are scowling at us now as well. Pub quiz passions can run high.

In a 2000 consumer survey, one in ten Britons self-identified as a "quizaholic," with hundreds of thousands playing in pubs every week. They take trivia seriously in the birthplace of Milton, Milne, and *Millionaire;* pub controversies over cellphone cheating or answer acceptability, combined with copious pints of lager, have led in the past to bare-fist brawls or, in one memorable case, to a £17,500 defamation of character lawsuit. So why is pub quiz still a niche activity in America when it's practically a national pastime—certainly up there with cricket, whining, and overcooking their food—in the United Kingdom?

Possibly because they're smarter and better-read than we are. This is, after all, a nation that broadcasts the Booker Prize ceremony—a literary prize!—over national TV, with the kind of pomp and splendor that we in the States reserve for the VH1 Music Awards. It doesn't take more than a single ride on the London tube to convince one that British commuters read many, many more books than their American counterparts, even in a land where tabloid newspapers have the added distracting appeal of naked women on page 3. Genuinely academic quiz shows such as *Mastermind, Fifteen to One,* and *University Challenge* thrive on the British telly decades after the United States collectively gave up and sank back in the couch to watch *Wheel of Fortune.* When Madonna wanted to seem smarter, what phony accent did she adopt? Bingo.

It's not just the British Isles, either. Quiz games are immensely more popular all over the British Commonwealth than they are Stateside. Ottawa's World Trivia Night, a Canadian charity event that attracts over twenty-five hundred players every November, is North America's largest live trivia gathering. You can find fifty pubs in Sydney, Australia, that host a quiz night every week, and India's major cities all have booming quiz communities, dating back to a quiz league that formed in Hyderabad way back in 1971.

But if there's one thing holding back the spread of live quiz nights in American bars, it's not the comparative loftiness of the British trivia IQ. It's the amazing success of NTN. The Carlsbad, California–based NTN (short for National Telecommunicator Network) pipes its interactive electronic games via satellite to screens at over three thousand seven hundred establishments all over North America. The technology debuted in 1984, during Super Bowl XVIII, with the "QB1" sports game, which rewarded sports bar denizens for predicting which plays teams would run during football games. In the beginning, trivia games were used as a cheap time-filler between the network's flagship sports contests. But today, trivia is the backbone of NTN's programming, with fifteen hours of games, almost all trivia-based, seen by over a million viewers every day.

Mindy and I have never played NTN trivia, Salt Lake City's bar scene not being exactly what you would call "hopping." But finally, a few weeks ago, we tracked down a steakhouse just south of town with NTN, and dropped in for an early dinner. When we tell the hostess we want to play NTN, she seats us in a corner table under a ceiling-mounted TV, and goes off in search of two "Playmakers." These turn out to be the blue handheld controllers, running over a wireless network connection, on which the game is played nationwide. Trivia appears on the TV screen, you select your answer on your Playmaker. In Countdown, NTN's most popular game, the multiple-choice trivia questions run for twenty seconds each, and wrong answers are gradually eliminated as time ticks off the clock. The quicker you answer, the more points you earn.

Over a million Americans have "Players' Plus" numbers, identifying them as registered NTN players who can rack up points cumulatively, but Mindy and I aren't among them. We choose screen names in happy anonymity, knowing that our scores won't be going down on our permanent record.

The questions seem designed to be as accessible as possible without crossing over the trivia DMZ into "boringly easy." What was banned by the Eighteenth Amendment?[8] What was the original theme song to

Happy Days?[9] What state is home to Guadalupe Mountains National Park?[10] I remember this last answer from a *Jeopardy!* clue on Guadalupe Peak that I'd recently botched.

Four questions in, I'm still boasting a perfect score of four thousand. I feel cocky, which is a funny way to feel just for sitting in an empty restaurant mashing down buttons on a glorified Speak & Spell. Mindy is annoyed that I won't share answers with her.

"Who originally sang 'When a Man Loves a Woman'? I don't know this one."

"Well, you have a one-in-five shot."

"You're mean! Why won't you tell me?"

She finally chooses (2), Sam Cooke, only to have that answer eliminated in typical NTN weak-pun fashion. "The band's not Cooke-ing!"

"You know, you can change your answer any time before the twenty seconds run out," says our teenaged waiter, Jared, who has been watching us struggle. We are embarrassed NTN rookies. Mindy quickly switches to (5), Otis Redding.

"Not Otis the elevator!" the screen immediately informs us. Mindy scowls.

I take pity on her now that she's dropped out of contention for the lead. "It's Percy Sledge."

Each question is followed by a fun little after-fact. "Sledge pushed 'Monday Monday' out of the top Billboard spot. Remember?"

"Uh, no, because I'm not, like, *eighty*!" answers a cranky Mindy.

"You're talking to the screen, honey."

"Hey, look, I made the top three!"

It's true. The running scoreboard for this restaurant shows Mindy in third. Unfortunately, there are only three players. It's a slow afternoon before the dinner crowd comes in, and the third player is the manager, who's been playing against us at the bar. He's good, too, in second place by only a razor-thin margin. Even better, there's nobody around to recognize me from *Jeopardy!* There's a lot of unwelcome pressure to get trivia answers right when you're *that nerd from TV*.

After seven questions, I have a perfect seven thousand points and anticipate easy victory, cheering crowds, the acclaim of millions. Then my ribs and Mindy's tilapia show up, interrupting us right as the eighth question begins. I fume quietly at Jared's poor NTN etiquette, though, to tell the truth, I didn't know the answer to this one anyway. "What is the company Zimmer famous for manufacturing?"

Mindy and I punch in answers and then compare notes. "I guessed 'golf tees,' " I tell her. She went with artificial joints.

Twenty seconds later, Mindy is vindicated. "Ha! Artificial joints! Take that."

"Lucky guess."

"I was going to tell you, but *you* didn't want to share answers. . . ."

Suddenly I notice that my controller isn't responding. "Wait, what's going on here? I think I logged off accidentally. Crap!"

Mindy is less than sympathetic in the face of my technical difficulties. "Looks like I just made the top two," she crows.

I finally figure out how to log back in, and the game ends with my Playmaker covered in rib sauce and my final score at a sort-of-lousy 11,889. This, the TV informs us, is good for twenty-fourth nationwide. I hope none of the other twenty-three ever show up against me on *Jeopardy!* Somebody at a Wild Wing Café in Charlotte won the round, with a near-perfect 14,906, for which he gets the grand prize of . . . absolutely nothing. (NTNers play for bragging rights, mostly.) As a team, our little steakhouse got its butt kicked by a T.G.I. Friday's in Tucson, Fletcher's Pub in Kalamazoo, and a couple hundred other establishments.

Mindy and I are unsuccessful at cleaning the barbecue sauce out of all the nooks and crannies of my Playmaker, so I leave poor Jared a very big tip.

Many NTN customers are like me: casual players who sit alone at a bar or corner table, idly passing the time with a few rounds of trivia. It's the perfect companion to a couple beers and a bowl of peanuts, at least on nights when there's no game on.

But there are also NTN players like Joel Suzuki (NTN handle LILJOL), a Bay Area maritime contracts negotiator who schedules his day job around his *real* calling—traveling the country playing NTN. He's racked up games at over a thousand locations nationwide, and posts site reviews on the Internet, along the lines of "Forty accessible boxes, but general setup of clubhouse area difficult to reconfigure for team play" or "Only openly gay site ever visited anywhere. . . . Suffers from poor lighting and other distractions (will provide details on request)." There's the Naples, Florida, NTN veteran who e-mailed NTN hoping for some help with his love life: "I would like nothing more than a proposal on the screen between the 8–8:30pm EST games that says, JADE—WILL YOU MARRY ME? I LOVE YOU ALWAYS—HAQQER." And there's Tampa's Ken "TENPIN" Bowling, who played 416 hours of NTN during March 2000 hoping to win the grand prize—two round-trip plane tickets—in an NTN endurance contest. That's over thirteen hours a day. Luckily, Ken was out of work and killing time between college and law school. Thirty-one days, 960 ounces of Pepsi, and 1,656 ounces of Guinness later, Ken had amassed 7,662,007 points and walked away with the prize. He used the plane tickets to fly down to— where else?—an NTN get-together in Phoenix.

Folks like these are part of NTN's core player community, people who play once a week or more. Most play not individually but in tightly knit local teams, and they are intensely loyal to their home NTN site, whose progress they follow on fan websites that obsessively track scores and standings. Many congregate on Internet forums like the "Bad Bart" message group, rehashing the previous night's questions and slinging barbs at cross-country rivals they feel they know intimately, though they may be thousands of miles away.

These hard-core fans have a strong idea of what *real* NTN play should be, and have evolved a whole slang dictionary to denigrate light-weights who don't measure up. "Sandbaggers" are players who insist on competing alone, mooching answers off the rest of the bar but offering none of their own. "Salad-eaters" or "tea-sippers" don't drink a healthy amount of beer, but instead nurse a single inexpensive menu item for hours while hunched over a Playmaker, thus souring managers on cheapskate NTN players. Worst of all are the "Borg," players who haul reference books, electronic encyclopedias, and even Internet-connected laptops into the bar to boost their scores. This kind of thing, I'm told, makes a mockery of everything NTN stands for.

And what does NTN stand for? To many of these players, NTN

provides a sense of instant community no matter where they go. If business takes them to a strange and faraway city, they'll hop in a cab and spend a few hours in the warm, dimly lit company of trivia pals they've never met but whose six-letter handles they've cursed for years. *"You're BBQGOD? No way! I'm RRICKY and this is ELDORK! Grab a seat!"* Some crisscross the country, like Ken Bowling did, to attend informal "bashes" in Houston or Tampa or Wichita, where dozens of players congregate for a weekend and propel a lucky local bar to the top of the NTN standings, albeit briefly. Fans organize their own yearly tourney, the McCarthy Cup, more elaborate than anything officially organized by NTN. There have even been two Carnival trivia cruises for NTN fans.

To demonstrate how tightly knit the community is, Bad Bart head honcho Darren "KAOS" Gasser, who calls himself the Internet group's "cat-herd-in-chief," tells me the story of Keith "MRDATA" Donnelly, a thirty-three-year-old Vegas casino supervisor and NTN nut who died unexpectedly in February 2001, leaving behind a young pregnant wife. Donnelly was legendary in NTN circles for his masterful play—he would often juggle games on a dozen Playmakers at the same time, deftly "splitting" answers on various boxes to cover different answer possibilities. NTNers nationwide were shocked at his loss, and that night, dozens of the top teams chose to play using his "MRDATA" handle in tribute. The national leaderboard showed "MRDATA" after "MRDATA" topping the standings, and many players shed tears and lifted glasses for a "friend" that most of them had never even met in person.

For others, the fierceness of the rivalry, not the cheer of the camaraderie, is the main attraction. The most prestigious NTN game is currently Showdown, the Tuesday-night "premium" general-knowledge game, and the two best Showdown teams in the country—and therefore the most elite rivals—are Grand Slam and A&M Roadhouse. The Grand Slam team, many of them high-powered Beltway lawyer types, play at the spacious sports bar in D.C.'s swanky Grand Hyatt hotel. The A&M Roadhouse, by contrast, is a small, funky, wood-floored blues joint in Manhattan's Financial District. Both teams boast their share of quiz show überchamps. The Roadhouse squad includes children's book author Tom Hoobler, who won $500,000 on *Who Wants to Be a Million-aire*, and the Grand Slam team includes *Jeopardy!* five-timer J. J. Todor and *Jeopardy!* and *Millionaire* champ Rick Grimes. Grand Slam has also recruited no fewer than ten former college quiz bowl players, including John Sheahan, the Chicago team captain considered the nation's best player back in my own quiz bowl days. It's amazing what a small world trivia is at its highest levels.

These teams are obviously a world apart—each has beaten the rest of the nation at Showdown thirteen times this year alone. The third-place team, somewhere in Manitoba, currently has just four wins. But apart from superteams like these, who have actually been known to watch for local faces on quiz shows so they can track them down and re-cruit them into the fold, NTN teams are a little unusual in the trivia world. Mostly, they aren't the glowering hotshots of college quiz bowl or the fastidious academics that dominate *Jeopardy!* Even the very good teams are just folks: nice matronly ladies with hoop earrings and murder mysteries sticking out of their purses, blue-collar guys with walrus mus-taches and beer bellies. They look like bowling leagues, not elite trivia death squads. NTN may squelch live quiz events, to some degree, but they've also reminded America that trivia can be for everyone. After all, we each have at least *one* area of useless expertise. If you don't know the hockey question, don't worry—there'll be a geography question or a *Buffy* question or a sixties music question coming along in a minute.

At Hajjar's, the Trolls and I are down to the final round. We've widened our lead over the no-longer-so-Intact Toads to twelve points, but you can wager up to ten points each on the final two questions. As in chess, the endgame is crucial.

"In 1793," begins the moderator, "the French government declared that what unit of length was equal to one-ten-millionth of the distance from the pole to the equator?"

Like an absent-minded professor in a movie, I'm sketching calcula-tions on the back of a napkin before the quizmaster even finishes the question. I've never heard this fact before, but hopefully we can make our guess as educated as possible. Let's see: the circumference of the earth is twenty-five thousand miles. That means the shortest distance from the pole to the equator is—

"Would you like some dessert?" asks the waitress, poking her head down between me and my scribbling.

"No!" Then, realizing that I've just yelled at the poor woman for no real reason: "Er, no. No, thank you."

Trivia and servers don't mix, I'm learning.

The Trolls are still tossing out possible answers while I finish my math. "Whatever it is, it's about six-ten-thousandths of a mile. That's—let's see—about a meter or a yard."

"In France, they use meters," says Danielle decisively. The team writes down "meter" on the answer sheet and argues over how much we should wager while I double-check my math.

The final question *seems* easy. "The largest crowd ever to witness a women's sports event did so in 1999. What was the sport?" We all immediately think it's soccer, since the United States hosted the women's World Cup that year. But is that too obvious?

Finally, we use game theory. "Everyone else is going to put soccer, and it seems so obvious that they'll all wager the full ten points," I figure. "Therefore we should do the same thing to protect our lead."

The quizmaster plays "Second Wind" by Billy Joel while he grades the final answers. Given our come-from-behind charge, maybe this song is a good omen.

"So why do you all keep coming back for pub trivia?" I ask the Trolls.

Everyone has a different answer. Mom and Dad enjoy the weekly family reunions. "We just like to go and be with the kids," says Albert simply. Al Jr. thrives on the competition. Danielle feels like trivia validates an expensive education. "I don't use any of that college stuff unless I come here," she says. "It's corny, but I just like learning new things," offers Cherie.

The emcee finishes adding up scores and clears his throat into the mike. "Our winner tonight, with 133 points," he announces, pausing dramatically, "is the Trolls!"

Our guesses of "meter" and "soccer" must have been right. We whoop and applaud. "I wouldn't want to go under their bridge!" bellows a noticeably pinker Dave Blowers, from behind his beer mug. He finished third; the Toads were a close second. Not wanting to blow my cover, I turn my head to study the napkin dispenser intently while the quizmaster comes round to hand us our prize: a thirty-dollar discount coupon to next week's trivia night. I'm sad that I'll be missing out on next week's game.

"You're welcome anytime," Albert tells me. That's what I like best about this kind of trivia, I guess: the teamwork. The sense that you're serving your fellow man when you chip in with "the meter" or "Max von Sydow" or "Rocinante." You're not just a cutthroat quiz mercenary perched on a barstool or behind a *Jeopardy!* podium. You're actually helping out the team.

And it's nice to have your teammates salute you for your contribution. That kind of recognition is much nicer than being gawked at in line at the supermarket. Tonight, for a change, I'm not "that *Jeopardy!* guy." Tonight I'm just one of the Trolls.

ANSWERS

1. **Nickelodeon** debuted on cable
in 1979 as "Pinwheel."

2. **George Clinton** founded Parliament
and Funkadelic.

3. The pH number of a neutral solution is **7.**

4. The birds who make a famous yearly
return to Capistrano are **swallows**
(cliff swallows, to be precise).

5. **Terry Gilliam** is the only American-born
Monty Python member.

6. Baroque composer **Johann Pachelbel** was largely
forgotten until his Canon in D became a hit at
twentieth-century weddings.

7. **Bing Crosby**'s last words were reportedly,
"Great game of golf, fellas."

8. **Alcohol** (well, more precisely, the manufacture,
transportation, and sale thereof) was banned
by the Eighteenth Amendment.

9. **"Rock Around the Clock"** by Bill Haley
and His Comets was the original
theme song to *Happy Days*.

10. **Texas** is home to Guadalupe
Mountains National Park.

CHAPTER 15

What is DEMOLITION?

Human beings are amazingly adaptable. The first time we sit down behind the wheel of a car, for example, we are overwhelmed by everything—by all the lights and doodads on the dashboard, by backing up, by parallel parking, by the possibility of accident and death at every turn. But after a few months of driver's ed, even the most neurotic teens can cruise blankly along, navigating without a second thought at speeds that would have shocked any pre-1900 human, totally unaware of their surroundings unless something goes wrong. The first astronauts to walk on the moon reveled in the almost religious experience, composing grandiose paeans to the diaphanous clockwork perfection of creation as seen from space. But just three moon missions later, astronauts were trudging around up there sniping crankily at each other about the endless rock samples NASA was forcing them to collect, and hoping they could knock off early and play a little golf. Even the most alien and demanding situations quickly become routine.

And so it goes with *Jeopardy!* For most contestants it's a roller coaster, a momentary thrill ride, but try staying on the same roller coaster for months at a time, and see if the thrills don't start to lose their edge. I've been standing behind this podium for seventy-odd "days," and by now it seems prosaic, even comfortable. Seventy games! That's fourteen games longer than Joe DiMaggio's storied hitting streak. It's twenty-one more matches than Rocky Marciano won in a row. It's eleven more shows than all the failed sitcoms of the *Seinfeld* alumni lasted, put together! In all, I've been in America's living rooms for nearly six months. That's a month longer than it took Jim Cameron to shoot the famously over-schedule *Titanic* (160 days). Two months longer than the Spanish-American War lasted (113 days). Three months longer than a year on planet Mercury (88 days). Five months longer than our ninth president lasted in office (thirty days).[1] By this time, even the most exciting-sounding thing possible—playing a fast-paced mental game against America's brightest people for big-money stakes—has started to feel routine.

That's not to say that every game has been a walk in the park. I'm not lounging idly at the podium, sipping a cup of tea and working a crossword puzzle while occasionally deigning to buzz in. No, these are still hard-fought battles against some very sharp cookies, especially since *Jeopardy!* came back from its summer hiatus. I have no idea if there were panicky backstage meetings about my residence on the show, à la *Champagne for Caesar,* but it must have been clear to all that twenty-eight locked games in a row make for TV about as exciting as that PBS guy with the soothing voice and the Afro painting trees and sunsets. Even Alex has been getting annoyed by all the runaways. "You are not here as Ken Jennings's fan club!" he berates two buzzer-challenged challengers on one show, with uncharacteristic terseness. "Think about *that* during the commercial break."

Jeopardy! thought about this during *their* season break, and when tapings started up again in August, a few changes had been made to the tape-day agenda, without explanation. All contestants now get much more on-set warm-up time to get used to the buzzer. During these rehearsals, the buzzers are now run by the same staffer who will control them during the actual games. Most pointedly, the longtime buzzer guy (*Jeopardy!* editorial supervisor Billy Wisse, whose timing I became *very* accustomed to) has been replaced by staff researcher Ryan Haas. Whether by personal preference, inexperience, or design, his buzzer-activation timing seems vastly different, and varies more from question to question.

In the abstract, I like these attempts to level the playing field, even though they lead, in practice, to closer finishes—even a handful of games that are still up in the air going into Final Jeopardy. After all, the NBA widened the free throw lane for George Mikan and Wilt Chamberlain. Major League Baseball shrank the strike zone to hamper pitchers like Bob Gibson. At least I'm in good company.

I'm also not especially worried about losing. I expected to lose my very first game, after all. Every win since February twenty-fourth has been just gravy. There's nothing wrong with gravy, but if you keep ladling it on, everything on your plate starts to taste the same after a while.

Back on my very first day of *Jeopardy!*, I had the spur-of-the-moment idea to write my name on my podium in a different style every game. Now that I've had to come up with over seventy ways to write the three letters in my name, I deeply regret this little whim. I'm sitting in the greenroom doodling new ways to write "Ken" on a napkin (a retro space font? Morse code? Ye olde English?) when one of my fellow contestants, a woman in a Technicolor-red blouse, plops down in the chair to my left and introduces herself. When she smiles, her arched eyebrows disappear behind a yardstick-straight helmet of dark bangs, making her look a little like an extraordinarily cheerful Vulcan.

"Hi, Ken. I'm Nancy Zerg."

Maybe her space-opera last name should set off warning bells in my brain—the "Zerg" are armored hive-mind space aliens that swarm players of the popular computer strategy game *StarCraft*, and "Zurg" is also, of course, the feared nemesis of a popular kiddie movie hero[2]—but it doesn't, mostly because she's so genuinely warm and good-humored. I happen to mention that Mindy and I want to use some of my winnings to see Europe, and Nancy is suddenly full of recommendations: where to find the most scenic walks in Tuscany or the best gelato in Rome. Soon we're chatting easily.

I lock up the first game of the day, but only barely; my rhythm seems off. My newfound fame is tiring and time-consuming and losing its glamour quickly. For the first time, I've flown directly into L.A. from the road—some business meetings in Toronto—and not from home. Mindy's not here, but her aunt and uncle have flown down from Utah to watch the taping. I don't know them well, but Mindy says that their self-described family relationship to me has been getting tighter and tighter the more games I win. Her parents and mine are both in the studio audience too.

The *Jeopardy!* media circus is intruding on my usual routine as well. For the first time in six months of tapings, I know that, win or lose, I'll be stuck in California until the end of the week, so I can do a series of satellite interviews with *Jeopardy!* affiliates nationwide, and then appear on Ellen DeGeneres's talk show. Winning ten games between now and then seems like an afterthought.

Nancy draws the second podium for the second game of the day, my seventy-fifth. I have recently discovered that Thom McKee's forty-three-game *Tic Tac Dough* streak is only an American record—the international game show mark seems to be held by a bloke named Ian Lygo, who won seventy-five times on a British quizzer called *100%* in 1998, before the show got tired of him and abruptly sent him on his way undefeated. I can tie his record by winning this, my seventy-fifth game.

"Good luck," says Nancy, smiling at me and third-podium challenger David Hankins. It's not the frightened, intimidated grin that many contestants have been wearing lately, I notice uneasily. She seems exhilarated to be here, with the perky, can-do spirit of a Shirley Temple movie.

"I want to welcome our newcomers Nancy and David," says Alex at the top of the show. "Good luck. You know what you're up against— Ken and our material. I don't know which is tougher right now."

Right from the start of the game, though, I don't feel especially tough. My timing is off, and I can't tell if I'm just logy and complacent, or if I'm trying to force it and am overthinking. Either way, Nancy is beating me to questions that have my name all over them. Peter Ueberroth and Larry Flynt were on the same ballot to become governor of what state?[3] Who told Congress, in 1951, "I now close my military career"?[4] Only an easy Daily Double, asking for the one state that Walter Mondale carried in the 1984 election,[5] saves my bacon. I end the first round with a $10,600-to-$4,800 lead over Nancy, and breathe a little easier.

The Double Jeopardy round is better, with Nancy answering only four questions during the entire round, but, as I should have learned from Anne Boyd's final game, *Jeopardy!* players who live by the Daily Doubles die by the Daily Doubles. I find both of them this time, and hoping to put pesky gelato-loving Nancy away for good, I bet big twice, around $5,000 each. On paper, it's a strategy that's worked for me before; my big mistake this time is getting both answers wrong.

"On December 26, 1944, Patton's forces relieved this town in Belgium's Ardennes; the Germans were driven out in January."[6]

I can remember this sequence from *Patton*, George C. Scott hearing about the general who said "Nuts!" when asked to surrender, but the name of the town isn't exactly on the tip of my tongue.

"What is Verdun?" I finally stammer, fairly sure I don't even have the right war.

Then, two clues later, I'm blindly optimistic enough to wager $4,800 on a fashion category, of all things: "Funny Hats."

"The name of this often brimless hat, popular in the 1920s, is French for 'bell,' after the shape of the hat."[7]

This one I've never even heard of. Getting either Daily Double correct would have locked the game up for me, but after both questions beat me like Ike Turner, I have only a $4,400 lead over Nancy going into the final question.

"It'll be a two-person Final Jeopardy," announces Alex, striding over to the game board. David Hankins has finished in the red. "The category: 'Business and Industry'!"

I've been in this exact same situation before, but everything seems surreal and wrong this time, like I'm in the middle of a dream where I'm taking a high school test naked. This is about as close as the final scores have been since Julia Lazarus made her two-minute-drill of a charge in my first game, and now the Final Jeopardy category is one of my weakest spots. I'm not a *Wall Street Journal* or *Fortune* reader. I can't win the game without answering this question, and things don't look good.

"Most of this firm's seventy thousand seasonal white-collar employees work only four months a year," reads Alex. "Thirty seconds. Good luck."

My mind is a blank as I stare at the clue, fixated on the word "seasonal." It must be either the holiday season or the summer vacation season, right? What other kinds of seasonal businesses are there?

Then, as Merv Griffin's sinecure of a music theme begins to play, I hear the worst possible sound—the tapping and swishing of Nancy Zerg's light-pen, immediately writing down an answer. *She knows it!* She knew the answer right off the bat, and I've got nothing. Somewhere, British quiz show prodigy Ian Lygo can safely breathe a big sigh of relief.

I hear the final heartbeat of Merv's timpani for what I'm increasingly sure will be the last time, and now Alex is standing center stage.

"Nancy, you wrote down your response rather quickly, I thought! I hope it's correct."

"I hope so too!"

"Let's take a look." I'm staring a hole into the monitor, waiting for her answer to be revealed. "What is H&R Block?" Alex pauses dramatically. "You're right."

Of course. The four-month season isn't summer or Christmas—it's tax season. I realize this is the kind of answer that millions of random people on the street would get right away—I've lost on the humanizingly easy question, just like Herbert Stempel losing on *Marty,* just like Beauregard Bottomley not knowing his own Social Security number. And yet I'm relieved. Having always done my own taxes, I was light-years away from coming up with "H&R Block," even as a possibility. This clue was an archetypal Puzzler, and I just couldn't frame it right. In fact, I probably could have pondered for hours without stumbling on the right answer. At least I won't be kicking myself over an answer I feel I *should* have known.

"You have a one-dollar lead over Ken Jennings," Alex is saying, and hearing my own name dredges me out of my thoughts. "And his final response was . . ."

I smile and shake my head, as my wrong answer—"What is FedEx?"—appears on my screen, drawing gasps from the audience. The appalled "No!" I hear from the stands sounds suspiciously like my parents. In hindsight, I'm glad they never came to Little League games.

"His wager was $5,601. He winds up in second place with $8,799, and Nancy Zerg, congratulations! You are indeed a giant-killer, our new *Jeopardy!* champion!"

I thought I wouldn't mind losing, but I was still playing hard, playing to win, and so there's a momentary stab of disappointment as I see something I've never seen before from behind this podium: somebody else's face on the monitor above the winner's total. But that's replaced by a sudden and surprising tidal wave of relief. For months, I've been living an escalatingly weird life as *Jeopardy!* and the attendant attention have crept in on me, with me never knowing how or when it was going to end. I was constantly bracing for an attack that might never come, or might come tomorrow. Now, at long last, I know the end of the story and can go home to my family. Maybe now I can stop being Ken Jennings, nerd folk icon, and just be Ken Jennings, nerd, like I was before. I have finally, as they say in drama classes and twelve-step programs, achieved *closure*.

Nancy still has both hands pressed to her mouth in shock. I give her a hug, which seems like the mature, I'm-okay-with-losing thing to do, and I see out of the corner of my eye that the studio audience is standing up and applauding. There's no confetti or balloons falling onto the convention floor, but a standing O is an odd enough occurrence on the well-oiled machine that is *Jeopardy!* Well, why not? I think. She just defeated the six-month champ. Who deserves it more? I start to clap appreciatively in Nancy's direction as well. It never occurs to me that the ovation might be for me too.

After the cameras stop, I'm suddenly swarmed by show staffers, allowed to greet me by name for the first time, now that I'm officially an ex-contestant. Lunch is called one game early, and Nancy Zerg is swooped up to be interviewed for a show press kit. She will fall victim to the same dazzling media spotlight that has been distracting me lately and, just as unable to recover, will be beaten handily in her very next game.

Even Alex wanders back onstage, with his tie loosened and in his shirtsleeves. I've been watching Alex Trebek since I was ten years old, and in two decades, I've never seen him out of a suit jacket. The effect is disconcerting and uncomfortable, a little like seeing your parents naked.

"Congratulations, Ken," he says, offering one final handshake. "We're going to miss you around here." I can't believe what I'm seeing: the normally sure-voiced Trebek seems to have a frog in his throat and his eyes are even a little moist! What do you know. All those months, the old guy did like me after all. I'm genuinely touched. And a little relieved that the Ken/Alex slash fiction bloggers aren't here to see this.

No matter how stupid your favorite hobby is, America will invent a "world championship" for you. We're accommodating that way. Do you like tossing cow patties around the pasture on misty mornings? Head to Beaver, Oklahoma, for the annual World Cow Chip Throwing Championship. ("World"? I don't know if the Bulgarians are going to send their team this year, but some guy in a pickup said he came all the way from Wichita.) Did your friends laugh and point when you'd spend hours stacking towers of cups in the school cafeteria? Come to Denver, Colorado, and let the like-minded OCDers at the World Sport Stacking Association dry your tears at their yearly Super Bowl of Stacking. Hot Springs, Arkansas, now holds the International Corned Beef Eating Championship. Anchorage, Alaska, is the recently chosen home of an upcoming World Beard and Mustache Championship. There's something for everyone.

This is equally true of more cerebral pursuits (assuming *arguendo* that there exist pursuits more cerebral than the quiet joys of cow-pie tossing). There's an elite national tournament for even the geekiest of endeavors. Crossword buffs converge on Stamford, Connecticut, every spring and speed-solve puzzles on big whiteboard grids. Google sponsors the U.S. Puzzle Team, whose best players head someplace like Croatia or Finland every year to solve the language-neutral brainteasers at the World Puzzle Championship. You can catch chess and Scrabble championships on ESPN. Even high schoolers who like their algebra problems no-holds-barred, mano a mano, can attempt to qualify for the International Mathematical Olympiad. "Gentleman, start your protractors!"

In fact, I can think of only one popular brain game that doesn't have its own national championship, and that's trivia. I'm as nerdy as the next guy, as long as the next guy isn't dressed as Green Lantern or speaking Klingon or something, and I'm a little surprised that my own little nerd niche, trivia, doesn't get the same respect as crosswords or Scrabble. Almost everyone in America plays along with trivia questions from time to time, whether it's from a board game, a drive-time DJ, or a sports-event JumboTron. It's fair to say that we as a people enjoy trivia more than, say, geometry problems. Or cow-pie throwing. And yet there's no prestigious World Trivia Championship.

This is why *Jeopardy!* means so much in the trivia world—it's the only elite tournament we have. While you're in college, you can study up for the national quiz tournaments held by College Bowl, NAQT, or ACF. But once you graduate, what are you going to do but mope around the house, annoying your spouse and kids with tales of how you coulda been a contender, how you once knew all the medieval Islamic dynasties and the five founding members of the Baseball Hall of Fame,[8] the longest book in the Bible,[9] and the shortest Shakespeare play,[10] and now it's gone, all gone? *Jeopardy!* is the only venue for real glory to which trivia geeks can aspire, and it's an astoundingly well-run and well-funded venue, with regular six-figure winners and supertournaments for champions.

In a nutshell, that's why I was so excited to make it on the show, and to somehow find more success there than I'd ever dreamed possible. For most people, even loyal viewers, *Jeopardy!* isn't much: a nursing home distraction, a kitchen-TV staple you can half-listen to while cooking dinner, a college dorm time-filler. But for trivia people, it's something much more serious: the World Series–meets–Powerball institution that lends real-world legitimacy to their little hobby, or obsession.

And so I'm not brokenhearted by my loss either. Only one in a thousand trivia fans gets to play at the level I did, much less win a game or two. I'm well aware that I'm no trivia superhero—at every college quiz bowl tournament I ever played in, there were other players who could double my score. *Jeopardy!* has had hundreds of champions who had to retire after five days but who, given the chance, might have rattled off long streaks of their own. Any one of those five-time champs could probably take me at *Jeopardy!*, given the right day, the right game board, and the right buzzer timing. I just happened to be the guy in the right place at the right time, with a few fortunate breaks besides. I got lucky.

In a sense, I got the same run that every *Jeopardy!* contestant gets: just one loss. No more, no less.

The next day, it hits me. Not "You lost on *Jeopardy!*" I'd already figured that one out. More like, "You don't get to hang out at *Jeopardy!* anymore." For most people, a *Jeopardy!* spot is a surreal half-day adventure, but for me, it was a lifestyle, and for six months I got used to it. It finally sinks in that I won't be back next week, joking around with Maggie and the gang, trying to find something edible at the Sony cafeteria, riding the adrenaline rush as Johnny Gilbert booms out the opening narration of each show. It's a lonely feeling, like watching all your friends climb onto the bus on the last day of summer camp.

Because of *Jeopardy!* media commitments, I have to spend two more days alone in L.A. pondering my last game and the *Jeopardy!*-shaped hole in my heart. Luckily, Mindy's parents are still in town, and they distract me by playing tourist for a day, visiting the La Brea Tar Pits and the space telescope on Mount Wilson (the nerd genes are, obviously, not all on my side of the family). Mindy's dad wants to see Griffith Park, and I smile when I remember that Earl and I did exactly the same thing the afternoon we both passed the *Jeopardy!* test, a year and a half ago. We drive up the steep, winding road into the Santa Monica Mountains, but the observatory is still closed.

ANSWERS

1. **William Henry Harrison,** the ninth U.S. president, lasted only thirty days in office.

2. Zurg is the nemesis of *Toy Story* spaceman **Buzz Lightyear.**

3. Peter Ueberroth and Larry Flynt both ran for governor in **California.**

4. "I now close my military career" is from the end of **General Douglas MacArthur**'s famous 1951 farewell speech to Congress.

5. **Minnesota** was the only state carried by Walter Mondale in the 1984 election.

6. Patton's forces relieved **Bastogne,** Belgium, on December 26, 1944.

7. The **cloche** is the brimless 1920s hat whose name is French for "bell."

8. **Ty Cobb, Babe Ruth, Honus Wagner, Christy Mathewson, and Walter Johnson** were the five founding members of the Baseball Hall of Fame.

9. **Psalms** is the longest book in the Bible.

10. *The Comedy of Errors* is Shakespeare's shortest play.

CHAPTER 16

What is REDEFINITION?

Jeopardy! may frog-march its contestants around like political prisoners, but the studio audience watching every game is under no such tight security. Johnny Gilbert usually asks them nicely not to give any game outcomes away in advance, but nobody has to sign a form or even gets lectured much. So it doesn't really surprise me when, by the next day, accounts of my last game start to leak onto the Internet. Wire services pick up on the rumor, which soon makes the CNN news crawl and a *USA Today* front page. Nobody seems to consider whether or not they should spoil the ending of a TV show that won't even air for three more months. This just in: Rosebud is the sled! Details at eleven.

As a result, the day of interviews I had lined up turns into one long "No comment," and I'm feeling worn out and irritable when the car finally arrives to take me to the airport. I'm not in a chatty mood, but the driver is a sociable old guy named Leonard, whose offhand manner puts me immediately at ease. Soon we're comparing notes on our jobs and our kids.

"Let me tell you how the Lord do," says Leonard, apropos of nothing, as we turn off the freeway and approach the terminal.

"When I was in high school, I saw a sign saying BAND PRACTICE. So I take up the band and I learn me the flute and the piccolo. And being as competitive as I am, I got pretty good at it. But I never liked wearing the band uniform. Just never much liked it.

"After graduation, I got drafted and shipped off to Vietnam. And the army's got me picking up cigarette butts on the front line when one day I see a sign on the base, says BAND TRYOUTS TODAY. So I spend the rest of my tour playing piccolo for Uncle Sam, but you have to understand, army band members, they have themselves some pretty bad attitudes, and I'm the worst. When I finally get out of the army, I burn my uniform, all the green dungarees." He pronounces it "dun-jer-eez." "And I swear to God, I say, 'God, I ain't never wearing a uniform again for the rest of my life.'

"Well, then, like I told you, I worked for the Los Angeles County Fire Department for the next thirty years. I was captain when I retired. Could have made chief too but one day I just couldn't take the uniform anymore. Just couldn't take it, so I quit and I told them why. And now here I am, a limo driver, and this gray suit is my uniform. I got fourteen of them in my closet, all alike. I'll be wearing a uniform of a kind for the rest of my life.

"He sure do work in mysterious ways. He can show you where you going and you can say, 'Hell no, Lord!' and sail away to Tarshish like Jonah, just to get away from Him. But He'll get back at you one of these days. He'll get you coming or going, and ain't nothing you can do about it."

I consider Leonard's sermon as I sit at my boarding gate, staring blearily at the blinking lights out on the dark runway. "Let me tell you how the Lord do." For Leonard, it was a uniform he couldn't run away from. For me, I guess it was trivia. I decided once upon a time that Knowing Weird Stuff, for want of a better name for it, was an annoying penchant, a kiddie game, and I spent years pretending I didn't care for it.

By winning on *Jeopardy!*, I fulfilled a childhood dream of mine in big, glitzy, bug-eyed Make-A-Wish Foundation style. How often does that happen? Most of my other fourth-grade pipe dreams never came true—the X-ray vision, the helicopter that could go into outer space, Mr. T at my birthday party—but no matter what happens to me now, I'll always have *Jeopardy!* It was nice to get back in touch with all the old friends who saw me on TV and tracked me down to say congrats. It was nice to chill with Grover and Big Bird. It was nice to give a brief boost to that endangered species, the American game show. It was nice to have someone on TV for a few months who was openly religious and yet wasn't (hopefully!) the usual stereotypical mouth-breather or nut job. And then there's the matter of the $2.5 million, which I'll admit is a fun little bonus.

But mostly, I'm grateful to *Jeopardy!* because it reintroduced me, at long last, to trivia. I came out of the trivia closet on national TV, in front of tens of millions of people. I can never again quietly pretend I don't remember the name of some band's bassist or of some old Angie Dickinson movie on late-night TV. What's more, I don't really *want* to pretend anymore. I'm okay with being the one in every room who might conceivably Know Weird Stuff. There's no excuse for being a jerk or a know-it-all about it, but I've decided that knowledge is a good thing—an absolute good, in fact. It's always better to know a thing than not to know it.

Yes, I've finally embraced my inner trivia geek. After all, you can't run away from who you are. "He'll get you coming or going, and ain't nothing you can do about it."

The next evening, I walk out onto our new deck to join Mindy, who is sipping a soda and watching the sun sink behind our neighbors' giant Manitoba maple, which provides our backyard with much-needed shade every summer and bushels of leaves to rake every fall. Despite our best projections, the deck turned out to be an all-summer project, which means that we're only using it for the first time now that the days are already shortening. After a year of *Jeopardy!* chaos and hubbub, the backyard seems mercifully quiet.

"Who was that on the phone?" asks Mindy.

"It was Earl. He's buying tickets for Wilco in November. You want to go?"

"Yeah, maybe. Did he tell you again how all his friends think you two should split the winnings?"

"He seems to be at peace with *Jeopardy!* He wants to drive down to L.A. next year to try out again."

The streetlight mounted on a telephone pole across the way buzzes on, bathing the leaves of the ivy-shrouded pole in a warm, sodium orange glow. The wooden planks under my bare feet are still warm from the heat of the day, but now a cool breeze moves through the yard and rustles the branches of the maple tree, reminding me of long autumn afternoons of leaf raking to come. I still miss *Jeopardy!*, but it's good to be home.

"So what are you going to do now?" asks Mindy, leaning her head on my shoulder.

"I don't know. Dylan needs a bath. Then I should probably check my e-mail."

Dylan is, in fact, leaning his head out of the kitchen door as if it were a locomotive cab and bellowing railroadisms like "All aboard!" and "Pull the throttle!" gleaned from *Thomas the Tank Engine*. At first, I was worried by the idea of Dylan as a precocious trivia-nerd-in-training. But as I've come to terms with my own trivia-geekiness, I've stopped worrying so much about Dylan. He's a healthy, normal kid, who just happens to be an obsessive information sponge. And there's nothing wrong with that. After all, we're currently living in a Bizarro society where teenagers are technology-obsessed, where the biggest sellers in every bookstore are fantasy novels about a boy wizard, and the blockbuster hit movies are all full of hobbits and elves or 1960s spandex superheroes. You don't have to go to a *Star Trek* convention to find geeks anymore. Today, almost everyone is an obsessive, well-informed aficionado of *something*. Pick your cult: there are food geeks and fashion geeks and *Desperate Housewives* geeks and David Mamet geeks and fantasy sports geeks. The list is endless. And since everyone today is some kind of trivia geek or other, there's not even any stigma anymore. Trivia is mainstream. "Nerd" is the new "cool."

I'm also reassured to see that Dylan is driving his imaginary train while wearing the dog's water dish on his head and eating a tube of cherry ChapStick, since I don't know if that's the kind of thing that superprodigies do. Mozart's biographers agree that he never ate much ChapStick.

"I didn't mean 'What are you going to do right this minute?'" says Mindy. "I meant, what happens now? What are you going to do with the rest of your life, *Jeopardy!* guy?"

I've been wondering that myself. "Do you remember," I begin slowly, "that old *Twilight Zone* with Burgess Meredith? He's the bookworm bank teller who never seems to find time in the day to read. Finally there's a nuclear war, and he's the lone survivor, remember? The last man on Earth?"

"I hate that episode. His glasses break, right? He's left all alone and totally blind. It seems so unfair."

"Right, but *before* his glasses break. This guy's been ground down by a tiresome, thankless office job his whole life. Suddenly a miracle occurs and he has the rest of his life all to himself, time enough at last for all his nerdy pursuits. 'All the time I need, and all the time I want.' That's how I feel now. Suddenly liberated."

"Not by nuclear war, though."

"No, not as such. By a game show, in fact. Vastly preferable."

"So what are you going to do with all the time in the world? Burgess Meredith just wanted to read Dickens. What nerdy pursuits are you going to pursue?"

That's where she's got me. I honestly don't know. I'll have a lot more time to spend with the family, at least. I could go back to school. I could write. I could take up painting again. I could build scale models of world landmarks out of Legos in our backyard. The world is wide, as my mom always used to tell us growing up.

I remember what Fred Worth said about retirement: he now had the same 24/7 that Stephen King does, or that anyone else does. Well, sign me up. I don't think I'm going to be assembling a six-thousand-page encyclopedia of Hollywood, but I wouldn't be surprised if trivia stays a big part of my life from here on out. Not just trivia in the sense of random questions, but trivia knowledge in the broader senses: cultural literacy, curiosity about the world, being an irritatingly encyclopedic authority on the things that I love.

Which reminds me. "In all the commotion, did you remember that next Thursday is our anniversary?" I ask Mindy.

"I did. Four years." We clink our Diet Coke cans together.

"I realized something on the plane yesterday. What would you say got us together in the first place?"

"Well, you kept pestering my roommates to set us up, and—"

"Trivia."

"Trivia got us together? What, did we play Trivial Pursuit or something?"

"What were the first two things we knew we had in common?"

Mindy thinks for a minute. "That we both knew all the words to the songs in *Once Upon a Mattress*?"

"That's one. You loaned me your CD."

"Knowing a lot about Broadway musicals doesn't necessarily mean you were into trivia. You could have been gay."

I soldier on. "And then the day after our first date, I saw you again, and we traded lines from *What's Up, Doc?*" We had both grown up on worn VHS tapes of this 1972 screwball comedy, a favorite in our respective families. That afternoon, Mindy had said, as I was leaving her house, "Let's not say good-bye. Let's say 'Au revoir.'" "No, let's say good-bye," I'd responded automatically. Then we'd gaped at each other, realizing we'd been quoting the same movie.

"Love at first sight."

"So maybe we never would have realized we were so compatible if we hadn't been trading song lyrics and movie dialogue. That's textbook trivia right there."

Mindy looks unconvinced. "But that's how *everybody* gets together. They find some dumb thing they both know a little about that they can talk about until the waiter brings dinner. According to you, there probably isn't a marriage or a relationship or a friendship anywhere today that wasn't jump-started by trivia."

"I think that's exactly right," I agree. "To trivia." We toast with our soda cans again as the sun dips behind the big maple tree.

Centuries before it was getting me a new deck, or stared at in Costco, or married to my wife, trivia was already fascinating a small coterie of devotees who couldn't get enough of Knowing Weird Stuff, even if they didn't quite know why. They submitted their puzzling questions to the *Athenian Mercury* in the 1690s and bought every volume of John Timbs's *Things Not Generally Known* in the 1850s. In the 1920s, they read Ripley and played along with *Ask Me Another!* In the 1950s they gathered around the electronic hearth to watch make-believe fortunes won and lost on *The $64,000 Question* and *Twenty-One*. In the 1980s they threw Trivial Pursuit parties until their friends had heard all the questions twice and started to become mysteriously unavailable on Friday nights.

Every twenty years or so, it seems, trivia repeats its boom-and-bust cycle for a whole new generation. I asked Ray Hamel why trivia keeps coming back, and he had a theory. "Trivia gives people something to do when the economy's doing well. People want entertainment. They want to reminisce. They have time for pastimes. When the economy's bad, you're too worried about what's coming up ahead to think about what's happened behind you." Every trivia fad in history, he said, was followed immediately by hard times, by economic collapse.

Looking at the dates myself, I can see that Ray is on to something. *Ask Me Another!* hit at the giddy height of the Jazz Age, just two years before the market crash that ushered in the Great Depression. TV quizzes peaked during the postwar prosperity of the Eisenhower years, and their collapse was followed by the bear markets of the late 1950s and early 1960s. Campus trivia flourished in the years just preceding the oil crisis and global recession of 1973–74. The Trivial Pursuit fad was over by 1987, just in time for "Black Monday" and the largest one-day drop in stock market history. When *Who Wants to Be a Millionaire* became a sensation in 1999, the Internet bubble was at its ready-to-pop peak.

If trivia's reemergence is indeed tied to economic cycles, the craze will no doubt come around again, just as it always has. But trivia is now so mainstream a phenomenon that it surrounds us daily, unnoticed, even when it's not grabbing headlines. What is the Information Age if not the final, righteous ascendancy of trivia? Maybe the trivialization of America will produce a rising generation of bright, curious, culturally literate citizens, conversant in every subject of learning under the sun, and trivia will thereby save the world. Or maybe it will just produce more couch potatoes full of ironic hipster regard for crappy old TV, and obsessed with niggling sports statistics and the detail-filled "bonus features" on their DVDs. Time will tell. But in either case, trivia is here to stay.

And now I'm part of it. I've attained the Holy Grail of trivia buffs: I'm now a trivia answer myself! Someday, decades hence, a Trivial Pursuit game (Remember the '00s? edition) may grind to a halt because of a People & Places question like:

"Who won $2.5 million during his record-breaking six-month run on the game show *Jeopardy!* back in 2004?"

And players will groan and strain and dig the heels of their palms into their furrowed brows. "You remember! That one Opie-looking guy, from Utah or Idaho or someplace. Grandma was always talking about him, the summer before we put her into the home. *What was his name?*"

I'm a trivia answer, just like dancer Bob May, who played the Robot on *Lost in Space,* or William Rufus King, who was Franklin Pierce's vice president for a mere forty-five days, nearly all of which he spent dying of tuberculosis in Cuba. I'm right up there with William Moulton Marston, the psychologist who created Wonder Woman and invented the lie detector, or Al Downing, the pitcher who gave up Hank Aaron's record-breaking 715th home run. Or, for that matter, Venetia Burney (the eleven-year-old who named the planet Pluto) or Elwood Edwards (the voice-over guy who says "You've got mail!" on AOL) or Robert Opal (the streaker at the 1974 Oscars).

And there's plenty of room, in the margins of history, for us trivial footnotes. Trivia, to borrow a phrase from Walt Whitman, is *large.* It contains multitudes. In fact, it contains everything.

That's what we love about it.

Am I the only one who turns straight to the Acknowledgments page of a book as soon as I buy it? It's a weird habit, and I'm not really sure why I do it. I guess I like the forbidden-fruit thrill of jumping ahead to the end of a book, but without running the risk of ruining the ending. (Spoilers: I lose to Nancy Zerg in game seventy-five of my *Jeopardy!* streak!) But if you're hoping these pages will provide some kind of fascinating meta-conclusion or meta-commentary on the book, I apologize: they do not. I'm not really an author, but I've studied a few of these things, and it's apparently supposed to be an unreadably boring string of paragraphs listing the names of people whom the reader has never heard of. Unless you think I might be thanking you personally, you can probably move along. Nothing to see here.

I started writing this book knowing next to nothing about the history and culture of trivia, so I'm deeply indebted to the literally hundreds of trivia people who agreed to be interviewed, or provided answers to questions, or suggested new avenues for research. Many of those interviews are described explicitly in preceding chapters, so I won't name everyone again, but I should note that the book simply couldn't have been written without all the quiz fans who were so hospitable in letting me into their communities: trivia writers of all stripes, high school and college quiz bowl players, the wonderful people of Stevens Point, the Trolls and their Hajjar's rivals, the whole "Bad Bart" message group of NTN fans, and at least three Internet message boards full of game show buffs.

Eileen Curran and John Topham helped me track down the late great John Timbs, and Eric Caren introduced me to the *Athenian Mercury*.

Internationally, Jo Meek at All Out Productions mailed me a copy of her fascinating BBC radio documentary on pub quiz; Paul Paquet gave me a revealing glimpse into the devious inner workings of the Canadian trivia mind; and Shreeram Shetty shared his experiences with Indian quiz leagues.

Bryan Boam, Ginger Ferniany, Matt Ottinger, and Robert McIelwein gathered archival material that I needed to reconstruct my own (sometimes hazily remembered) *Jeopardy!* experience. Maggie Speak at *Jeopardy!* was kind enough to answer a few background questions for me, unless revealing such violates some arcane *Jeopardy!* security protocol for either of us, in which case, we never ever spoke.

Thanks also to Greg Hallinan at NTN (now called Buzztime, after a 2005 name change), Jim Ware at Horn Abbot, *Quiz Craze* author Thomas DeLong, game show guru Steve Beverly, game inventor Richard Levy, and anyone else I've forgotten.

Everyone I spoke to was incredibly helpful and generous with their time. Any errors, of course, are mine and not theirs.

I'm even more grateful to all those who provided valuable feedback by slogging through early drafts of the manuscript: Earl Cahill, A. J. Jacobs, Nathan and Faith Jennings, and Gwyn Nichol. My agent, Jud Laghi, and my editor, Ben Loehnen, deserve thanks not only for expert and professional services rendered, but for helping shape the concept of this book from the beginning. If I'd had my way, this would have been just another quickie C-list celeb cash-in, full of my shallow ghostwritten thoughts on why tolerance is good and pollution is bad, filled out with some baby pictures and holiday recipes. But *no,* said Jud and Ben, why not a book *about trivia?* Or we're withholding your advance. Well, okay, I said. But it sounds like a lot more work.

My parents, Ken and Cathi Jennings, fed, housed, clothed, and educated me for almost twenty years, in addition to helping out here and there with the book, so what thanks can I give in a single paragraph that would be worthy of all their trouble and sacrifice? Maybe I'll send them a nice gift basket. I mean one of the expensive ones, the kind with cashews instead of peanuts. Speaking of people who provided me shelter against the elements, thanks also to the Cannons, the Fewkes, the

Hentzels, the Johnsons, and the Thompsons, who let me sleep on their respective floors or guest beds during my trivial adventures.

On acknowledgments pages, writers' wives are always "long-suffering." What does that even mean? Writers forget anniversaries? Writers spend long nights hunched in front of a computer screen instead of coming to bed? Writers are cranky when a chapter isn't going well? Writers beat their wives? I'm sure I'm guilty of at least two of those, so thank you Mindy, the love of my life. She is certainly "long-suffering," and a top-notch proofreader, but those are the least of her many, many virtues.

Christopher Robin Milne supposedly never forgave his father for immortalizing his embarrassing stuffed-animal games in the Winnie-the-Pooh books. Apparently it got him beaten up a lot at boarding school or something. As a result, I thought long and hard before including my son Dylan's winsome childhood antics in this book. But never fear, Dylan. I've cleverly made sure this book is so lightweight and mediocre that it'll be long out of print by the time you're of school age.

And yes, Daddy is *now* done with the book, kiddo. We can go play Legos.

Ken Jennings
Behind a messy desk
In snowy Utah
January 2006

TRIVIA TIMELINE:
A BRIEF HISTORY
OF TIME-WASTING

1691

March 17: The *Athenian Mercury,* a coffeehouse biweekly, begins publication. Over the next seven years, it will answer over six thousand reader queries, many of them general-knowledge questions on trivia staples like bodily functions and weird animal facts.

1716

January 26: John Gay publishes his poem "Trivia; or, The Art of Walking the Streets of London."

1849

November 3: Victorian scholars begin *Notes and Queries,* a threepenny weekly where they can ask and answer one another's most obscure questions. The periodical is subtitled "A Medium of Inter-Communication for Literary Men, Artists, Antiquaries, Genealogists, Etc."

1856

March: John Timbs publishes *Things Not Generally Known*. This is not his first book of "curiosities in natural history, peculiarities in popular superstition, &c. &c.," but it will be by far his most successful, selling over forty thousand copies.

1875

March 6: Timbs dies in abject poverty.

1884

Albert Plympton Southwick publishes *Quizzism; and Its Key*, a Timbs-inspired patchwork of facts in question-answer form. Similar American compilations, like Sarah Killikelly's *Curious Questions in History, Literature, Art and Social Life* and Robert Thorne's *Fugitive Facts*, follow in the same decade.

1901

September: Essayist Logan Pearsall Smith completes *Trivia*, a slim collection of epigrams. When he self-publishes it the following year, it sells a whopping thirty copies, but a successful 1917 reprinting helps popularize the word "trivia."

1916

Frederic J. Haskin begins his "Answers to Questions" newspaper column. The "Haskin Information Bureau" is soon receiving a thousand questions daily.

1917

October 8: The U.S. Army begins administering Robert Yerkes's "Alpha" intelligence test to all recruits. Almost two million men take the test by the end of World War I, sparking an interest in intelligence testing in American classrooms and industries and helping to launch the earliest trivia quizzes.

1918

December 19: The *New York Globe* prints Robert L. Ripley's first *Champs and Chumps* cartoon, the odd-facts panel that will soon become *Believe It or Not!*

1921

May 6: Thomas Edison ignites a media firestorm when he tells *The New York Times* that America's college graduates are "utterly incompetent," since they are failing his "exceedingly simple" job questionnaire, composed of one hundred fifty general-knowledge questions, by the thousands.

1924

April 18: A nascent publishing house called Simon & Schuster prints its first book: the industry's first-ever crossword compilation. It will sell a half million copies and help fuel the puzzle epidemic of the mid-1920s.

1925

Minister Ralph Albertson ends his puzzle collection, *The Mental Agility Book,* with a 602-question "General Information Quiz." It is the first known trivia quiz in book form.

1927

February 5: Justin Spafford and Lucian Esty ignite the first trivia fad when *Ask Me Another!* comes off the press, and sells one hundred thousand copies in its first month alone.

1929

January 18: Albert Southwick dies in abject poverty, and is buried in a mass grave on Hart Island.

1936

May 9: *Professor Quiz,* the first radio game show with a quiz format, airs from Washington, D.C., on a limited CBS hookup.

1938

May 17: The erudite panel-quiz *Information Please* debuts. It will last until 1952 and become the megahit of the radio quiz era.

1941

July 1: Quiz shows come to television, the very night that commercial broadcasting itself begins. NBC airs *Uncle Jim's Question Bee* at 9:15 Eastern, followed by *Truth or Consequences.*

1953

October 10: Allen Ludden hosts the very first *College Bowl* event on NBC radio. Northwestern defeats Columbia 135–60.

1955

June 7: The first "big money" quiz show, *The $64,000 Question,* debuts on CBS. Staten Island police officer Redmond O'Hanlon wins $16,000 for his knowledge of Shakespeare.

September 13: The show awards its first grand prize: culinary expert Richard McCutchen wins $64,000 in front of fifty-five million viewers. The show leads the Nielsen ratings for the 1955–56 season.

1956

September 12: The umpteenth *$64,000* clone, *Twenty-One,* comes to NBC.

October 17: Herbert Stempel begins his *Twenty-One* run.

December 5: Charles Van Doren "defeats" Herbert Stempel in their fifth game.

1957

February 11: Charles Van Doren makes the cover of *Time,* a first (and last) for any game show contestant or trivia celebrity.

March 11: Van Doren loses to contestant Vivienne Nearing.

1958

August 25: The New York District Attorney's office announces that it's investigating allegations that the quiz hit *Dotto* is fixed.

August 28: Newspapers print Herbert Stempel's accusations that his loss to Charles Van Doren was rigged.

1959

Ten teams form the world's first pub quiz league, in Bootle, Merseyside, England.

January 4: *G.E. College Bowl* premieres on Sunday afternoon TV.

July 30: A month after the New York grand jury findings are expunged from the public record, Congress announces it will hold hearings on the quiz show scandal.

November 2: Charles Van Doren finally testifies as to his complicity in the rigging.

1963

On a long plane flight, Merv and Julann Griffin reverse the traditional quiz show question-answer format and come up with the idea for a show they call *What's the Question?*

1964

March 30: *What's the Question?*, now retitled *Jeopardy!*, debuts on NBC daytime.

1965

February: Dan Carlinsky and Ed Goodgold announce plans for a nostalgic quiz tournament at Columbia University. They call their game "Trivia."

1966

March: Dell publishes *Trivia*, Goodgold and Carlinsky's companion to their popular campus game. *Trivia* and its September sequel will sell over half a million copies.

1967

March: Carlinsky and Goodgold hold their second and final Ivy League–Seven Sisters Trivia Contest.

1968

April 16: Students at the University of Colorado in Boulder hold their first annual Trivia Bowl.

1969

February: WSUS, the student-run radio station at the University of Wisconsin at Stevens Point, holds a sixteen-hour trivia event. The contest becomes an annual tradition, and today bills itself as the world's largest trivia contest.

1970

June 14: *G.E. College Bowl* ends its television run, but the game lives on as a yearly live campus tournament.

1974

Fred Worth publishes his first edition of *The Trivia Encyclopedia*.

1975

January 3: The last *Jeopardy!* of the original Art Fleming run airs.

1979

December 15: Journalists Chris Haney and Scott Abbott come up with the idea for Trivial Pursuit over a Scrabble game in their Montreal kitchen.

1980

April: Navy pilot Thom McKee begins his record-breaking run on *Tic Tac Dough*, eventually winning forty-three games and $312,700.

1981

April: The Trivial Pursuit founders form Horn Abbot Ltd. to produce their game.

November: Trivial Pursuit rolls off the presses, selling over a thousand games in its Canadian trial run.

1982

November: Selchow & Righter agrees to distribute Trivial Pursuit in the United States.

1984

January 22: NTN debuts during Super Bowl XVIII, with their interactive "QB1" football game. Trivia games will soon become their programming mainstay.

September 17: The current, syndicated version of *Jeopardy!*, hosted by Alex Trebek, makes its debut.

October 23: Fred Worth files suit against Trivial Pursuit's inventors and distributors, asking for $300 million in damages for using his trivia.

December: By the time the Christmas shopping season ends, Trivial Pursuit has sold twenty-two million copies in the United States that year alone.

1986

May 6: Selchow & Righter, unable to bounce back from the popping of the Trivial Pursuit bubble, is sold to Coleco for $75 million.

1987

September 8: The Ninth Circuit Court of Appeals rules against Fred Worth in the Trivial Pursuit case.

1988

July 13: Struggling Coleco, having already lost its Trivial Pursuit license in May, files for bankruptcy. The Trivial Pursuit rights are snatched up by Parker Brothers, which is then purchased by Hasbro.

1990

September: The Academic Competition Federation, or ACF, incorporates. Their university quiz tournaments provide the first officially organized alternative to College Bowl events.

1993

February 6: The Kiwanis clubs of Ottawa, Canada, hold their first trivia fundraiser. The event has since grown into World Trivia Night, and attracts twenty-five hundred players yearly to North America's largest live trivia event.

1996

January 19: The august *New York Times* begins its "Noodle Nudgers" trivia column, with questions provided by Ray Hamel.

January 27: Quiz bowl players at Philadelphia's annual Penn Bowl meet to discuss a new college quiz organization to compete with College Bowl. Their organization will become NAQT.

1998

September 4: *Who Wants to Be a Millionaire?* premieres on British TV. Over the next five years, seventy versions of the show will be licensed overseas, including one for the United States.

1999

August 16: *Who Wants to Be a Millionaire* with Regis Philbin debuts on ABC as a summer event. The show is an immediate smash and soon becomes the linchpin of ABC's schedule, and spawns a legion of imitators.

2001

June: The first issue of *mental_floss*, the trivia magazine brainchild of Duke University seniors Will Pearson and Mangesh Hattikudur, hits newsstands.

2002

January: One hundred nine trivia factoids begin to appear on the underside of Snapple caps, beginning the beverage company's Real Facts campaign.

June 28: Its ratings slashed by overexposure and by a spate of celebrity stunt weeks in the wake of the September 11, 2001, terrorist attacks, *Who Wants to Be a Millionaire* is canceled by ABC. It will soon return in syndicated form, with Meredith Vieira replacing Regis.

2004

May 20: Procter & Gamble announces the world's first edible trivia: Trivial Pursuit questions will appear on Pringles chips beginning that summer.

June 2: Ken Jennings, an Opie-looking computer programmer from Utah, appears on *Jeopardy!* for the first of his seventy-five consecutive appearances.

Chapter 2

16 "Five thousand two hundred and eighty" Alessandra Stanley, "O.K., Alex, Smart News for $1 Million," *The New York Times*, July 13, 2005.

16 executives thought the questions Merv Griffin, *The Jeopardy! Challenge* (New York: Harper Perennial, 1992), p. xi.

Chapter 3

28 the answer to a Trivial Pursuit question Some locals are apparently convinced this is true, though the question is certainly not in the original Genus set of the game, as the most common version of the story has it.

29 eight students sit grouped around two tables I only recently discovered an article Bruce Weber wrote for the April 4, 1999, *New York Times*, which *also* begins with a reporter attending a quiz bowl practice in the Carleton College library and documenting the quick-buzz acumen of the participants by transcribing some sample questions, cut off where they were answered. I can understand the reasons for the coincidence (Carleton has one of the best-run quiz bowl programs in the country, and all quiz bowl practices are similar enough that descriptions of them are bound to echo one another), but I was still amazed by the co-incidence.

31 oversized second place trophy I later learned that this was a trophy for the tourna-ment's undergrads-only division, however. Carleton took eleventh overall nationally, still very impressive.

34 "The players on these teams" Noel Holston, "Gopher Gray Will Take on Cornell in Revival of College Bowl on TV," Minneapolis *Star Tribune*, Sept. 12, 1987.

42 the surprised moderator Interestingly, the moderator for that match was no less than original *Jeopardy!* host Art Fleming, who was hosting a series of College Bowl matches that year for broadcast on CBS radio. Waters credits Fleming's impeccable delivery, which punched up the word "Extremism" as if it were an important clue, with helping him answer the question on just one word.

Chapter 4

55   plenty of geeky pastimes   The Chinese were constructing "magic squares" as early as 2800 B.C. Acrostics appear in the Old Testament, anagrams were known to the ancient Greeks, and a palindromic word square, in Latin, was pulled from the ruins of Pompeii. Jigsaw puzzles date back to the mid-1700s, as do picture rebuses and some of the earliest parlor games, like charades.

56   "Italian warehousemen"   "John Timbs, F.S.A.," *Illustrated London News*, vol. xxvi, Feb. 10, 1855.

56   he printed his own school newspaper   John Timbs, "My Autobiography: Incidental Notes and Personal Recollections III—Schooldays in Hertfordshire," *Leisure Hour,* 1817.

56   "could not now be built"   John Timbs, *Things Not Generally Known* (London: Kent & Co., 1859), p. 232.

56   selling forty thousand copies   John Timbs documents, *Archives of the Royal Literary Fund, 1790-1918,* compiled by Nigel Cross (London: World Microforms Pub., 1982), reel 69, case 1775.

56   more copies of the latest Harry Potter   Simon Freeman, "Harry Potter Casts Spell at Checkouts," *Times Online,* July 18, 2005. The chain Asda sold sixty-six thousand copies of *Harry Potter and the Half-Blood Prince* in one hour.

56   Dickens . . . averaged only fifty thousand readers   Steven Johnson, *Everything Bad Is Good for You* (New York: Riverhead Books, 2005), p. 134.

57   Wilkie Collins . . . wrote an essay   Wilkie Collins, "Deep Design on Society," *Household Words,* Jan. 2, 1858.

57   refused a £40 yearly pension   "John Timbs," *Academy,* vol. 7, Mar. 13, 1875.

57   "into a singularly sour and cantankerous individual"   Henry Vizetelly, *Glances Back Through Seventy Years* (London: Kegan Paul, Trench, Trubner, 1893), vol. 1, p. 86.

57   the gowned "Poor Brethren"   "Mr. John Timbs," *The Times,* Mar. 6, 1875.

58   Albert Plympton Southwick   Southwick was no relation to the other famous A. P. Southwick of his day: Buffalo dentist Alfred Porter Southwick, who invented the electric chair.

58   modern trivia questions   Albert P. Southwick, *Quizzism; and Its Key: Quirks and Quibbles from Queer Quarters* (Boston: New England Publishing Co., 1884), pp. 63, 10, and 22.

59   the potter's field on Hart Island   "Author to Potter's Field; but Southwick's Relatives Say They Had Promise of Delay," *The New York Times,* Feb. 2, 1929.

59   "Can toads live enclosed"   Timbs, *Things Not Generally Known,* p. 88.

59   "Is there any word"   Southwick, p. 116.

59   tireless researcher, Norbert Pearlroth   The New York Public Library, "Fun Facts," http://www.nypl.org/research/chss/about/funfacts.html.

59   Eighty million readers enjoyed the strip   Michael Freedman, "True Story," *Forbes,* Mar. 17, 2003.

59 over two million pieces of fan mail   Ripley's Believe It or Not! Museum, St. Augustine, Fla., "Robert Ripley: Biography," http://www.staugustine-ripleys.com/about/bio.php.

60 "Whether a tender Friendship"   John Dunton, ed., *The Athenian Gazette; or, Casuistical Mercury* microform (Ann Arbor, Mich.: University Microfilms, 1950), English literary periodicals series, reel 594.

60 a fifth of the six thousand questions   Gilbert D. McEwen, *The Oracle of the Coffee House: John Dunton's Athenian Mercury* (San Marino, Cal.: Huntington Library, 1972), p. 114.

60 over a thousand questions a day   Fred C. Kelly, "What People Are Inquisitive About," *American Magazine,* May 1922.

60 Haskin's three most commonly asked questions   Ibid.

61 the new idea of measuring brainpower   Many observers of the time saw the nascent trivia boom as an outgrowth of intelligence tests in the military, in classrooms, and in industry. Foster Ware, in *The New York Times,* commented: "When psychology gave to the world the intelligence test, few dreamed that at that moment was being laid the foundation of a popular fad—that the world was, in a sense, being made safe for a deluge of question books" ("The Answer to Those Who Ask Another," May 1, 1927). Ralph Albertson specifically credited "the vast attempt at army intelligence tests" when he wrote *The Mental Agility Book,* though he already saw trivia as a social pursuit and not an academic one. "These questions will afford many an interesting and profitable evening's entertainment . . . [but] do not let one or two forward persons do all the answering!" (New York: Albert & Charles Boni, Inc., 1925), p. 175.

61 Albertson was an odd duck   Catherine Roach, "Guide to the Ralph Albertson Papers" (New Haven: Yale University Library, 2004), p. 1.

61 two out-of-work Amherst alumni   Rosa Strider Reilly, "What! You Don't Know That? Then I'll Ask You Another," *American Magazine,* Sept. 1927.

62 immediately broke sales records   Ibid.

62 almost as many copies as . . . Charles Lindbergh   *People Entertainment Almanac, 2000* (New York: Cader Books, 1999), p. 314.

Chapter 5

70 His historic first question   Thomas DeLong, *Quiz Craze: America's Infatuation with Game Shows* (New York: Praeger, 1991), p. 20.

70 ten thousand letters   Ibid., p. 25.

70 fifteen million listeners   Martin Grams, Jr., *Information Please* (Boalsburg, Penn.: Bear Manor Media, 2003), p. 58.

70 boosted annual sales of its sponsor   DeLong, p. 30.

71 "Suddenly, intelligent men and women"   DeLong, p. 32.

71 1,366 copies of the *Encyclopaedia*   Grams, p. 121.

71   a quarter of all radio programs   "Quiz Shows Blitz Actors," *Variety*, July 10, 1940.

71   Game show taglines   These catchphrases are from *Pot o' Gold, Dr. I.Q., Information Please,* and *Take It or Leave It,* respectively.

71   the program *Transatlantic Quiz*   "Stumpers Across the Sea," *Time,* Feb. 12, 1945.

71   a record $5,220 on *Break the Bank*   DeLong, p. 109.

71   the Brooklyn public library system   "Quiz Crazy," *Time,* Oct. 7, 1946.

72   DeLong credits the postwar GI Bill   DeLong, p. 167.

73   culling contestants from a lengthy search-and-testing process   DeLong, p. 179.

74   would all drop measurably on Tuesday nights   DeLong, p. 202.

74   Fifty-five million television viewers were watching   J. P. Shanley, "Marine Wins $64,000 TV Quiz; Aided by Father in Food Queries," *The New York Times,* Sept. 14, 1955.

74   Victor Bernardo won seven hundred dollars   "The Jackpot," *Time,* June 5, 1950.

74   Britain's biggest quiz champ   "British Quiz Champ," *Time,* Nov. 28, 1955.

74   *The 64,000-Peso Question*   "Quiz Crazy," *Time,* Feb. 27, 1956.

74   beauty queen Marisa Zocchi   "Tearjerker," *Time,* July 9, 1956.

75   his own 1958 appearance   David Schwartz, Steve Ryan, and Fred Wostbrock, *The Encyclopedia of TV Game Shows* (New York: Checkmark Books, 1999), p. 176. Redford wasn't a contestant, however. He was one of the young actors the show used to demonstrate tasks at which the contestants had to guess. A young James Dean held a similar job backstage on *Beat the Clock.*

75   thousands of fan letters a week   "The Quiz Show Scandal," *The American Experience,* PBS, May 16, 2005.

76   quiz ratings had already been sagging   Paul Gray, "Those Old Good Games," *Time,* Jan. 17, 2000. Nevertheless, most of the key quiz show cancellations came *after* the announcement of the grand jury investigation.

76   "I was involved, deeply involved, in a deception"   *Investigation of Television Quiz Shows: Hearings Before a Subcommittee of the Committee on Interstate and Foreign Commerce, House of Representatives, 86th Congress, 1st Session* (Washington, D.C.: U.S. Government Printing Office, 1960), p. 624.

77   producers made him flub answers he really knew   "Quiz Scandal (Contd.)," *Time,* Sept. 8, 1958.

77   McCutchen merely had to *describe* the dishes   Shanley, *The New York Times.* This final question is misdescribed in nearly every subsequent retelling of the event. It stretches the credulity of even 1950s audiences to suggest that McCutchen would have known, off the top of his head, five dishes and two wines from a British state dinner of two decades earlier. Thomas DeLong tries to explain this away by stating—wrongly, as far as I can tell—that producers publicly gave McCutchen books to study for the $64,000 question. Both confusions may arise from a contemporary *Time* account, which reported the final question somewhat ambiguously and mentioned McCutchen's cramming.

85   Snodgrass was instructed by producers   *Investigation of Television Quiz Shows,*
p. 63.

Chapter 6

89   Susanne Thurber, *Jeopardy!*'s head contestant coordinator   Susanne, who had been
with *Jeopardy!* for almost two decades, recently retired from the show. The redoubtable Maggie Speak now ringmasters the contestant circus at *Jeopardy!*

89   behind our podiums   Yes, these should more correctly be called lecterns, as the more
pedantic *Jeopardy!* contestants occasionally point out. (The podium is technically the thing a
speaker stands *on,* not behind.) But *Jeopardy!* calls the contestant lecterns "podiums," so I'll
follow suit.

91   some well-timed coughing by confederates   The "cheating major," Charles Ingram,
was caught almost immediately. Transcripts reveal that his coughing scheme was far from
subtle: often a sudden, mysterious audience cough would make him return to an answer he
had previously discounted to the host. The major was convicted, and he and the plot's ring-
leader, his wife, Diana, were given suspended eighteen-month prison sentences. He was also
forced to resign his army commission, though he continues, implausibly, to protest his innocence.

95   I wince on-camera   Most "Hometown Howdies" appear briefly on the *Jeopardy!*
website and then disappear into the ether. You play it once for your buddies at work, and
that's about it. In my case, though, the humiliating "Howdy" ended up staying on the site for
months, pained cringe and all.

99   $80 million in royalties   Lola Ogunnaike, "In the Chatting Olympics, Look for
Merv Griffin," *The New York Times,* May 26, 2005.

Chapter 7

104   "the flower of trivia and the weed of minutiae"   Edwin Goodgold and Dan Carlinsky, *More Trivial Trivia* (New York: Dell, 1966), p. 8.

106   his buddy Frank Sinatra's shoes   This story is most famously told in Don DeLillo's
1997 novel *Underworld,* which reveals that Sinatra and Gleason had J. Edgar Hoover, of all
people, with them at the game. But DeLillo didn't invent the story—it was apparently a favorite anecdote that Sinatra himself used to tell.

107   "TRIVIA with an *I* was taken"   By a player in the Stevens Point, Wisconsin, trivia
contest, I later discovered.

108   *both* a Nobel Prize *and* an Oscar   2005 Nobel laureate Harold Pinter was twice
Oscar-nominated but has never won the statuette.

110   back to high school time and time again   "One in a Million Trillion," *First Person,*
Bravo, Sept. 4, 2001.

111   "overall Obscurity Rating"   Richard Rosner, "Three Letters of Protest Regarding
Who Wants to Be a Millionaire," *Noesis: The Journal of the Mega Society,* Oct. 2000.

111   "final and binding"   *Rosner v. Valleycrest Productions,* B165004 (Cal. Ct. App. May 26, 2004).

Chapter 8

125   Paul Graham has also wondered   "Why Nerds Are Unpopular," *Hackers and Painters: Big Ideas from the Computer Age* (Sebastopol, Cal.: O'Reilly Media, 2004).

128   ex-*Jeopardy!* producer Harry Eisenberg claimed   "What Is 'Affirmative Action'?" *Time,* June 7, 1993. The book in question is *Inside Jeopardy!: What Really Goes On at TV's Top Quiz Show* (Salt Lake City: Northwest Publishing, 1993) and was originally released by a crooked vanity publisher. The mass-market 1997 edition, from Lifetime Books, is entitled *Jeopardy!: A Revealing Look Inside TV's Top Quiz Show* and omits most of the juicy (and potentially actionable) details.

Chapter 9

134   a green forty-nine-cent mixing bowl   "Triviaddiction," *Time,* Mar. 10, 1967.

135   buffs who would drive from both coasts   At least two of the trivia luminaries in this book have won the Colorado Trivia Bowl: Fred Worth (in 1978) and Ray Hamel (in 1986).

136   "'Voivode' in Romanian just means 'Count'!"   "Voivode" *is* a title, but it might be more accurate to translate it as "warlord" or "prince," or even "governor."

137   "The sensibility of high culture"   Susan Sontag, "Notes on 'Camp'," *Against Interpretation and Other Essays* (New York: Picador USA, 2001), p. 291.

Chapter 10

148   "amazingly ignorant"   "Edison on College Men," *The New York Times,* May 6, 1921. The best summary of the media firestorm over Edison's job quiz is Paul M. Dennis, "The Edison Questionnaire," *Journal of the History of the Behavioral Sciences,* January 1984.

148   Albert Einstein himself took a shot   "Einstein Sees Boston; Fails on Edison Test," *The New York Times,* May 18, 1921.

148   "exceedingly simple"   "Why Do So Many Men Never Amount to Anything?" *American Magazine,* January 1921.

148   "alertness of mind"   "Mr. Edison's Brain Meter," *Literary Digest,* May 28, 1921.

148   those were the *easy* questions   The questions are taken from *New York Times* reconstructions of Edison's questionnaire, as remembered by disappointed job seekers. "Edison Questions Stir up a Storm," *The New York Times,* May 11, 1921.

149   specific kinds of craftsmen   Harold Evans, Gail Buckland, and David Lefer, *They Made America* (New York: Little, Brown, 2004), p. 171. Interestingly, one of the few people to pass Edison's test was a young Bill Wilson, who later went on to cofound Alcoholics Anonymous. I bet he *aced* that martini question.

149   a series of general-knowledge questions   *FSWE: The Foreign Service Officer Written Examination and Oral Assessment Procedure Study Guide* (Iowa City: ACT, Inc., 2005), pp. 7–9.

150   ***mental_floss*** magazine   Full disclosure: I now write a column for ***mental_floss***, as a result of the conversation with Will Pearson recounted here.

150   selling six thousand five hundred copies   Adam Tschorn, "If It's Trivial, Magazine Is in Pursuit," *Los Angeles Times*, Sept. 1, 2003.

150   reader base in the hundreds of thousands   Ibid.

150   a 2003 episode of *Friends*   "It's Brain Food for the Fun at Heart," *NBC 13 News*, NBC 13 Birmingham, April 24, 2003.

151   "Life with the dull bits cut out"   Charlotte Chandler, *It's Only a Movie: Alfred Hitchcock—A Personal Biography* (New York: Simon & Schuster, 2005), p. 297.

156   "Knowledge and intelligence"   A. J. Jacobs, *The Know-It-All* (New York: Simon & Schuster, 2004), p. 369.

157   self-confessed trivia fans   Virtually every obituary of the late Chief Justice Rehnquist mentioned his penchant for trivia—he would often spring trivia questions on his law clerks in morning meetings. Tom Hanks is a *Jeopardy!* nut, as he's confessed in many interviews, including in a 2004 *Oprah* appearance. Bill Clinton brought Trivial Pursuit with him to the White House after his 1992 election, and called it his favorite board game (possibly "nude Twister" was not an option on the survey). Thomas Edison's trivia tests are detailed earlier in this chapter. In November 1995, Maya Angelou went public with her *Jeopardy!* habit, though it was in the context of telling an interviewer that she was going to begin boycotting the program for not featuring enough contestants of color.

Chapter 11

159   "The answer is . . . yes!"   Holly E. Thomas, "The Answer Is 'Jeopardy!'" *The Washington Post*, November 6, 2005.

159   I can still picture the entry   Fred L. Worth, *The Complete Unabridged Super Trivia Encyclopedia* (New York: Warner Books, 1977), p. 514.

162   "fourteen years from the time Elvis became popular"   This is a slight exaggeration, but Fred's on to something here. Of the hundreds of books that have been written about the King, the 1950s really produced none at all, and the 1960s only a few, nearly all originating in the United Kingdom.

164   a young Andy Williams   Film critic Pauline Kael is one of many who swore by this story, but it's not true. That's actually Bacall's voice you hear in the movie. The legend may be *almost* true, however. Howard Hawks claimed that he planned to have Andy Williams dub her singing, and may even have used Williams's voice for playback when the scene was shot, but then he learned Bacall's own voice sounded fine. Joseph McBride, *Hawks on Hawks* (Berkeley: University of California Press, 1982), p. 130.

164   Iron Eyes Cody   Iron Eyes Cody, who played the famed "crying Indian" in the popular ecology PSAs of 1971, impersonated a Native American almost his entire life, but he

was in reality Espera DeCorti, the Louisiana-born son of Sicilian immigrants. Angela Aleiss, "Native Son," New Orleans *Times-Picayune,* May 26, 1996.

165   the world's leading Thoreau scholar   The late Professor Harding made the claim in *The Days of Henry Thoreau* (Princeton, N.J.: Princeton University Press, 1965), p. 183, and recanted in "Thoreau and Raisin Bread," *Thoreau Society Bulletin* 191, 1990, pp. 1–2.

166   Bugs Bunny voice actor Mel Blanc   "I don't especially like carrots, at least not raw," wrote Blanc in *That's Not All Folks!: My Life in the Golden Age of Cartoons and Radio* (New York: Warner Books, 1988), p. 87.

166   Sir Isaac Newton   Literally dozens of books make this claim, as do the tour guides at Newton's boyhood home, but I'm skeptical. The oldest citation I can find makes this sound like a typical the-English-are-dumb-too joke told by Irish novelist Maria Edgeworth: "Sir Isaac Newton . . . after he had made a large hole in his study-door for his cat to creep through, made a small hole beside it for the kitten." Ha ha! And you'll never believe how many Isaac Newtons it takes to change a lightbulb. *Essay on Irish Bulls* (London, 1802), p. 240.

166   an amateur etymologist named Barry Popik   Cecil Adams, "Why Can't Cecil Get His Facts Straight About the Origin of 'Big Apple'?" *The Straight Dope* syndicated column, Sept. 17, 1999.

167   Chris Haney and Scott Abbott   The best retelling of the Trivial Pursuit origin, which I have heavily relied upon here, is Louise Bernikou, "Trivia Inc.," *Esquire,* Mar. 1985.

168   "We were the world's largest game publisher"   Quoted anonymously in Richard C. Levy and Ronald O. Weingartner, *The Toy and Game Inventor's Handbook* (Indianapolis: Alpha Books, 2003), p. 204.

169   fifty copycat trivia board games   "Trivia Mania," *Fortune,* Nov. 12, 1984.

170   Both entries are utter fakes   Henry Alford, "Not a Word," *The New Yorker,* Aug. 29, 2005.

170   "It's like tagging and releasing giant turtles"   Ibid.

170   Fred's lawyers put the count   *Worth v. Selchow & Righter, Horn Abbot, Ltd.,* 827 F. 2d 569 (9th Cir. 1987).

171   one in five American game closets   "Seeking Board Game Bonanza," *The New York Times,* Dec. 30, 1986.

171   The abrupt sales plunge   Eva Pomice, "Not So Trivial Problems," *Forbes,* Apr. 7, 1986.

Chapter 12

177   an old Donald Duck comic   Donald's appearance on *We Say—You Pay* was originally published in *Walt Disney's Comics and Stories* 99, in December 1948. That issue featured uncredited work by two legendary cartoonists: Carl (*Uncle Scrooge*) Barks co-wrote and drew the quiz show story, and Walt (*Pogo*) Kelly drew the cover.

182   every eighteen months   Robert Anton Wilson credits this estimate to Vallee in *Cosmic Trigger II: Down to Earth* (Tempe, Ariz.: New Falcon, 1996), p. 274. Wilson and Vallee each have their share of odd beliefs, but other estimates of information growth track Vallee's quite closely.

Chapter 13

188   largest student-run radio station   Gene Kemmeter, "Movie Kicks Off Trivia Events," *Portage County Gazette*, Mar. 5, 2005.

189   "The World's Largest Trivia Contest"   "A Look at the Man Behind World's Largest Trivia Contest," *Milwaukee Journal-Sentinel*, Apr. 16, 2001.

189   a simple one-day affair   Kemmeter, "Movie Kicks Off Trivia Events."

189   The first Lawrence question ever   Heather LaRoi, "Annual Contest Is Not a Trivial Matter," *Appleton Post-Crescent*, Jan. 28, 2005.

189   an *even earlier* contest at Beloit   LaRoi, "Annual Contest."

205   don't buy a single book   Paul Collins, *Sixpence House: Lost in a Town of Books* (New York: Bloomsbury, 2004), p. 4.

Chapter 14

212   "the most annoying man"   Stanley, *The New York Times*.

212   running for the Senate   Having just turned thirty a few months before, I was barely constitutionally eligible.

215   Britain's first quiz league   Nicholas Parsons, "Masters of the Quiz," BBC Radio Four, February 26, 2005.

219   In a 2000 consumer survey   By Britain's Consumer Analysis Group. Ibid.

219   a £17,500 defamation of character lawsuit   "Pub Quizmaster Wins Libel Action," *BBC News*, Jan. 11, 2005. A Bedford pub quiz player missed a question about the first five hosts of Britain's National Lottery show, and insisted his answer had been right, berating the quizmaster at the pub and then on his website. The quizmaster sued for libel and won.

219   fifty pubs in Sydney   Joe Nickell, "Pub Smart," *The Missoulian*, Oct. 16, 2003.

Chapter 15

229   sniping crankily at each other   "Alan Shepard Was 'a Pretty Cool Customer,'" *CNN News*, July 22, 1998. True story. Alan Shepard and Ed Mitchell were the cussing sleep-deprived malcontents aboard Apollo 14.

229   failed sitcoms of the *Seinfeld* alumni   For those of you keeping score at home, through early 2006: *Bob Patterson*, ten shows; *Listen Up*, twenty-eight shows; *Watching Ellie*, nineteen shows; *The Michael Richards Show*, eight shows.

KEN JENNINGS spent much of his childhood
in Seoul, South Korea. A graduate of Brigham Young
University in Provo, Utah, he worked as a computer
programmer until becoming an unlikely celebrity due
to his unprecedented, record-breaking streak on the
television quiz show *Jeopardy!* He lives outside Seattle
with his wife and two children. For more
information, visit www.ken-jennings.com.

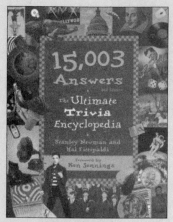